THE *NEW* TEXTILES TRENDS+ TRADITIONS

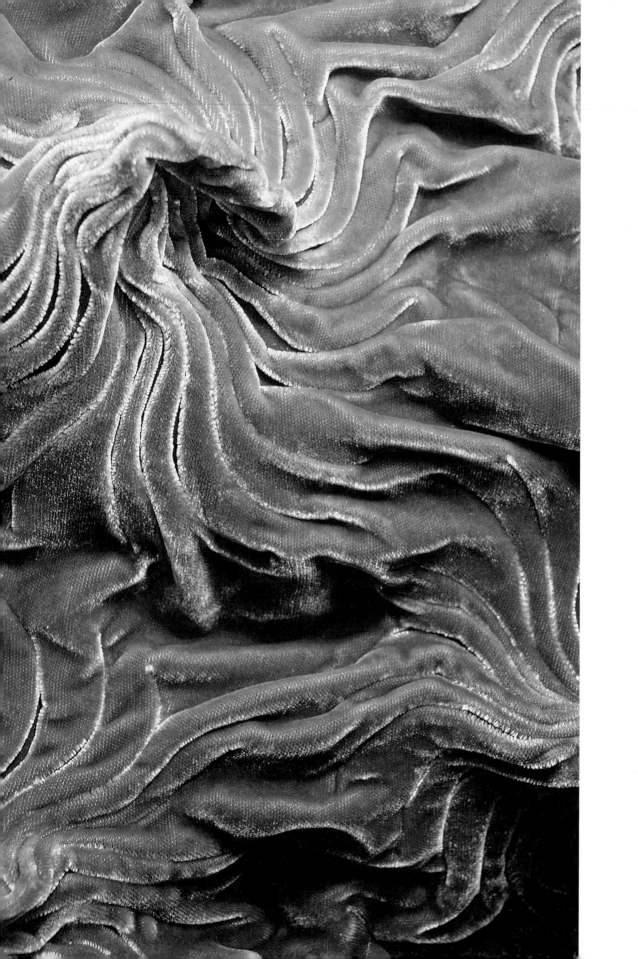

CHLOË COLCHESTER

THE *NEW* TEXTILES

TRENDS+TRADITIONS

with over 250 illustrations,
153 in colour

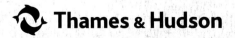
Thames & Hudson

Acknowledgments

I wish to thank the following people and organizations for their considerable help: Design Analysis International for their continued advice and administrative support as well as for tolerating all the disruption to their office space; Belinda Rowland for all the work that she put into assembling and controlling information for this book; and Vibeke Riisberg for her support and advice. I would also like to thank especially: Kiyoji Tsuji and his staff at The Office in Kyoto; the American critic Janet Koplos; the Nederlands Texteilmuseum, Tilburg; Hodge and Sellers; the staff at Tee Pee and Michel Thomas at Comtexte in Paris; Victoria Fernandez; *Textilforum*; *Crafts* Magazine; and for the plate illustrations Andy White (1, 2); Jean-Yves Ledorlot (3-6); the Fashion Foundation (22, 36); Du Pont de Nemours (23); Peter Williams (26, 28); Jeffrey Kong (33, 34); Makiko Minagawa (38, 39); Ralph Schandiljah (45, 46) and Cindy Palmano (53, 54, 64, 65).

Finally, particular thanks are due to Peter Dormer, without whose intelligent advice, patience and support this book would not have been possible, and to Helen Drutt for sharing her invaluable experience and expertise.

Frontispiece:
'Jellyfish', heat-moulded velvet. Nigel Atkinson, UK, 1990

First published in the United Kingdom in 1991 by Thames & Hudson Ltd, 181A High Holborn, London WC1V 7QX

www.thamesandhudson.com

ISBN 0-500-27737-0

Printed and bound in Singapore by C.S. Graphics

CONTENTS

Introduction · 6

Textile Design · 13
Textiles in Fashion • 13
Fabrics at Home • 27

Craft Textiles · 105

Textile Art · 137

Biographies • 170
Galleries and Museums • 181
Exhibitions • 185
Publications • 187
Glossary • 188
Index • 191

INTRODUCTION

THE design and manufacture of textiles is one of our oldest industries. It caters for the fundamental human need for clothing and for protection and fulfils a basic demand for decoration. But although textile making is an ancient activity it is not a conservative one. The very centrality of fabric in human culture has ensured that it is at the forefront of both technological and artistic development. Weaving was the first industry to be fully mechanized; it was the catalyst to the Industrial Revolution, and today the possibilities that have been created as a consequence of the advances in synthetics engineering, micro-electronics and dyes have yielded a new and hitherto undreamed of area of 'intelligent' fabrics. Yet, despite the technological and manufacturing changes in textile production, the industry remains diverse in production techniques and pluralistic in terms of the designs, styles and patterns that make up the contemporary designer's modern vocabulary.

The importance of the textile industry has meant that fabric has been taken seriously by the male-dominated world of commerce as a major merchandizing commodity. But within this industry there is a core of aesthetic concerns which have failed to receive their due regard for the reason that textiles are still so strongly associated with the home, homemaking and women. Neither textile design nor textile art has enjoyed the interest or acclaim (let alone status) that products within a more masculine sphere, or, of course, fine art, have been accorded. Part of the reason for this disregard stems from the fact that although thousands of women are still employed in both textile manufacture and design, there are still very few women playing an active role in textile management. Textile design still has strong roots in the home, however, and textile art in part stems from post-war feminist art practice. Both are given some weight in this book.

In recent years textile design has grown in status. It is simultaneously both futuristic and traditional, reflecting the tensions of a number of different forces coming together in the market place, which have led, in turn, to a new generation of hybrid products. Textile design today is influenced on the one hand by major, broad-based industrial research projects into new fibre technologies for sportswear and industrial textiles, and also by the development of automation and flexible manufacturing systems; and on the other, by the luxury markets and their revival of elaborate, decorative and ancient craft techniques and traditional patterns.

Parallel to the strengthening of the art market, the 1980s also witnessed a boom in the collecting of craft textiles and fibre arts, and a vast increase in the number of specialized galleries in

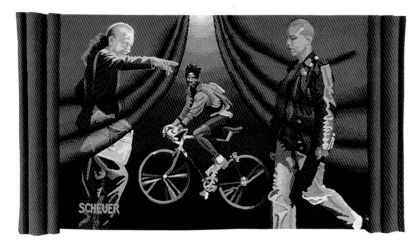

'Veils'
Gobelin tapestry
Ruth Scheuer
USA, 1989

Europe, Japan and America to supply it. Craft collecting thrived due to affluence at the top end of the market; but affluence itself, and the growing desire to display affluence, has had its effect upon the style of work produced. At one end of the scale, there has been a clear move towards work which displays virtuoso skills, rich materials embellished with expensive-looking surface patina. At the other, crafts have become more artlike, more diverse. This new market for craft and art textiles, which values the work of patient hands, has prompted a second renaissance of traditional flat tapestry work, and it is in this field, after years of surviving at low ebb, that narrative content has become important again. At the same time Japan, encouraged by its textile industry, which recognizes the value of the fibre arts as an image-bank and as a promotional tool, has become a new arena for the more abstract side of fibre art. It could be suggested that there is something atavistic about tapestry, a medium that has appealed to traders and merchants throughout history. Although tapestries are genuinely non-functional, their attraction lies in the fact that they speak of the great labour and time that was spent in their construction: this is part of their enduring allure.

It needs to be understood that since 1960 the textile industry in the West has developed in an unnatural economy. Protectionism has existed for the past thirty years in the textile trade and the last seventeen of those have been regulated by a system called the Multifibre Arrangement. This is a system of trade tariffs and export quotas of Byzantine complexity which in effect exists to protect the Western textile and clothing industries from market disruption, dumping or tactical undercutting from the low-wage developing countries. Put simply, this agreement has had the effect of blocking a significant number of imports from advanced developing countries, with the consequence that Western textiles and Western clothing are sold at an artificially high price. It is widely believed that without the support of this system the textile industry in the West would be unable to continue at its current level.

In the 1960s and 1970s textile manufacture was perhaps more affected than any other industry in the West by the idea of mass production that was so typified by the photographs of the endless chains of cars lined up on the Fiat production lines in the late 1950s. Industrialists, particularly in France, America and Britain, became a little mesmerized by the idea of mass production, imagining that engorging vast yardages of cloth at speed would provide a lasting solution to the problem of overseas competition. This was a mistake, and it was exacerbated by the first oil crisis of the 1970s. The specialized skills and character of the smaller family-run businesses were lost, as they went under or were amalgamated into large, unwieldy, featureless conglomerates, and textile products became standardized and dull.

This process of amalgamation and consolidation was not an even one across all Western nations – it was especially prominent in Britain and the USA. In both countries, but in particular in Britain, the manufacturing and retail industries (regardless of what was made or sold) became dominated by a few very large companies. Indeed, it was the rapidly emerging mono-culture of the 1970s that spurred rebellion. The reason why the crafts revival, and later, the street-style movements, were so striking in Britain was that they were part of a general mood of resistance which combined with a search for smaller, more individual options, whether it be in textiles, food, clothing or design generally.

So, although the 1970s recession may have put a stop to much interesting and experimental design work, it did provide the space for a number of alternative movements in textiles to flourish which questioned the role and status of textiles in contemporary society. The 1970s are generally viewed as the hangover after the party of the 1960s. This view is of course a simplification of the facts. Nonetheless, for the first time since the Second World War there was a crisis of confidence in the values of the dominant culture – technology, science and mass production. This scepticism revealed itself in a number of ways, but of special interest here was the rise of arts and crafts textiles and the flourishing of fibre art in the 1970s.

Influenced by the increasingly fashionable science of anthropology, textiles were analysed as a revealing material facet of culture – terms such as 'textile culture' and 'textile language' came into being. Themes as various as the meaning of textiles in the home, the link between textiles and nature, textiles in folk and tribal art, and the meaning and etymology of motifs, became the subject not only of publications but of fibre art works as well. This period of introspection provided the groundwork for many contemporary fibre arts and crafts. It also led to a new trend of what ceramicist and critic Alison Britton so aptly described as 'self-consciousness' or 'self-reflection' in textiles, which prompted both designers and craftspeople to make textiles not only the substance but also the subject of their work. Together with the trend in conceptualizing textiles, the 1960s and 1970s also witnessed a widescale revival of interest in ancient textile-making techniques, from pre-Columbian textiles to South-East Asian resist-dyeing techniques. The development of a fibre art movement in America and Europe, and the strengthening of an arts and crafts movement in Britain and Scandinavia created therefore an idea-bank of images and techniques which a new generation of designers were able to exploit.

The early 1980s saw the rapid rise of a new ideology across the field of design under the general umbrella of post-modernism; the idea of pluralism, individuality and decoration was exploited in everything from product design and furnishings to architecture. In textiles, particularly in the young, experimental style-based design movements, the spirit of innovation, humour and rebellion led the textiles industry out of the static conservative spirit that it had sunk into during the 1970s. Then, in the late 1980s, it started adopting craft techniques.

As with any historical overview, it is easy to succumb to the simplest diagnosis of change in fashion or ideology as being merely the swing of the pendulum, each phase a reaction against its predecessor. Change in design in the 1980s was not simply a response to a 'natural' perennial

'Verone'
Deposit printing on velvet
Andrée Putman
Edmond Petit, France, 1990

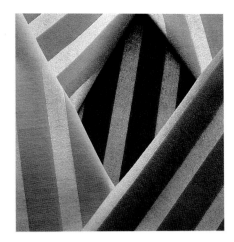

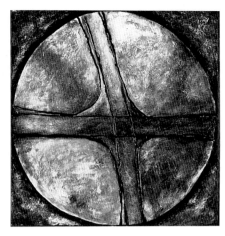

A non-woven fabric (detail, artist's impression). Two heterofil fibres are thermally bonded together. The nylon 6·6 core has a higher melting point, whilst the nylon 6 sheath melts to form a protective bond.

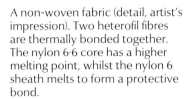

demand for new styles. The boom in information technology accelerated the flow of visual information around the world to such an extent that fashion itself became accelerated with it; also, more importantly, it democratized information. Suddenly it dawned on design theorists that people had their own news, that there was no longer any need for them to fortell what was to happen in the future. Hitherto, in both design and architecture, there had been an assumption among professionals that they knew best about what looked good and what was good. Yet, it was realized, after decades of designers and architects preaching that this or that style was 'correct' both aesthetically, and, often, morally, it was seen that both in clothing and dress people still selected what they liked and ignored the rest. Designers especially, and architects to an extent, stopped trying to work to an ideology but, like food manufacturers, started experimenting with new 'lines' to see what might be palatable. The boom in the availability of style choices coincided with a change of attitude by the industry; it was realized that specialization, not just automization, was the answer to overseas competition. And because there were few other sources to draw from, the industry began to recognize the potential of craft and the independent designer-makers as a means of sophisticating their products.

In the 1970s Japan and, to a lesser extent, Europe and America, sensing the danger of being undercut by rapidly developing countries – South Korea, for example – embarked on an extensive research programme to develop new, technology-rich products which would overcome the shortcomings of the first generation of synthetics, diversify markets and be difficult to imitate. Both manufactured and art or craft textiles have been affected by the new interest in fibre technologies. The presence of synthetics in engineering and even, in the case of vascular grafts and ligament repair, our bodies, is becoming increasingly important. Non-corrosive, lighter and stronger than metal, second and third generation synthetics, highly prized for their lightness and strength, are now used to build space, air and marine craft – they are woven into fabrics which can withstand bullets and extremes of heat and cold, they are used in earthworks, in bridges and in rooves, or they are extruded at high speed into non-woven fabrics for uses as diverse as car-battery linings and babies' disposable nappies. The hype surrounding the synthetics industries' performance fibres, which have the elasticity of human skin, absorbing or repelling heat as body temperature fluctuates, have made the natural fibre industry consider ways to bring out the qualities of its products. The industry has started to pour more design resources into yarn-spinning techniques

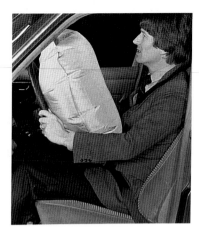

New fibre technologies and safety: this electronically triggered airbag, developed by Mercedes-Benz, inflates within thirty milliseconds in the event of a car crash.

to maximize, for example, the natural springiness of silk. This is an example of the way in which artificial materials are bringing about a change not only in the way that we see but also in the way we use and perceive natural materials. Yarn spinners are now considering ways in which they can maximize or better express natural fibres' 'performance' qualities.

Computerized weaving provides the space in which the full creative potential of these new inventions can be explored and tested – fast. Just as the arrival (1930) and mechanization (1950) of screen printing changed attitudes towards the established methods, so the advent of computer-automated jacquard looms has transformed woven fabrics. The results are fascinating because computerization, synthetic textiles and now a new generation of natural fibre production methods mean that the textile industry can make use of ideas developed by artists, designer-makers and craftspeople. Indeed the very fact of flexibility means that choice – diverse ranges of designs and fabrics – becomes a market necessity. The small, individual crafts-based artist or designer has therefore been given a new sense of purpose through the development of new technology.

The New Textiles focuses on the work of individuals, in craft, in art and at the fringes of mainstream design. This is a selective approach: much of textile design is and must be a collective, collaborative venture. Yet creatively, however, the work of individual designer-makers and artist-craftspeople does have an important role to play. They are free to take imaginative leaps and break the rules; they have fewer commercial or marketing constraints and they are prepared to take risks. But above all, their work is important because they create dazzling image-building objects that not only raise the status of textile design but also encourage interest in it as well. This book looks at the role that these independent textile makers have had in textile design, craft and art, and within fashion design, in the 1980s. It analyses the revival of the textile artisanal heritage in the French couture system, the development of a radical, alternative approach to textiles as an applied art in Britain and the fusion between high technology and craft which took place in Japan. It traces the role that craftspeople have had to play in the shift from simple printed fabrics which dominated textile production in the 1960s and 1970s to more complex, woven fabrics and prints in both fashion and furnishing fabrics. It also examines the manner in which a new decorative language of pattern has developed from independent art-based designers on the one hand, and the fusion of craft and technology on the other. The chapter on craft traces the development of

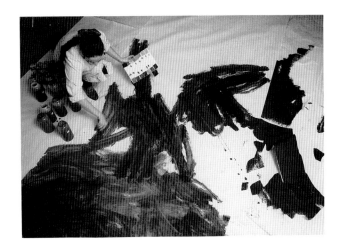

Applying art to cloth: Sylvie Skinazi prepares a transfer to be heat-printed on to fabric for Christian Lacroix at Patou in 1986.

the post-war contemporary craft movement in textiles, the flowering of 'alternative' movements in the 1960s and 1970s and the impact that these ideas had upon it, focusing on the way in which familiar domestic crafts, such as embroidery, quilting and later basketry, have been adapted and transformed by contemporary sensibilities. The discussion of textile art in the final chapter charts the development of the fibre art movement in America, alongside its equivalent on the European continent, and takes a look at the growing interest in tapestry.

Divisions between design, craft and art, even for practical purposes, may seem brutal and somewhat rash, given the volumes of debate that these particularly controversial boundaries have generated. Indeed, so much cross-referencing has taken place between artists, craftspeople and designers that it has been argued that the old categories of art, craft and design are splitting into hybrids of various sorts. This book certainly covers some of the complexities that exist: multimedia artists; artists who explore the metaphoric content of designed manufactured products; tapestry makers who skilfully reproduce artists' work; independent tapestry makers; applied artists and designer makers; that hybrid of art and design; the applied arts; and more recently, famous artists who are now adding a new 'design' dimension to art.

The debate continues, not so much for the ideological reasons which may have been its primary motivation in the 1970s, but more because there is still a lot of money at stake – especially in America. One of the central problems of the issue is a general lack of honesty as to what is actually being discussed. Decorative artists and craftspeople are now employing writers to 'talk up' their work into something more allusive and philosophical than it actually is. Look at it hard and it begins to seem that the debate about art, craft and design is about pretensions motivated by ambition, perhaps even greed, and the desire for personal glory. A more diplomatic approach, as Nancy Corwin suggested in her review of the 'Fiber R/Evolution' exhibition at the American Craft Museum in 1986, is to adopt an 'inclusive aesthetic'. As she puts it, 'Contemporary fiber art . . . is interesting and vital precisely because it exists between the old categories of craft and art as two things at once. It defines a new art form by merging old separate ones.' Overall, however, *The New Textiles* seeks to show a balance of design and craft, recognizing that whilst the avant-garde is always important in leading the way, there is also a need for good, sober contemporary work that satisfies the mass of consumer design. This book celebrates textiles as both an artistic and a service enterprise.

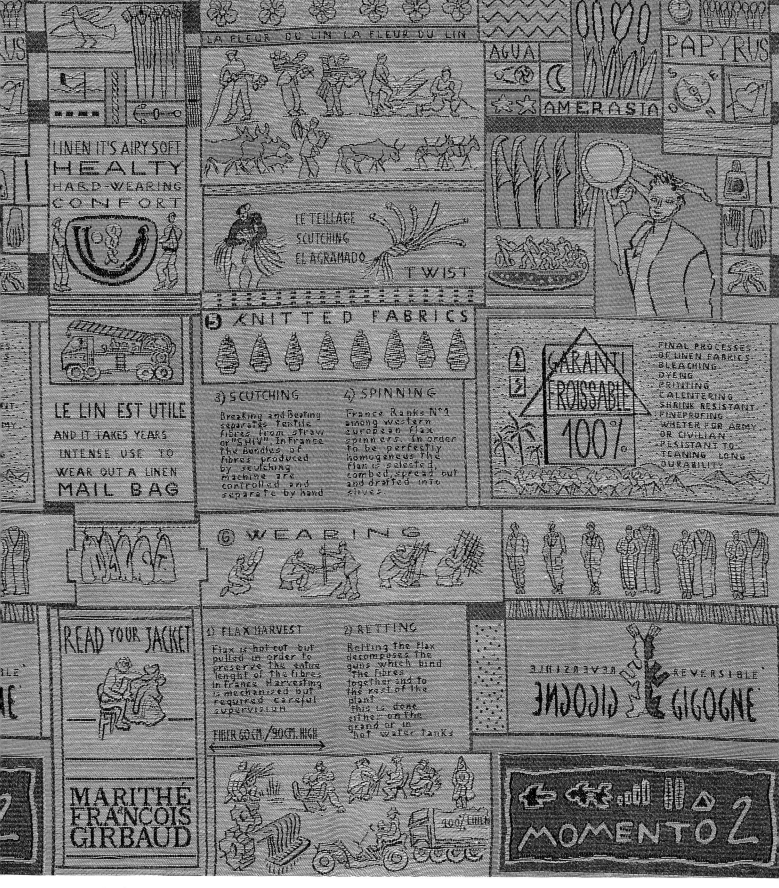

'Read Your Jacket', jacquard double cloth. François Girbaud for Marithé and François Girbaud. France, 1986

TEXTILE DESIGN

Textiles in Fashion

IN 1986, the French fashion designer François Girbaud, celebrated for his fifteen attempts at restyling a pair of blue jeans, used an Egyptian cotton jacket to summarize neatly the predicament faced by the fashion and textile designers at that time. Egyptian cotton had once been renowned for its softness, but with the advent of synthetics, this had been forgotten. In the jacquard pattern of the jacket, Girbaud wove a cartoon that bluntly indicated the value of the jacket to the consumer: 'Feel this jacket' is written in large letters on its sleeve, and various images showed cotton being harvested in Egypt, Egyptian hieroglyphs, people feeling the jacket on display and admiring it at home. The message behind Girbaud's cartoon, that the consumer had to some extent lost contact with the goods he bought, playfully reiterated the concerns expressed by William Morris a century before: that the industrialization of textile production has led to a decline in standards expressed in the lack of 'authenticity' of the product.

Girbaud's anxieties were shared by many. In 1987 Micheline Alland, the director for the exhibition mounted at La Villette in Paris entitled 'La Mode: Une Industrie de Pointe', expressed similar concerns. 'Today', she said, 'we impose a colour fabric and design standard on the consumer who no longer has any idea of what fabric is about. He buys a grey suit or a red dress, and that's it.' In France it was realized that the restructuring of the textile industry during the late 1970s had, by the mid-1980s, all but obliterated specialist production. The French textile industry had become a manufacturer of commodities and as such was made vulnerable by overseas imports. French conservationists in particular woke up to the fact that the 'big is beautiful' approach to industrial production was placing their cultural heritage in peril.

In 1988, the conservative Parisians' concern for the loss of their *patrimoine* prompted a vast exhibition called 'De Main de Maître', held at the Grand Palais, on the use of traditional craft skills to create luxury products. For the next three years the luxury market was extensively promoted as the bastion of France's artisanal heritage. Financial investment and a flurry of attention revived the flagging interest in the haute couture system, and for the first time the doors of its suppliers opened to the public. Thus exposed to new scrutiny, 'les petites mains' (as the hundreds of anonymous artisans behind the great names of the Parisian couturiers were habitually called) were suddenly heaped with awards for their years of devoted service.

The embroideries of the master *parurier* François Lesage, Director of Lesage S.A., were particularly admired and sought after by the thousand or so women in the world that could afford

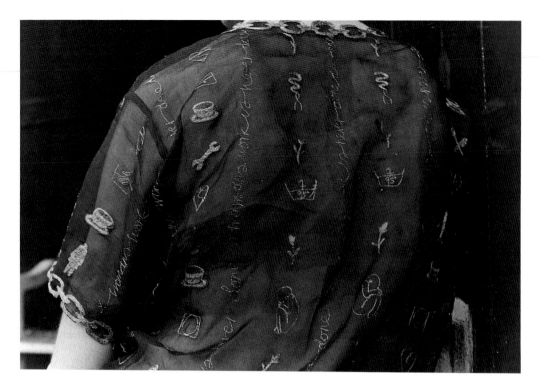

'A Woman's Work Is Never Done'
T-shirt (one-off)
Machine-embroidered organza with
    metallic thread
Carolyn Corben
UK, 1990

them, since they represented the pinnacle of exclusivity – hand-embellished fabrics for hand-made clothes. Lesage remains the leading supplier of embellishment to the Parisian couturiers. Each season he provides them with a 'palette' of materials, patterns and embroidery styles which he hopes will anticipate the mood of their collections. After lengthy discussions with Lesage the couturiers present their sketches which Lesage and his team of embellishers must then translate. Lesage's skill resides in his capacity to provide innovation each season within a restricted and conservative idiom. He must embellish fabrics using constantly new and enticing combinations of materials: raffia, semi-precious stones and leather one season, cockerel feathers, beetle wings and Czechoslovakian jet the next. Such materials, taken from Lesage's stocks underneath his workshops, are, like the skills that went into assembling them, unique, and therefore all the more valuable. They are also what makes his work a 'heritage' craft, essentially disarticulated from industrial production. Lesage's atelier, filled with seamstresses apprenticed from the age of fourteen working at wooden work benches, was described in *Le Figaro* as a haven of pre-revolutionary France.

By 1987 Lesage's embroideries had come to be seen as the hallmark of exclusivity, a metaphor for the society of the Reagan era, desiring conspicuous consumption. Lesage knowingly manipulated this need in his creations for couturiers who reached out directly to the booming art market. Yves Saint Laurent dressed up his models as status symbols in sequined copies of Braques, Picassos, and Van Gogh's *Irises*, which had just been sold for a record price in London; earlier, in 1984, Karl Lagerfeld, working for Chanel, dressed his leading model Inès de la Fressange in a bodice that copied a Ming vase made of thousands of seed pearls. What confirmed Lesage's embroidery as an object of status was the amount of time, often hundreds of hours, lavished on each piece, time thrown into relief, as it were, by the accelerating pace of the world outside.

In the couturier Christian Lacroix's first independent collection in 1987, his fabric assistant Sylvie Skinazi provided an interesting, rapid alternative to this time-consuming method of creating art fabrics for fashion. Using a relatively new technique called heat-transfer printing developed by the Swiss chemical company Ciba Geigy, Skinazi was able to create large painterly prints. By sublimating pigment and solvent on to cloth, this technique gave an exceptionally high-fidelity print, recording the full gestural vitality of Skinazi's designs. Describing these painting-dresses in an interview, Lacroix took care to lay special emphasis on the most important point, the fact that each transfer could only work once. A relevant consideration, in view of the fact that his dresses cost as much as a luxury car.

The couture revival had a strong impact on textile design in general. For example, the British designer Carolyn Corben, working outside the conservative idiom of couture, embroidered a telling commentary on it. On the reverse of a shirt machine-embroidered with various different currencies she stitched the words 'Greed is Virtuous'.

Radical Prints: British Fashion Textiles in the 1980s

Corben's roughly made, satirical embroideries are characteristic of the subversive, art-based textile designs that emerged from Britain in the 1980s, as the country clambered its way out of the 1980–83 recession. The stagnation of the economy during the late 1970s that had had such a deadening effect on architecture, fashion and design also dealt a body blow to the ailing British textile industry. It had been the first textile industry in the world to undergo mechanization, but now it was collapsing from a lack of modern management, sufficient capital investment in new machinery and a poor understanding of the value of good design. Not all companies were so ·inept, but many of the stronger ones grouped together in ever larger conglomerates in an attempt to protect themselves from cheaper imports from developing countries. This resulted in an inevitable loss of individuality and character amongst the independent design companies.

One of the consequences of the textile industry's weakness was a failure of nerve. Instead of attempting to open new markets or revive moribund ones with good new design, it tamely allowed the retailers – often a conservative group – to dictate style. And what the retailers demanded were large orders of trivial, bland fabrics. In Britain, perhaps uniquely, the retail world in all categories of consumer products – including food, clothing and furnishing fabrics – is dominated by a few very large companies with shops and stores in every city and town in the land. This means that the retailers are very powerful and are able to dictate to manufacturers.

Yet against this background of uniformity and compliance in design, Britain witnessed the explosion of punk, which revolutionized music, fashion and design. It was successfully marketed by Malcolm McLaren (manager of the Sex Pistols) and Vivienne Westwood from their shop Seditionaries in the World's End, Chelsea. In the early 1980s, graduate fashion students from London art colleges became street-style celebrities overnight. These new designers had no money and no business experience. However much credibility they had in 'the street', they had none in the corporate board rooms. Unable to muster sufficiently large orders from the textile manufacturers, who were geared up to supply the retailers, they were forced to rely on their own resources. So they turned to friends working in textiles for imaginative designs. For the surplus of textile students that issued from Britain's thirty-odd textile courses each year, the possibility of forging such partnerships provided a tempting alternative to producing standardized designs on paper for the conservative taste of the mass market. New 'studios' for independent fashion and textile designers were established in the crumbling warehouses and disused Victorian factories of East London.

Much of the strength of street-style fashion was derived from these collaborations between fashion and textile designers. Compared to the rest of the fashion design industry, which was separate from textile production in terms of both time and space, these young fashion designers enjoyed a unique relationship with their textile counterparts. The only approximate equivalent was the interaction between the Continental suppliers and the Parisian and Milanese couturiers, but even this was totally different in approach. The British fashion and textile designers matched independence for independence. Their designs were conceived together so that they went well together, manifesting similar intentions and, above all, equal irreverence towards the accepted canons of high fashion. The fashion designers' radical experiments in cut were matched by the textile designers' muscular prints.

Many of the patterns were crudely designed and roughly printed (the textiles were all produced by students), but these qualities complemented the prevalent fashion aesthetic which was intended, above all, to read dramatically at a distance, on the pop promo or the fashion pages of the style magazines. The more subtle designs exhibited a tendency towards self-parody that tapped into the nation's sense of humour and provided a good record of the 'no future' generation's first contact with the commercial world. Working with the young fashion partnership Body Map (who hit the headlines with their graduation show from Middlesex Polytechnic in 1983), their contemporary, Hilde Smith, made painstakingly – by hand – oversize two-tone simulations of computer graphics. Both Helen Lipman, working for the fashion company English Eccentrics, and the young print-design partnership Hodge and Sellers, made mock of the nascent craze for designer clothing with print designs made from famous people's signatures and the reverse side of couturiers' labels – a wry parody of the growing trend of sporting a designer's or couturier's label as a means of accruing status.

Encouraged by the success of their peers, subsequent generations of students followed suit. The confusion of contradictory styles and looks that resulted from this influx of independent talent in textile design was artfully marketed by the menswear designer Paul Smith, who made a medley of strong patterns into a fashionable look. As the decade wore on, the increasing numbers of designers who had set up on their own, not only in textiles and fashion but also in graphics, furniture and interiors, began to shift towards a more craft-based approach. Despite the fact, however, that these designers made most of their work themselves and that much of it was conceived as a 'one-off', never intended for mass production, most vehemently rejected the label 'craftspeople'. 'Craft' in their eyes was a word that carried a stigma, fatally associated with the 'cloying' concerns of the early 1970s back-to-naturists. The designer-makers' ideas were quite different, inspired by urban style culture. They were less-than-concerned with the display of virtuoso techniques, as their designs were conceived to be used rather than displayed in a gallery. In search of an alternative aesthetic to the pristine cleanliness of high-tech design, experiments

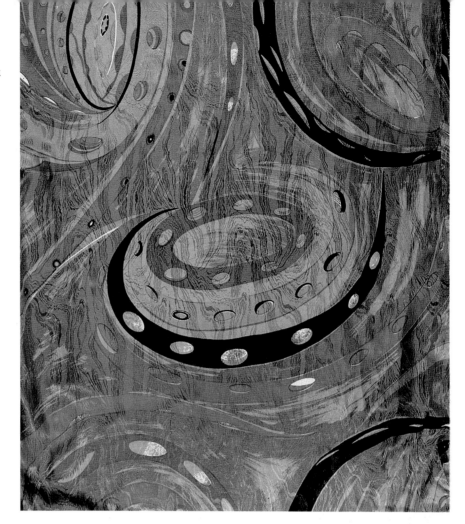

'Tempest'
Screen-printed damask silk
Georgina von Etzdorf
UK, 1990

were conducted using recycling and techniques for creating surface patina and depth. The layered print emerged as a decorative fabric equivalent to the distressed, oxidized surfaces favoured by British 'one-off' furniture makers such as Ron Arad and Tom Dixon. Working for Katherine Hamnett and John Galliano, the London-based Venezuelan designer Luiven Rivas Sanchez embroidered amorphous amoebic shapes over camouflaged prints of 1970s pin-ups. The rigorously craft-based West Surrey College of Art produced several generations of students, notably Joanna Gordon and Victoria Richards, who repetitively screen-printed and bleached their fabrics to create dense, painterly prints with shifting surfaces and depths – 'distressed' versions of conventional English chintzes.

For many of these designers who set up on their own, securing an adequate market for their esoteric designs presented a problem. Of the few textile designers who did manage to put their business on a firm financial footing, Georgina von Etzdorf was the only one to establish a substantial overseas market for her finely crafted designs. Working within the more conventional British idiom of romantic naturalism, her painstakingly constructed patterns such as 'Fritillary' (1985) and 'Tempest' (1990), which each took a year to perfect, were more accessible to overseas buyers from America and Italy who felt that their finesse offered value for money. By the end of the 1980s this approach to quality was an attitude that the British fashion designers, educated by several years of exposure to the fashion market, had come to share.

High-Tech and Texture: The Japan Aesthetic

JAPAN has exerted a strong and enduring influence on Western ceramics and textiles this century, one result of the standing that these crafts enjoy in Japan, where potters, dyers and weavers are held in greater esteem than their native fine artists. This traditional respect for textile craftsmen which leads the Japanese to award veteran kimono makers with the title 'National Living Treasure' explains the global strength of Japanese fabrics. Consistent investment since the Second World War has also given Japan the most sophisticated technological base for textile manufacture in the world. This modern industry, coexisting alongside an active folkcraft tradition, has put Japanese textile production in a unique position. In terms of attitude, technology and tradition Japan is the closest thing on this planet to a textile paradise for designers.

Since there is little historical precedent for interior furnishing fabrics in Japan it is the fashion designers who have provided the arena for textile development. During the first half of the 1980s designers such as Issey Miyake, Rei Kawakubo and Yoji Yamamoto made fashion an area of synthesis between digital technologies and craft. In particular, Issey Miyake, whose Miyake Design Studio in Tokyo opened in 1971, pioneered a new approach to fashion with his more extravagant and expressive use of dramatic fabrics inspired by Japanese craft textiles. His cutting method, influenced by the strict geometry of the kimono and Madeleine Vionnet's innovatory use of the bias cut in the 1920s and 1930s, introduced a looser way of draping fabric around the body, freeing it from the constriction of French tailoring. His ideas turned Tokyo into a fashion capital and generated the interest and the financial support to initiate an extensive research programme into textile design.

Miyake's, Rei Kawakubo's and, later, Yoji Yamamoto's patronage of textile research led to a number of innovations. In 1977 the Miyake Design Studio, in cooperation with a Japanese dye printer, developed laser-beam printing, which produced beautiful geometric prints of graduated colours. During the course of the 1980s Miyake's in-house designer, the master-weaver Makiko Minagawa, endeavoured to simulate traditional hand-woven fabrics gathered on visits to craft-weavers from the Japanese outback on state-of-the-art computer-driven looms. To do this he used random generators to create built-in flaws during weaving – an interesting use of robotics to respond to the human desire for the accidental. Other methods were evolved to achieve similar effects. In 1986 an article published in *Le Monde* described how Rei Kawakubo's knitwear designers loosened screws on sophisticated knitting machines, or left perfect lengths of machine-knitted fabric to bleach in the sun for a whole summer long in order to achieve the desired surface effects. And although they looked raw, the Japanese fabrics were a strongly tactile experience: they felt extraordinary.

In terms of the quality of the result these experiments were far removed from, though influenced by, the hobo look of 'post-holocaust chic' made fashionable by the British designer Vivienne Westwood in 1983. For although the Japanese textile designers' experiments with fabric were often quite brutal (Miyake, for instance, melted high-quality synthetic fur on heated rollers), they were separated from European trends by a gulf of technological know-how and national tradition of respect, embodied, for example, in the refined aesthetics of the tea ceremony. Sensing the mood of the market, however, the Japanese designers were quick to capitalize on it.

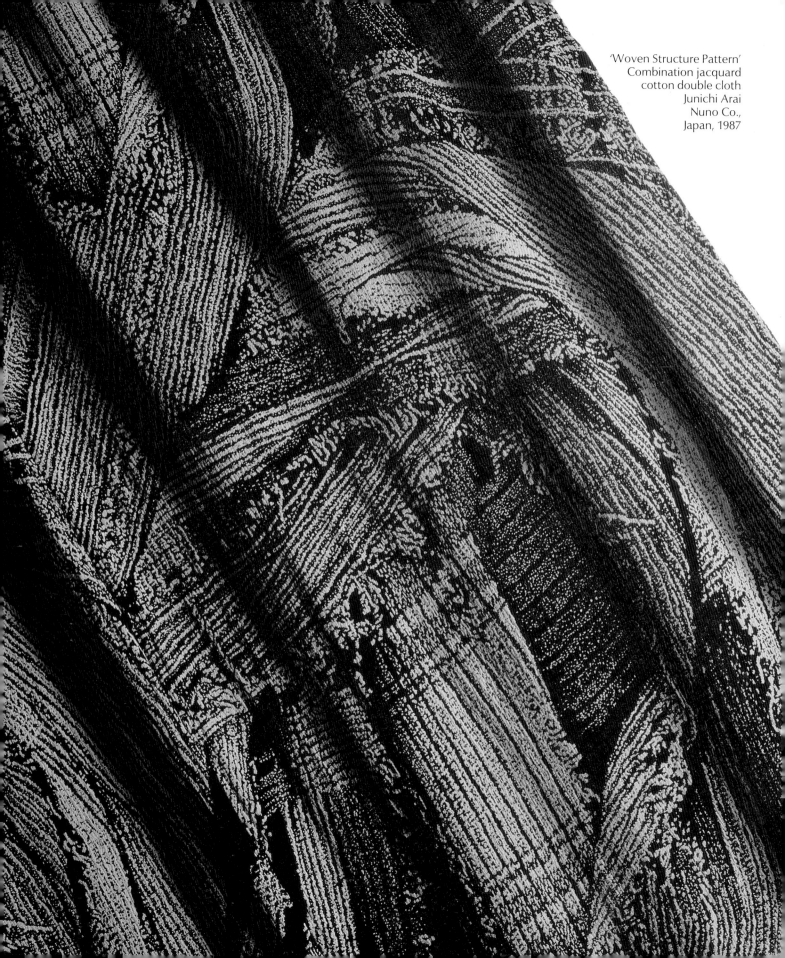

'Woven Structure Pattern'
Combination jacquard
cotton double cloth
Junichi Arai
Nuno Co.,
Japan, 1987

In the West, there was a mixed reception to this new 'humility' look, which, after all, cost the same as more conservative luxury. Japanese design was expensive. One of Miyake's favourite axioms, quoted in Leonard Koren's Japanese design manual, *New Fashion Japan*, was 'The price is part of the design'. There is no doubt that Nicholas Coleridge, author of the *The Fashion Conspiracy* (who clearly sided with shiny brass buttons against the intricacies of weave structure), spoke for many when he disparagingly described the fashion design scene in Japan as the 'Wabi Lobby'.

Junichi Arai's remarkable genius as a weaver is an indication of just how much the West still has to learn from Japan. Arai supplied some of the most dramatic, image-building fabrics to Miyake, Kawakubo and Yamamoto in the 1980s. It is a tribute to Miyake that he understood his genius and prompted it with provocative Zen-like design briefs to make a textile 'like clouds', or 'like poison'. Arai's approach to weave design is unusual. For most weavers, design is a graphic process which is completed on paper before work starts on the loom. Arai never draws his designs but regards weaving as a three-dimensional construction, a sensual form of engineering with fibres. Indeed, he is interested in the orchestration of stress through balancing the properties of materials through structure in the same way as an engineer would be. Expressed through cloth, Arai's own brand of engineering is an intimate, tactile and vital form of physics. All woven fabrics are tension structures of a sort, though most aim for controlled tension and stability. Arai's designs are based on destabilizing fabrics and releasing rather than controlling tension. He weaves loosely, with high-twist yarns (similar to those traditionally used to make crêpe fabrics in the West) to create cloth with a bouncy texture and feel which seems to spring with life.

The basis of Arai's palette during the mid-1980s consisted of a hundred and fifty different synthetic and natural yarns – almost entirely black and white – which were distinguished by different characteristics of twist, sheen, stability and shrinkage. He is known to be extremely exacting in his demands from spinners. He plays the qualities of the yarns off against one another to achieve a vast variety of effects, experimenting with their behaviour at every stage in the manufacturing process. Arai's experiments with the most naturally springy fibre – wool – have been both a revelation and a source of dismay to the West (Japan's woollen industry is only twelve years old). By combining wool and cotton yarns, for example, which react quite differently to extreme heat, and hurling the freshly woven fabric into a heated dryer, it is made to distort into sculptural relief according to the weave structure and pattern.

The Arai family has a tradition of weaving. Arai's father was a weaver and his grandfather a spinner; he grew up and now lives in the traditional Japanese craft-weaving centre of Kiryu, a small town to the north of Tokyo which specializes in high-twist yarns. This, to some extent, accounts for his thorough knowledge of his craft. During the 1980s, trading under the name of Anthologie, Arai created fabrics that were the result of his experiments with a network of small family businesses of spinners, weavers and finishers of the Kiryu district. What has made him outstanding as a designer is his use and understanding of contemporary manufacturing technologies – he designs with manufacturing processes rather than for manufacture. This has led to some substantial innovations. Kiryu has always specialized in jacquard weaving, and Arai pioneered the idea of creating with the aid of a computer far more complex jacquard punch-cards than the traditional ones. This idea has a neat, circular logic to it – the jacquard loom, with its system of punched cards, was after all the forerunner of the computer. It is also an interesting example of the way in which the intangible – electronic data processing – can be used to heighten our awareness of the tangible. Arai has pioneered a technique called combination jacquard which allows yarns of various thicknesses to be woven into textural pattern – an idea which has now been adopted by designers from all over the world.

Landscaping the Fabric Surface: 3-D Fabrics

Towards the end of the 1980s and the beginning of the 1990s, the fashion market has become increasingly fragmented, reflecting the plurality of cultures in the West. As a result, high-fashion designers of womenswear no longer impose a consensus of opinion as to whether hemlines are to be low or high and jeans broad or narrow, and where there once was an agreed strategy concerning the lines, looks and colours of the season, there now exists a fractured market of designers, each attempting to establish their independent mark. It is generally agreed that the frenetic succession of different looks during the 1970s and 1980s finished by saturating the consumer in terms of cut. When, by the end of the 1980s changes in fashion had become so accelerated that shapes only remained 'in' for a matter of weeks, this method of stimulating consumption stopped working. Style no longer had time to accrue social value and so people lost interest. In the aftermath of this, fashion has turned its attention to its materials for inspiration and innovation.

Fabrics have responded by becoming more prominent and have started to assert themselves dimensionally on the fashion silhouette. Taking their inspiration from traditional craft techniques of pleating and smocking, and the ruched effects achieved by Japanese Shibori resist-dyeing processes, designers have begun to explore surface relief. Research into finely crafted surfaces indicates a shift from the individualist, art-based, expressionist prints of the 1980s towards a more observant, skill-orientated approach. Designers are less concerned with imposing an image (their mark) on fabric, but rather explore the behaviour of the cloth itself.

Relief effects, or dimensionality, can change the role of print from that of applying pattern on a surface to describing form. By screen printing stripes across a length of fabric, for example, British designer Bridget Bailey brings out the spines of her steam-pleated organzas in contrasting colours – a simple but effective method of highlighting the fluidity with which these pleated fabrics move. Another British designer, Nigel Atkinson (who supplies Romeo Gigli, Issey Miyake and Martine Sitbon, as well as interior and costume designers), has gone a step further, using industrial printing processes of his own devising to create form. A series of corrugated lines printed in rubber paste along a stretch of fabric creates pleats; a swirling, aqueous rubber print gives a fabric a stiffer texture, like creased paper; in each case the fabric's behaviour is adapted by the pattern he prints. Atkinson has also developed a techique for baking fabrics at high temperature, which moulds them into permanent shape – another industrial process which rapidly achieves effects it would have taken hours to create by hand. Inspired by nineteenth-century prints of fossils and plants, Atkinson explores natural textures and forms. He moulds his fabric into deep relief; velvets are furrowed with spiralling crevices, or are transformed into a downy lilac landscape of whipped

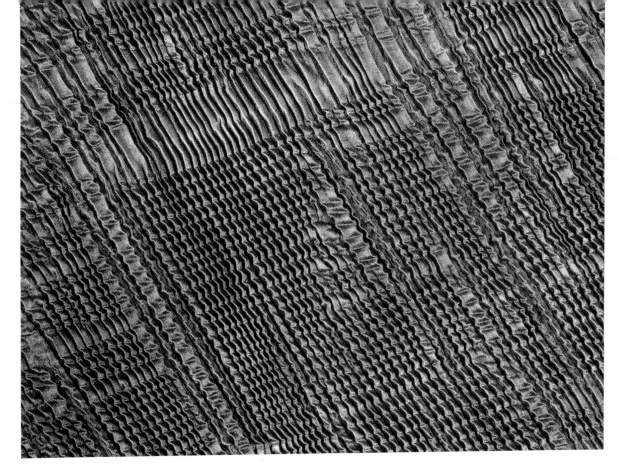

peaks. Atkinson's work is sensual, perhaps even pretty, and is favoured by the most romantic of the Italian fashion designers, Romeo Gigli. That said, it offers an altogether more forceful view of nature than the often bland, diluted and stylized florals one tends to associate with textile prints.

Perhaps the stunning photography of modern wildlife documentaries has revitalized our vision of animals and plants by bringing a rawer form of nature into the domestic environment. Certainly the growing concern over the future of the planet would seem to have made designers re-evaluate nature as a source of inspiration. The bold, semi-abstract prints of the French textile artist and designer Patrick Pinon provide a clear, harrowing articulation of nature in peril.

The work of the British artist and designer Alida Efstratiou takes a more decorative and celebratory approach towards the natural world. She weaves fine metallic filaments into striped iridescent lamé which can then be teased into delicate, undulating forms with her fingers. Efstratiou uses these metal meshes to make shimmering one-off clothes, hats and sculptural objects. Like Atkinson, Efstratiou does not treat the natural world figuratively but analyses its surfaces. Her sculptural work suggests close-up impressions of microscopic marine life – zooplankton with their wildly waving filia.

The work of American D'Arcie Beytebiere conveys a similar impression of the world being pulled into focus, as a finer, more detailed observation is brought to bear upon it. Beytebiere is a craftswoman and her approach (a mélange of discharge and Japanese Shibori) is labour-intensive. But the finesse of the results, with their sensitive modulations of rhythm and relief, provides a reminder of the way in which imagination and fine workmanship can serve both textile and fashion design.

A Battle of Wills: Fashion versus Textile

Most of the textiles featured here are the work of independent fabric designers, who in the fiercely competitive world of fashion enjoy, at best, a very precarious position. One much-discussed reason for this is what has become known as the 'rip-off' factor. As the British fashion designer Georgina Godley points out, 'the rag trade is notorious for confusing innovation with changes in style'; new ideas are devalued by superficial imitations appearing in the shops a couple of months later.

A more insidious problem exists in the delicate balance of power between fashion and fabric designers. Today, many top fashion designers have begun to adopt the Italian system of working with a team of in-house designers and commissioning state-of-the-art suppliers to manufacture fabrics to their specifications. The computerization of the textile industry has succeeded in making manufacture sufficiently flexible to supply short lengths of fabrics to fashon designers on demand. The industry is now divided into three tiers: companies with lengthy cycles of production that concentrate on equally lengthy programmes of research; middle-of-the-range companies with faster cycles capable of supplying large quantities of fabrics to the mass market; and small, specialized companies capable of responding to the spasmodic eruptions of the avant-garde. Once industry is capable of a quick response, the alternatives for craft production are reduced, and the space for the independent textile designer becomes restricted. As the Japanese textile designers have shown, the possibility of an industrially produced 'one-off' is now a reality, and the division between industrial design and the couture has become blurred.

Clearly, this eats into the territory of the independent designer, who must now offer a product that is increasingly remarkable – something that the fashion designer still couldn't get anywhere else. However, in a market where it has become more and more important for fashion designers to establish a strong individual identity, textile designers must provide fabrics that are both interesting and diplomatic. Today, remarkable fabrics are commissioned by fashion designers to boost their own name rather than that of their suppliers. The flexibility of the industry has put fashion designers in such a position of power that they are free to choose.

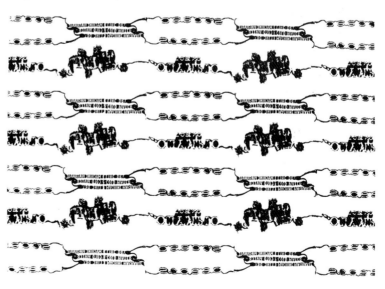

Opposite:
Hand-painted, tie-dyed and
    discharged silk charmeuse
D'Arcie Beytebiere
USA, 1987

'Labels'
Design for shirt fabric based on
    reversed designer labels
Hodge and Sellers for Cerruti
UK, 1983/84

The highly successful print-design partnership Hodge and Sellers (UK), which has launched a number of other designers, including Atkinson, on successful careers, provides evidence that it is possible to negotiate these problems and still create interesting work. It is highly adept at slipping into the idiom of different fashion designers. The partnership comprises a good combination of skills – Hodge's approach to print is graphic, Sellers' more textural. In a celebrated design for Azzedine Alaïa, they applied Sellers' research into finely ridged and textured rubber laminates for product design to tulle, thus creating a clever, modern rethink of lace.

The Danish-French print/weave partnership Tastemain and Riisberg provides a good example of another market in which rather more thoughtful design can greatly enhance the product. They operate a craft-based design studio in Paris and specialize in using their broad knowledge of design skills to revitalize the production of manufacturers of specific fabrics.

Despite the 'peacock revolution' of the early 1980s which was supposed to reliberate the male wardrobe, men's shirts remain a sensitive area in textile design. In an inspired move Tastemain and Riisberg supplied intelligent weave-designs to the top-quality French shirt manufacturer Jean Passot, which looked acceptably conventional at a distance, but proved rather more intriguing when seen close to. Needless to say, their designs revitalized Passot's production, and within three seasons had substantially increased its profit.

Fabric Futures, New Fibre Technologies: Second Skins

NEW fibre technologies present the most advanced and uncompromisingly modern aspect of textile production today. After a decade in which the more conservative and hierarchical codes of dress were re-established, the growing popularity of sportswear, leisurewear or activewear marks a welcome return to a more democratic attitude to dress. The current fashion interest in technology-rich textiles, originally designed to meet the performance demands of professional sportswear market, presents fibre manufacturers with new opportunities for research. In terms of fabric design, fibre engineering signals the most exciting prospect for the future, presenting the possibility of a fusion between craft, history and new technology.

Many of these new textile technologies are, in fact, quite old; what is recent is their inception on the fashion, leisurewear and activewear markets. Lycra had been present in swimsuits and women's underwear since its invention in the 1960s, but it was not until the British fashion partnership Body Map removed the protective crotch padding from cycling shorts and put them on the catwalk that lycra made its debut on the fashion market. Lycra introduced to ordinary clothing the qualities of mobility, functionality and comfort that the urban fitness craze of the 1970s had made fashionable. Used in combination with natural fibres, it modernized traditional fabrics: suddenly chiffon could stretch and no longer required ironing. Moreover, for designers of ready-to-wear clothing, lycra presented an easy solution to some of the problems of industrial tailoring, and created, according to fashion designer Georgina Godley, who intends to experiment with stretch worsteds at her new partnership in Saville Row, a new, hybrid approach to clothing based on a mix of formal dress and leisurewear. Lycra's success has been so remarkable – Du Pont de Nemours of America are still failing to satisfy demand – that other manufacturers of

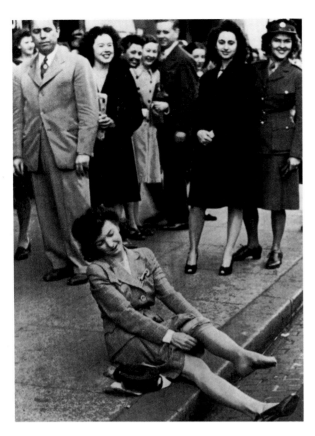

Nylon was given an enthusiastic welcome home when it made its post-war reappearance in ladies' hosiery.

One of a series of advertisements designed by Hans Schleger to introduce ICI's new fabric 'Terylene' in the 1950s.

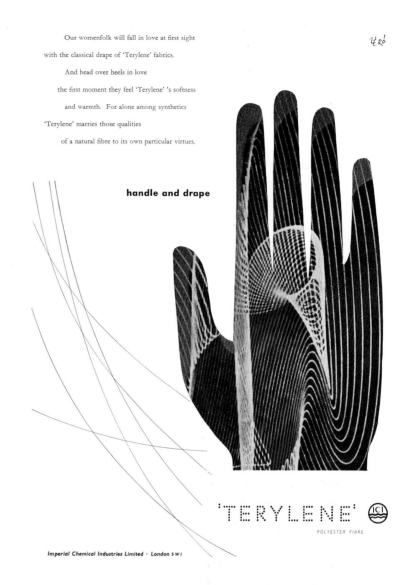

Our womenfolk will fall in love at first sight
with the classical drape of 'Terylene' fabrics.
And head over heels in love
the first moment they feel 'Terylene' 's softness
and warmth. For alone among synthetics
'Terylene' marries those qualities
of a natural fibre to its own particular virtues.

handle and drape

'TERYLENE' ICI

POLYESTER FIBRE

Imperial Chemical Industries Limited · London S W I

technology-rich textiles have been encouraged to follow suit. For protection from the wet, the current Cadillac of the performance fabric market is Gore-tex, the miracle material that protects the feet of the streetsmart Timberland boot wearers. The Gore-tex microporous membrane, manufactured by the American company W.L. Gore, is an expanded version of PTFE (properly called Polytetrafluorothylene), derived from the same petrochemical products by a similar technique as its well-known cousin, Teflon. It was originally designed for the NASA Space Programme, and was later developed to withstand Arctic conditions and to prevent the passage of bacteria in surgeon's gowns, but can now be found on the fashion market. Gore-tex is totally windproof and waterproof but allows the body to sweat and breathe in comfort: it is perforated with holes so fine that they will only allow the passage of water vapour. What makes the Gore-tex membrane interesting in terms of fashion is that it can be laminated to almost any material, including lycra (demonstrated by Godley's prototype for the 'Sport '90' exhibition' at the Design Museum, London), without losing its performance qualities.

Gore-tex made possible clothes that are light and yet capable of resisting extremes of temperature. Microfibres, fibres of less than 0.1 decitex in diameter, which is to say sixty times finer than a human hair, can offer similar performance qualities combined with a silky soft finish – and they are machine-washable. When tightly woven together, microfibres are also impermeable to wind and water and are ideal for lightweight coats for wear throughout the year.

New materials can go out of fashion, however, when so much is claimed for them. When nylon was launched in 1940 it was marketed as a wonderfibre. During the 1950s and into the 1960s nylon shirts, socks and sheets were promoted because of their 'easy care' characteristics – no ironing needed. Unfortunately feet and armpits clad in nylon sweated horribly, and nylon sheets were unpleasant to sleep on – you slithered and sweated and even itched. Nylon was passé by 1970 for chic sheets or anything else, but the situation is now changing again because manufacturers have resolved many of the problems concerning comfort. ICI have successfully introduced a double-layered knitted sports fabric called Aquator, incorporating their nylon microfibre Tactel, which draws sweat from the body and disperses it on the outer layer of the fabric for speedy evaporation, keeping the layer next to the skin dry and therefore comfortable at all times.

In the late nineteenth century, the chemists who made the first attempts to extrude filaments from cellulosic pulp were driven by alchemical ambitions – they wanted to find a cheaper alternative to silk. In Japan, the current world leader in new textile technology, producers are confident that they have successfully simulated the look and feel of silk and are now experimenting with imitating its sound. A leading Japanese fibre manufacturer, Teijin, has developed a fibre that simulates not only the feel but 'the "scrooping" russle of wild tussah silk', whilst another major Japanese synthetics company, Toyobo, has developed a new polymer partly derived from milk, whose molecular structure is actually similar to that of silk.

Creating such complex, non-biodegradable fabrics from petrochemical products may seem wilfully foolhardy given our increasing concern for the environment, not to mention the often precarious position of the petroleum market. But in the case of artificial silk such developments are balanced by humanitarian concerns. The production of all fine natural silk yarns relies on the filaments from the silk moths' cocoons being reeled on to spools by hand after they have been immersed in boiling water – a highly skilled, and extremely painful process which permanently maims the hands of the workers.

Heat- and light-sensitive dyes are, perhaps, the most new-age aesthetic to have come from the sportswear market. A technique called 'microencapsulation' creates micron-sized bubbles that attach themselves along the length of a fibre. These can be filled with bactericides, jasmine essence or heat-reactive liquid crystals, which create the possibility of clothes that not only adapt to the temperature of the environment but also change colour as the wearer passes from sunlight into shadow, from exterior to interior. So far, these new aesthetics have still mainly been used in sportswear – heat-reactive dyes are particularly effective in swimsuits, which change colour as they dry in the sun. The American textile and leisurewear designer Jhane Barnes has experimented with weaving fluorescent and light-sensitive yarns into men's shirts. Barnes is celebrated in America for her experiments with the surface puckering effects that can be achieved with lycra.

Tactile design looks set to become another area of research in the 1990s. The aesthetic is so new that its formal vocabulary has yet to be established. New microfinishes created by micropowders, crimping, or combining polyester fibres with widely different shrinkage rates, are described, vaguely, as being dryer than apricot, or softer than washed silk, peach skin, or even (and this one is an Italian invention) 'angel skin'.

Developing such sophisticated, technology-rich fibres is an expensive and time-consuming operation; its true purpose is, once again, to produce competitive products. Another reason for the decline of the synthetics industry in the West in the early 1970s was that the developing countries created synthetics industries themselves, thereby devaluing Western products. It managed to recover by specializing in new markets, notably geotextiles (specialized polyester fabrics used as foundations in earthworks) and textiles for specific industrial engineering technologies.

The heavy investment in new fibre technology for the sportswear market has implications for textile designers. Having learnt their lessons from the past, fibre manufacturers are keen to use design as a means of communicating the value of their products. But fibres must be spun into yarns, woven into cloth, finished, and made up into clothes before they reach the consumer. Sloppy production at any one of these stages may affect the performance qualities of the fibres and therefore reduce their value.

This danger has had the effect of tightening the industry's vertical structure (the chain of manufacturers and suppliers, as opposed to the horizontal structure, which is the field of competitors – weavers, for example) at any one stratum. In order to protect the value of its product, the American company W.L. Gore has started to award a seal of approval to products that have met its manufacturing specifications at every level of the production process. In Japan, fibre manufacturers now commission spinners, weavers and textile designers to experiment with their products. This research-based attitude to design demands increasing finesse from textile designers who must achieve a delicate balance between the conflicting demands of performance, comfort, feel and look.

The work of the Japanese-based British designer Rosemary Moore is representative of the future potential created by the fusion between history, craft and new technology. As a graduate student at the Royal College of Art, Moore patented her invention for a crinkle-knit lycra, made famous by the swimwear 'Liza Bruce'. Moore's new composite fabrics, manufactured under licence in Japan, are exotic, hybrid creations that combine dimensionality, performance and pattern. As with Arai's fabrics, Moore's designs rely on playing off yarns with different degrees of elasticity against one another – state-of-the-art synthetics are combined with natural fibres and knitted into patterns taken from Ancient Greek masks.

Not all textile design using new technology need rely on weaving such intricate structures with yarns. The Dutch milliner and theatrical designer Maria Blaisse has made design experiments in an area of current extensive research – nonwovens. Blaisse's designs are an essay in simplicity; her 'flexicap', designed for Issey Miyake in 1988, was a heat-moulded envelope of neoprene rubber with a single incision in it, which enabled it to be worn in a variety of ways. Blaisse has created equally lucid designs for the dance company Iso. Made from closed-cell foam polyamides, Blaisse's designs use processes such as vacuum moulding and lamination to create geometrically formed ultralight costumes reminiscent of those used by the German artist and Bauhaus tutor Oscar Schlemmer for the Triadic Ballet in 1926 and 1927.

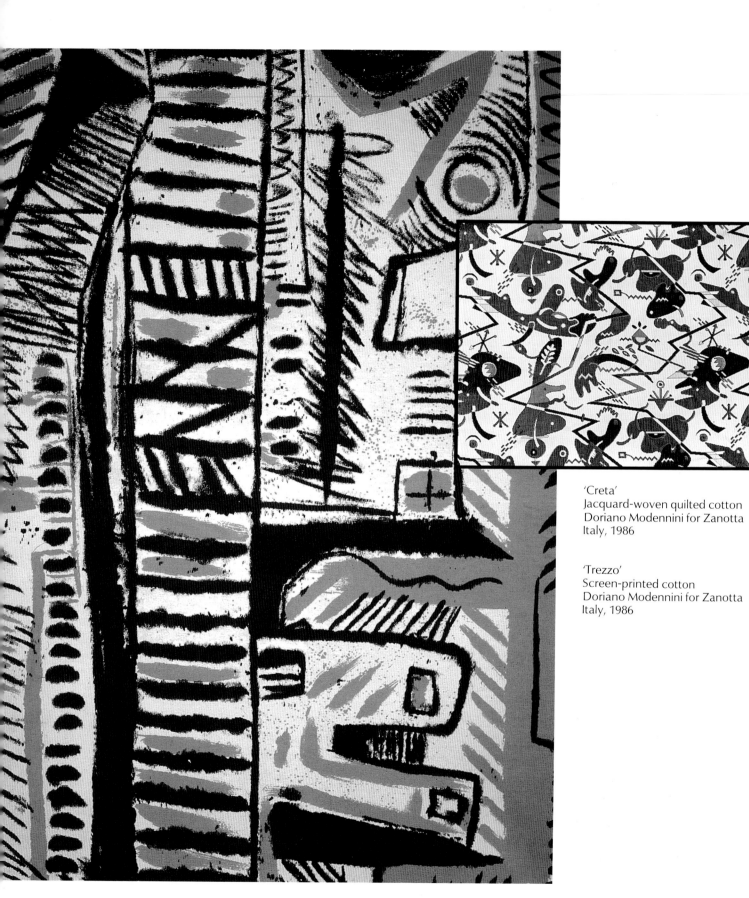

'Creta'
Jacquard-woven quilted cotton
Doriano Modennini for Zanotta
Italy, 1986

'Trezzo'
Screen-printed cotton
Doriano Modennini for Zanotta
Italy, 1986

Fabrics at Home

Sᴉɴᴄᴇ the Second World War, prints have been overridingly the most popular form of furnishing fabric. Screen printing in particular, introduced to the West in the 1930s and mechanized during the 1950s and 1960s, did much to change attitudes towards both furnishing fabrics and their manufacture. Printed fabrics do not wear as well as woven designs, but since they are cheaper to replace consumers soon warmed to the idea of changing the appearance of their home interiors every year or so rather than once every decade. Furnishing fabrics thus became susceptible to the rapid changes in fashion and design. From the industrialists' point of view, screen printing was an easy way out. Compared with the expense of setting up a roller, or even a loom, screen printing was cheap and offered a quick and flexible method of bestowing upon vast yardages of standard mass-produced cotton the latest style of the moment.

Fabric printing holds an ambiguous place in the history of modernist design. Along with other methods of embellishing fabrics, such as embroidery, printing was excluded from the Bauhaus curriculum: the application of decoration to sound materials went against the tenets of modernist ideology. The development of the contemporary print was greatly influenced by another school of modernist thought, however, which was central to the art and design movements in the USSR, the Netherlands and Germany at the beginning of the century. This held that contemporary social issues should inform the development of a new idiom of design. These ideas, combined with the dearth of ornament in the houses and buildings created by modernist architects, meant that from the 1930s onwards contemporary art came to exert a stronger influence on fabric printing than ever before.

Screen printing lent itself most accommodatingly to the task of applying art to fabric. If an artist's print could be reproduced on paper, then why not on cloth? In 1946 the experimental Czech printers Zika and Lida Ascher hit upon the idea of commissioning celebrated artists of the time – including Henri Matisse and Henry Moore – to create designs which they then editioned on silk and sold as scarves.

In the 1950s the linear graphics characteristic of the work of Paul Klee, Joan Miró and Alexander Calder inspired a new movement in furnishing fabric design. During the 1960s and 1970s fabric design reflected the rapid succession of movements in art – abstract expressionism, Op and then Pop Art – before finally looking to folk art for inspiration. Writing in 1957, the British print designer Lucienne Day (celebrated for her upholstery fabric 'Calyx', which was first shown at the Festival of Britain in 1951) expressed her belief that the influence of abstract painting had inspired an entirely new style of furnishing fabric design, which had finally broken away from floral themes to focus exclusively on modern art. The idea of textile design as an applied art flourished in the mid-1980s when roughness started to be valued as an aesthetic by both artists and designers. The gestural, roughly sketched patterns by designers such as The Cloth, in London, and Doriano Modennini in Milan, are examples of this approach. It was in Scandinavia, however, that this art-based approach fostered a lasting contemporary style in fabric design. Before the 1930s, Finland and Sweden had relied on imported print designs, largely from France, but the advent of screen printing prompted designers from both these countries to experiment with print for the first time; the resultant brilliant colours and dynamism of their designs reflected the excitement this new medium inspired. At the great Italian design Triennales of the 1950s the fresh, brightly coloured Scandinavian prints together with the stripped pine furniture of the 'contemporary' look were warmly received by people eager to forget the past and the drabness of wartime products.

The two leading forces behind the development of contemporary Scandinavian prints were women. In Sweden, Astrid Sampe (RSDI), who was appointed director of the newly created textile design studio at Nordiska Kompaniet in 1936, became a forceful advocate of an innovatory approach to fabric design. For her most celebrated collection of fabrics, called 'Signed Textiles', printed by Eric Ljunbergs in 1954, Sampe commissioned designs from leading artists and contemporary architects such as Alvar Aalto and Arne Jacobsen. As a mark of its enduring popularity this collection has recently been re-edited by Ljunbergs. Swedish contemporary-style furniture is now available through hypermarkets throughout Europe and its printed fabrics are now mass produced by large companies such as Borås, Almedahls, Kinnasand and Ikea.

In Finland in 1951, Armi Ratia founded her fashion and furnishing fabric company, Marimekko Oy, along similar principles to Sampe's experiments at Nordiska Kompaniet. Marimekko, which means 'Mary's dress', also drew its inspiration from contemporary art and placed an emphasis on the individuality and autonomy of the designer. This approach to fabric design was not without its problems. When, in 1964, one of Marimekko's leading designers, Vuokko Eskolin Nurmesniemi, left Marimekko to found her own company, Vuokko Oy, Marimekko's identity as a company was threatened. It survived this upset, however, and still pursues a similar policy to this day, albeit more tactically. It employs seven independent designers whose fabric designs range from the rich abstract patterns of Inka Kivalo to the evocations of rock and landscape by the celebrated Japanese designer, Fujiwo Ishimoto. Ishimoto is a distinctive fabric designer, but his presence at Marimekko also serves a different purpose — to promote Marimekko's fabrics in the rapidly developing market of Japan, which shares this enthusiasm for brilliantly coloured fabrics.

Denmark has been slower to develop a distinctive contemporary idiom in print than either Finland or Sweden, but since the mid-1980s it has started to contribute some original fabrics made by independent designer-makers who are able to maintain a degree of control of their craft. Unlike pattern designers, who do not produce their own work, the designer-makers can also experiment with printing techniques. This approach to design does, however, impose certain restrictions and many Danish designers continue to favour simple geometric forms because they are easier to print by hand. Nevertheless, the designer-makers gain certain freedoms as well. Else Kallesøe's hand-printed geometric fabric uses basic geometric forms, but they are printed in a spectrum of colours (something that a manufacturer would be unlikely to permit) to great effect — the colour creates a pattern of shifting rhythms. Elsewhere, this new hybrid approach to fabric design that fuses traditional craft techniques and geometric pattern has softened the familiar modernist look. The surface of Bitten Hegelund Sørensen's grid-printed banners is enlivened by using batik, and Sharon Fisher softens the stark geometry of her designs with the ikat technique. The work of both these designers has attracted the attention of the leading Danish fabric manufacturer Kvadrat who has realized that these designers' innovative approach to traditional craft techniques could be used to broaden their technical vocabulary.

This indicates a shift in thinking by the industry. Instead of adapting patterns, or paintings, to commonly used production techniques, machines are now being adapted to recreate technical effects as well as the specified designs. This progression, from machine-made fabrics to craft, and from craft back to industry, was one of the most important developments in textile design in the late 1980s.

Textiles or Design?

ONE peculiarity of textile design in the 1980s was that, despite the boom in design of domestic products on the one hand and of the interior decoration market on the other, these two areas, which one would have expected to complement one another, by and large developed quite separate, if not antithetical, aesthetics. A crisis in confidence in the future, combined with an increase in demand for luxury, meant that the major trend in interior decoration was retrospection. Luxury became associated with the past. From the mid-1980s onwards – particularly in America, France, Italy and Britain – the style of furnishing fabric responded to the mounting interest in conservation and restoration with a widescale revival of eighteenth- and nineteenth-century prints.

The old furnishing fabric houses, such as Brunshwig and Fils (USA), Berger (France), Rubelli (Italy) and G. P. and J. Baker, of London, which had survived on low ebb since the 1960s, responded with alacrity to the growing demand for archive prints. Even the new companies who achieved success at this time, such as Ted Tyler in New York, and the Designer's Guild and Osbourne and Little in London, took much of their inspiration from the archive. This mood of retrospection was succinctly illustrated in 1987, when Bernard Neville, the then head tutor of textiles at the Royal College of Art (Britain's leading postgraduate college of art and design), admitted in a magazine interview that there was not a single piece of contemporary fabric in his home. The revival of English country-house and American colonial styles also led to an increasingly lavish use of fabric. Chairs, tables and beds were upholstered with flounces and frills, and interior designers framed windows with swags, elaborate drapes and billowing festoons.

In stark contrast to this, designers tended to use little or no fabric in their interiors. Architects' memories of the fabric installations of the 1970s may have made them particularly wary of this medium during the 1980s. More seriously, contemporary fabrics were seen to date faster than interior design, and the many styles of furniture which emerged during the 1980s were also extremely limited in their use of textiles, the notable exceptions being those designed by the Milanese group, Memphis, and the Catalonian design movement, which were both strong advocates of comprehensive design.

One problem may have been that the different marketing strategies in textile and furniture design promoted designs of different intention. As a rule, furnishing fabrics are marketed in coordinated collections which correspond to the style, or handwriting, of a fabric house, whilst in furniture design more emphasis is placed on the individual name of the designer. The tendency of designers during the 1980s to view furniture as if it were an individual sculptural statement also discouraged the use of fabrics. With chairs masquerading as sculpture, stripped down to the armature in order better to express their form, furnishing fabrics, with their humdrum associations of the living room, were banned from the vocabulary of avant-garde design. Star furniture designers who emerged during the 1980s, such as Shiro Kuramata of Japan, and Philippe Starck of France, favoured pure, hard materials, such as carbon fibre, wood, metal and plastic.

A number of style commentators have remarked on the fact that much of design in the 1980s showed a worryingly persistent tendency to conform to masculine stereotypes. The high-tech interior that emerged at the turn of the 1970s which went on to become the advertising cliché of the mid-1980s – 'decorated' typically with gun-metal venetian blinds and a video console – was replaced by a series of anti-industrial looks that tended, however, to be no less overtly masculine in feel. This trend reached its most extreme in 1988, when the fashionable Milan-based design team Pallucco designed a coffee table in the shape of a caterpillar wheel from a tank. The machine aesthetics and 'butch' posturing of so much design might explain why so many women were less enthusiastic about the design boom than their male counterparts, and also why so few of them were attracted to the design profession. But if design hastened towards a masculine stereotype, interior decoration, taking its inspiration from the late nineteenth century when the home was described as a sanctuary of feminine leisure, presented an equally stereotypical vision.

The polarization of furnishing fabrics away from the rest of design was also marked by the decline in coverage and support that textile design received from the design press and institutions. The split has, however, strengthened the links between fashion and fabric designers. Furnishing fabric designers are greatly influenced by the more sophisticated market research conducted by the fashion trade. In Italy particularly a number of leading fashion designers, such as Gianfranco Ferre, Gianni Versace and, above all, the Missoni family, have started to apply their extensive knowlege of fabrics to furnishing fabric design.

Art At Your Feet

CARPETS are one of the few areas of textile design in which the design profession as a whole shows an active interest, and they have therefore become the focus for its experiments in pattern and ornament. These experiments have injected a new sense of excitement into an area of furnishing that, since the 1960s, had become standardized and dull. The carpet's return to popularity was prompted by the revival of modernist-style furniture in the early 1980s. One of the first notable collections was a limited re-edition, produced by Andrée Putman in 1983, of Eileen Gray's (UK) designs from the 1920s and 1930s, when carpets assumed the pinnacle of their importance as the decorative focus of a room.

These experiments were much encouraged by the invention of the pistol tufter in the early 1980s – a highly versatile tool that allows wool to be literally shot through canvas webbing before being fixed into place with a gum backing. This technique was (and still is) not quite as simple as it sounds; the pistol tufter is not a tool for hobbyists – it requires a degree of skill to manipulate it – and various technical complications have yet to be met. Yet it effectively offers designers a flexible graphic tool for drawing in wool that is immeasurably faster and of course less expensive than weaving a tapestry.

Since the mid-1980s a number of small companies have sprung up in Paris, Milan and Barcelona that operate on an exclusive basis, offering 'limited editions' of carpets by artists, designers and architects, and making carpet design a high-status area. Certain designs from this time took the analogy with art too far, creating visually busy carpets that had the antisocial effect of riveting one's attention to the floor; designers overlooked the fact that carpets serve a different function to paintings, their proper purpose being to decorate, rather than dominate, a floor. The rich and traditional use of symbols and the complex decorative motifs in Persian carpet design have also shaped our conception of carpets and raise a specific challenge to the contemporary designer. The Spanish architect Oscar Tusquets designs carpets that offer an interesting response to these demands. His computer-generated images of the earth and planets, made into hand-knotted circular carpets by the small Spanish manufacturer B. D. Ediciones, suggest an astronaut's view of the world, and it seems appropriate to look down at them. Another basic requirement of a good carpet is that it should withstand scrutiny from different vantage points, and lead the eye around the room. The Milanese design-team Oxido's carpet 'Di Mano in Mani' uses the hand of the title, repeated in gestural poses indicating different directions, to embody and symbolize multiple viewpoints both literally and metaphorically.

Marie Christine Dorner's elegant and sensitively conceived designs are also alert to the carpet's main function of decorating a room. Her carpets do not demand attention but instead reward it. One, for instance, features an ambiguous, semi-figurative central motif that suggests different forms from different angles. Seen from one position it resembles the gesture of a hand, from another it can be read as a dove of peace, and from a distance it recalls the shadows that might be thrown by a pair of lovers.

The decorative frame, frowned upon by modernist practice and banished from windows, doors, paintings and, of course, carpets, has started to reappear. Andrée Putman's most recent collection of carpets, 'Linera', is dominated by flamboyant baroque frames.

The success of these small independent companies has encouraged industrial carpet manufacturers to follow suit at a competitive price. The Paris-based Vietnamese designer Christian Duc has his carpets mass produced by the traditional Belgian carpet manufacturer Toulemonde Bochard. Woven on a broad loom, these carpets have the advantage of a greater density of wool than pistol-tufted carpets. More importantly, they are cheap to produce and can be sold for a quarter of the price. The success of Duc's carpets in Europe, America and Japan is an indication of how popular this area of design has become. It is estimated that he sells eight carpets a day.

Since 1988, Vorwerk, another traditional carpet manufacturer based in Germany, has started to invite leading architects, designers and artists, including David Hockney, Roy Lichtenstein, Matteo Thun, Zaha Hadid, Arata Isozaki and Sol LeWitt, to design wall-to-wall carpets. The list of names involved in the project is deliberately impressive, a good example of instant provenance where the artist's, architect's or designer's status or fame has been used to reassure people that they are right to invest in these new works. It is interesting to note that for the first 'Dialog' collection in 1988, Vorwerk went to great pains to reproduce the marks of authentication – the dribbles of paint, slight errors of brushstroke – in a characteristic design of graphic squiggles by David Hockney.

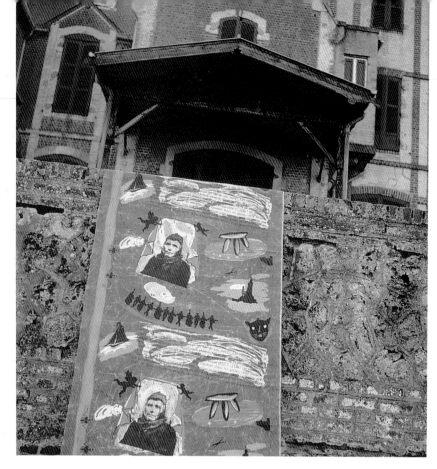

'Le Pilleur d'Epaves'
Glazed and screen-printed linen
Robert le Héros
Nobilis Fontain, France, 1989/90

Opposite
Left:
Design for an interior
George Sowden
Memphis, Italy, 1984

Right:
'Japan'
Hand-knotted wool carpet
Palmissano Edizioni Tessili
UK/Italy, 1989

Far right:
Screen-printed silk
George Sowden
Memphis, Italy, 1988

That said, Vorwerk's initiative, to produce dramatic designs by celebrities at an affordable price, is laudable. The 'Dialog' collections contain designs which would be suitable both for the domestic and contract markets. And, after the more exclusive approach to carpet companies during the 1980s, the idea of seeing, say, an airport carpeted with a Roy Lichtenstein design, seems comparatively democratic.

Citing the Past

ONE of the theses suggested by the art historian Ernst Gombrich, in his superb account of the history and theory of decorative ornament, *The Sense of Order*, was that human beings are creatures of habit and that decoration is a product of evolution, the result of a gradual process of mimesis, repetition, fusion and adaptation. His fascinating chapter on the etymology of decorative motifs describes, for example, how the border of a seventeenth-century Persian carpet could be traced back via the acanthus scroll found in the classical architectural ornament from ancient Greece to the lotus friezes from ancient Egypt.

By opposing decoration, modernism severed the decorative tradition, but now that modernism itself has been reassessed, designers have once again started to see the value of creatively borrowing from the storehouse of past decorative motifs. And whereas the computer as a design tool is hampered by speed, it offers great potential as a means of *adapting* designs. It should not be long before designers will be able to afford the technology which will allow them to store and

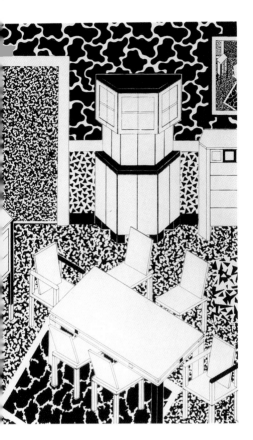 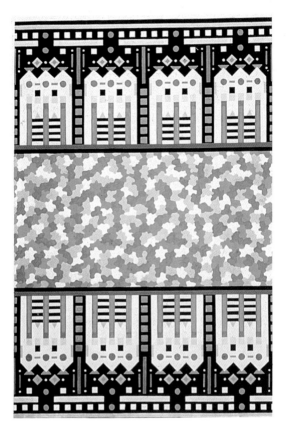 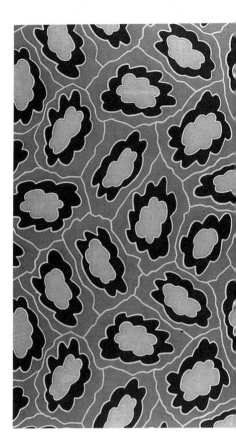

transport a virtually limitless archive of patterns on disk. This is one way in which digital technologies promise to transform our view and use of the past and, since it would seem textile design develops generally through a process of evolution rather than revolution, they should also have an impact on shaping the designs of the present.

These technologies may also offer the possibility of revealing hitherto inaccessible museum collections to the public. The Musée de l'Impression sur Etoffes, which houses the largest collection of eighteenth- and nineteenth-century prints in Europe, has recently completed a visual archive of five million fabric samples on fibre-optic disk. As a source of inspiration, the past will soon be more readily available to designers than ever before.

This may not necessarily be a recipe for unrestrained nostalgia: parallel to the general move towards retrospection, certain designers in the 1980s began to quote from tradition with a view to creating a decorative idiom that was relevant to the present. During the early 1980s, companies such as Timney Fowler (UK) reflected the renewed interest in classical motifs in monochrome prints taken from enlarged and distorted engravings of classical motifs. The French design group Robert le Héros also achieved considerable success with their painterly reworkings of French baroque and High Renaissance patterns.

Textiles, as with all other aspects of cultural production, reflect something of the attitudes and sometimes the beliefs of the societies that produce them. The initiative of the Italian design group Memphis was interesting in that it tried to infuse its objects with meaning deliberately. It held that giving an object meaning was more important than the technique by which it was made. George Sowden (UK) and Nathalie du Pasquier (France) in particular did much to create a decorative

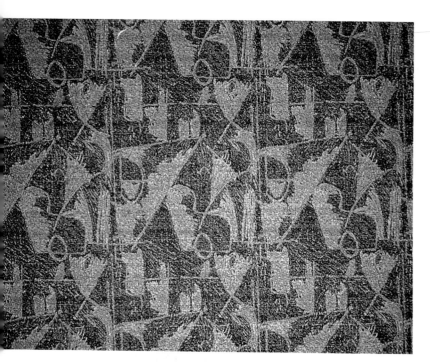

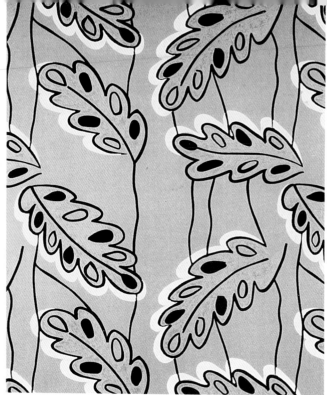

language of contemporary relevance that they hoped would provide a playful and humorous alternative to the market-led, functional style of international modernism. In the context of 1980s design, their work was also important because it bridged a number of disciplines; as well as creating designs for textiles and carpets, they applied their patterns to shoes, clocks, ceramics, and furniture.

Sowden and Du Pasquier's designs from the mid-1980s are of enduring interest because they signal how electronic media can allow fragments of the graphic environment to be combined into a contemporary style. Du Pasquier's approach to pattern was the visual equivalent of a 'remix' in music. She used her computer to synthesize and layer decorative signs, symbols and surface patterns from urban, ethnic, historic and – all importantly – both high and low cultures. Her designs for Esprit, Lorenz and the carpet manufacturer Palmissano in the mid-1980s registered surface patterns from disparate sources, such as cartoon imagery, graffiti, 1950s laminates, architecture, Persian carpets and Navajo blankets, which she fused into luminous psychedelic patterns.

Du Pasquier's work was alert to the evocative potential of pattern: by caricaturing and superimposing decorative styles she created designs that were rich in metaphor. Her work remains one of the high points of the many attempts during the late 1980s to piece together a new decorative idiom by a process of collage that exploited unlikely conjunctions to create meaning. Her designs for Palmissano stressed the tensions inherent in her pluralist approach to design, where floral and architectural motifs strain against one another.

The new generation of designers to emerge from Barcelona during the 1980s were also advocates of comprehensive design strongly inspired, in this case, by the styles of the 1950s. Their designs for a few adventurous Spanish textile companies, such as Marieta, Traficó de Modas,

Transstam and Nicky Bosch, have injected a new sense of humour and enthusiasm into furnishing fabrics. Like so many of the Spanish architects who put Barcelona on the map in the 1980s, Javier Mariscal's work bridges a number of disciplines, including furniture, ceramics and product design. But in Mariscal's case it is his training as a cartoonist that informs the rest of his work with comedy and confidence.

Mariscal's work is figurative and fun, and deals with familiar themes, such as animals, and the urban environment. His cartoonist's eye animates his subjects humorously: cats grin out from his fabrics, cockerels attempt to outstare one another, goggle-eyed fish swim in shoals; or a New York cityscape is given a smog effect with a warp-printed ikat. But above all, his work is interesting because it shows how mimicry and adaptation, which is the very stuff of decorative language, can themselves become creative acts, even when they are focused on the most familiar of themes. He quotes openly and therefore audaciously from both high and low cultures – William Morris, Mickey Mouse, Persian miniatures, cashmere patterns and 1950s graphics are reworked and 'updated' with disarming directness. His work is distinguished by an idiosyncratic, deceptively loose style which enables him to appropriate pattern from different sources. Many of the archive prints look stuffy and overworked in comparison.

Opposite
Left:
'Coches'
Screen-printed cotton
Silvia Gubern
Transtam, Spain, 1989

Right:
'Clorofila'
Screen-printed cotton
Silvia Gubern
Transtam, Spain, 1989

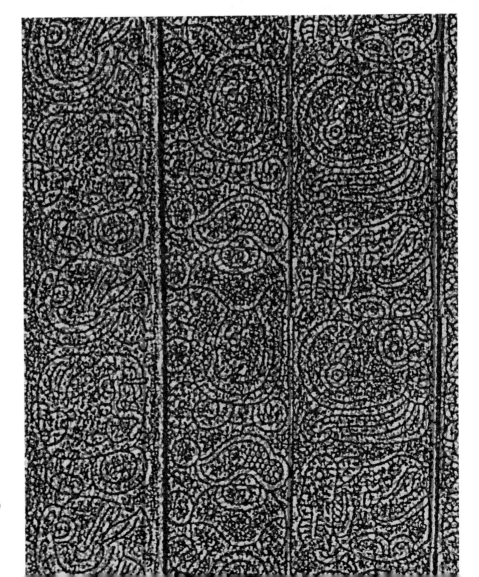

'Smaragd'
Screen-printed viscose
Maryan Klomp
Zeebra, Holland, 1988/89

Futuristic Fabrics: Transparent and Light-sensitive Surfaces

TRANSLUCENCE and iridescence are among the more modern concerns of aesthetics that express contemporary techniques now being explored by textile designers. They offer a means of 'dematerializing' materials into a play of light, reflections and transparency, which not only evokes a contemporary response to the intangibles of the computer but also enables fabrics to be designed in such a way that they 'react' to the increasingly sophisticated methods of manipulating light in an interior. Metallic pigments, light-sensitive pigments, new techniques of vacuum-bonding metals on to yarn or cloth, highly reflective polyester slit films and printed lacquers can all create fabrics that are 'sensitive' to changes in light frequency.

The decorative manipulation of light upon or through the fabric surface was the theme of an exhibition at the Cooper-Hewitt Museum in 1990 called 'Colour, Light, Surface'. As the exhibition's curator Milton Sonday pointed out, this is an area of research that fabric designers seem to have started to explore simultaneously all over the world.

One reason why some textile designers find working with computer-aided design frustrating is because of the way in which the electronic iridescence of the computer screen distorts colour relationships which seem disappointingly flat and dull when translated on to cloth. Transparency and iridescence are a means of recapturing the shimmer of suspended images on a hologram or on screen. Jack Lenor Larsen's gauze fabric 'Hologram Square' is self-explanatory. 'Scritto', a fabric from the Swiss design team at Création Baumann, uses contrasting high-gloss slit film and matt yarns in a design that refers to archaic calligraphy as well as to its present-day counterpart, on-screen text with its persistent glare.

The Scottish designer Stephen French is interested in exploring new applications for technical effects normally used at the bottom end of the market, and has created a series of fabrics that change colour as the viewer moves around the room. His 'Lenticular Screen Upholstery' fabric was made from an offset litho-printed fabric laminated with a fine plastic film embossed with lenses that refract different areas of pattern as the viewer shifts position. This technique is borrowed from 3D-animated postcards – the sort that have kitsch images of saints that raise their arms and eyes to heaven as you wiggle the card backwards and forwards. French has also explored the optical effects of working with holograms on curved surfaces – his holographic blinds transform light into dazzling bands of colour.

Synthetic fibres offer similar advantages to plastics – transparency combined with performance. They also offer means of controlling the flow of light: through a fabric, it is possible to project into a room decorative patterns of light and shadow.

The recent developments in 'devoré' techniques, which are now more suitable for large-scale production, have given a new lease of life to the lace curtain, a virtual anathema in Britain but popular both on the European continent and in America. 'Devoré', a word derived from the French verb meaning 'to devour', is a chemical preparation which can be printed and then baked at high temperature to 'burn out' patterns from a length of cloth, thereby creating a modern, cheaper and more adaptable alternative to lace. Used on a combination cloth – of cotton and polyester, for example – it can be used to remove selectively areas of cotton, leaving a translucent pattern of polyester net.

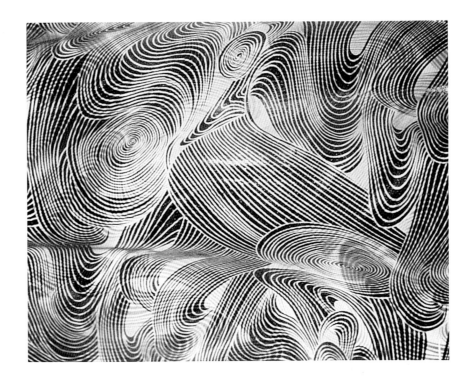

'Melting Off'
Polyester yarns coated in
 metal devoré pattern
Junichi Arai
Nuno Co., Japan, 1989/90

Using this technique, it is possible to create a wide variety of effects. In their design 'Oggi', the German company Intair has used devoré to burn out large areas of cloth in the shape of brushstrokes through which one can catch glimpses of the world outside. Junichi Arai's beautiful design 'Melting Off' uses a variation of this technique to etch a swirling pattern in a titanium-bonded fabric that recreates both the translucence and play of light upon the surface of running water.

Colour printed on fine fabrics can also be used to project colour into a room, much in the manner of a stained-glass window. Sally Greaves Lord's silk banners are concise essays in colour, tone and light. Greaves Lord's palette is based on a variation between black and white achieved by the carefully timed chemical reaction between black procion dye and bleach. Left for a couple of minutes the dye produces a powder blue; left a little longer it gives a rich gold. These banners work well against a wall, but they are best placed in front of light so that they project faintly tinted geometric patterns on to the floor.

Another method of manipulating the light on cloth is by adding to, rather than subtracting from, the fabric surface. Acids applied to cloth can be used to elongate fibres, thereby achieving blistered and puckered surfaces known as 'crêpe plissé'. The American designer and manufacturer Gretchen Bellinger, who was one of the first designers to introduce a range of fabrics that not only used dimensionality but catered to the performance and fire-security standards of the contract market produces similar results with double-woven fabrics, whilst a fabric by Création Baumann uses machine-stitching to achieve a honeycomb effect.

Western Germany and Switzerland currently lead the rest of Europe in terms of technically innovatory fabrics for the interior market. In Switzerland, companies such as Création Baumann, Christian Fischbacher and Zumsteg are some of the most technologically advanced in Europe. Création Baumann is celebrated for supplying precise fabric solutions to the contract market. The

Baumann factory is a precise and economic mechanism for textile production which offers a vision of the factory of the future. The gleaming white modernist building set in a green park houses facilities for yarn spinning, weaving, dyeing and printing, as well as design studios and offices. The factory is also energy efficient. The hot water used for dyeing also heats the building before it is piped to a refining plant. There it is filtered of harmful chemical residues before it re-enters the system.

Western Germany is the greatest consumer and producer of textiles in Europe. Its strong modernist traditions, combined with a highly affluent market, have placed it at the forefront of the development of a new, hybrid aesthetic of contemporary luxury. This aesthetic developed with the boom in the hotel industry during the 1980s but went on to become popular with the domestic market as well. It is characterized by its rich vocabulary of textile techniques which are layered or superimposed to create opulent effects. Renata Weisz is an in-house designer for one of the leading fabric houses in Germany called Zimmer und Rohde. It has brought out a number of different designs which overlay patterned woven fabrics with printed designs.

The hospitality market – hotels and restaurants – also prompted a revival in complex jacquard-woven fabrics. It is fairly well known that the jacquard pattern-making device, based on a sequence of punched cards, was the forerunner of the British punch-card tabulator of the 1930s which led, in turn, to the development of the first electronic computer. All are operated by a system of binary, yes/no logic. Surprisingly it was not until the mid-1980s that a fully automated jacquard system was first brought out by the British company Bonas, a system which was perfected in 1987. The computerization of jacquard weaving has meant that the richness of colour and pattern characteristic of woven jacquard fabrics are for the first time available at speed. By linking a computerized – or automated – jacquard loom to a CAD (computer-aided design) system with a scanning device, a photograph can be translated from paper to digital information on a floppy disk to woven fabric in a matter of hours.

The automation of the jacquard weaving process has brought it into line with the accelerations in the rest of weaving production. Yarns can be spun twenty times faster now, shuttleless looms can weave at sixty times the speed. The speed and flexibility of automated jacquard weaving means that it is fast becoming an area of experimental design. Formerly the prohibitive costs and time involved in setting up a jacquard loom meant that jacquard patterns tended to be conservative and dull.

The designs by the experimental Japanese firm Nuno are an illustration of the way in which the intangible technologies of CAD linked to a CAM system can be used in an innovatory way. Nuno is both a shop as well as a group of skilled designers, managed by the enterprising designer Reiko Sudo. Junichi Arai joined Reiko Sudo in 1987, when he decided to transfer the focus of his attention from fashion to furnishing fabrics. Both Arai and Reiko Sudo have applied his pioneering experiments in combination jacquard to create furnishing fabrics that achieve the sensuality of hand-crafted fabrics. Arai is both a futurist and a historicist; his work is as much inspired by Peruvian textile masterpieces as by new textile manufacturing technologies. Nuno's fabrics provide one of the most significant pointers yet towards the future: the gradual fusion of history, craft, diverse cultural influences and new textile and digital technologies that indicate that design has become the true successor of the traditional crafts.

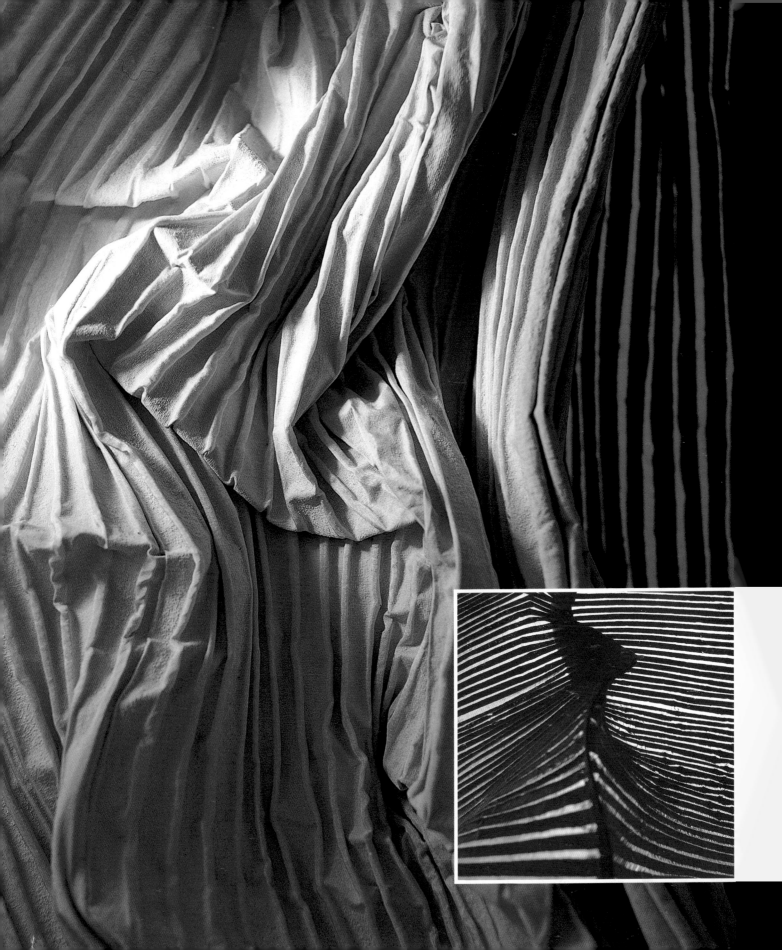

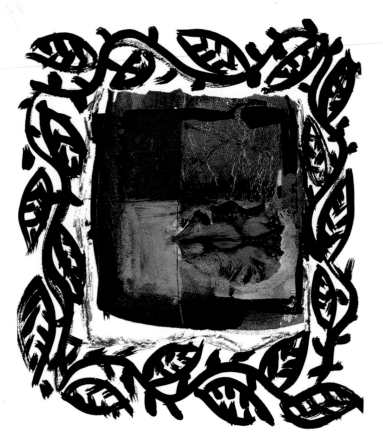
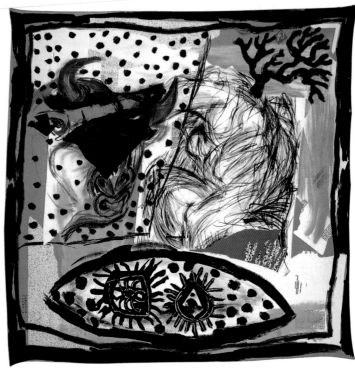
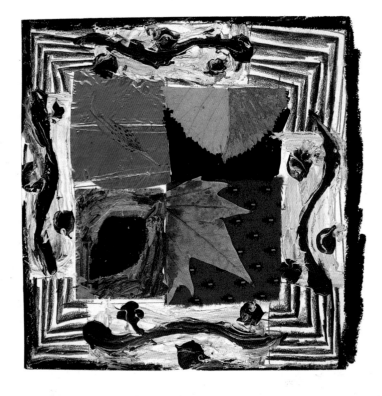
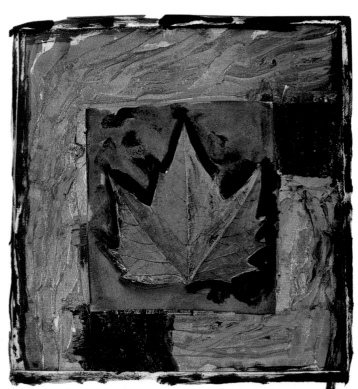

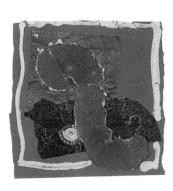

3, 5–7
  Preparatory studies for
4 Heat-transfer printed
   'Minotaur' scarf
   Sylvie Skinazi for
      Christian Lacroix Prêt-
      a-Porter
   France 1988/9

8 Heat-transfer printed
   lycra swimsuit
   Sylvie Skinazi for
      Christian Lacroix
   France, 1988

Page 41:
1,2 Heat-moulded fabrics
    Rubber printed and
       baked on silk
    and (inset)
    Rubber printed on
       cotton and chiffon
    Nigel Atkinson
    UK, 1989/90

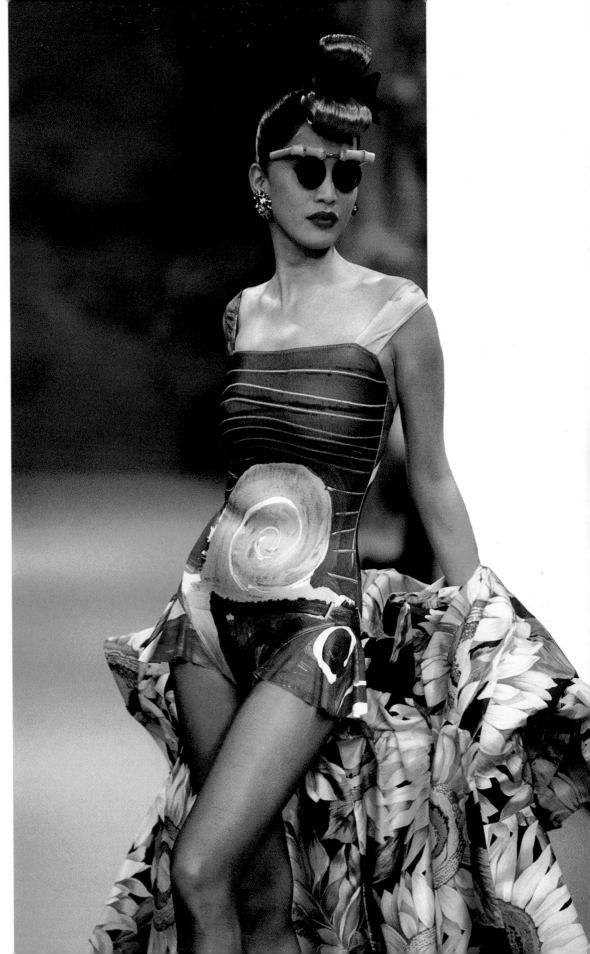

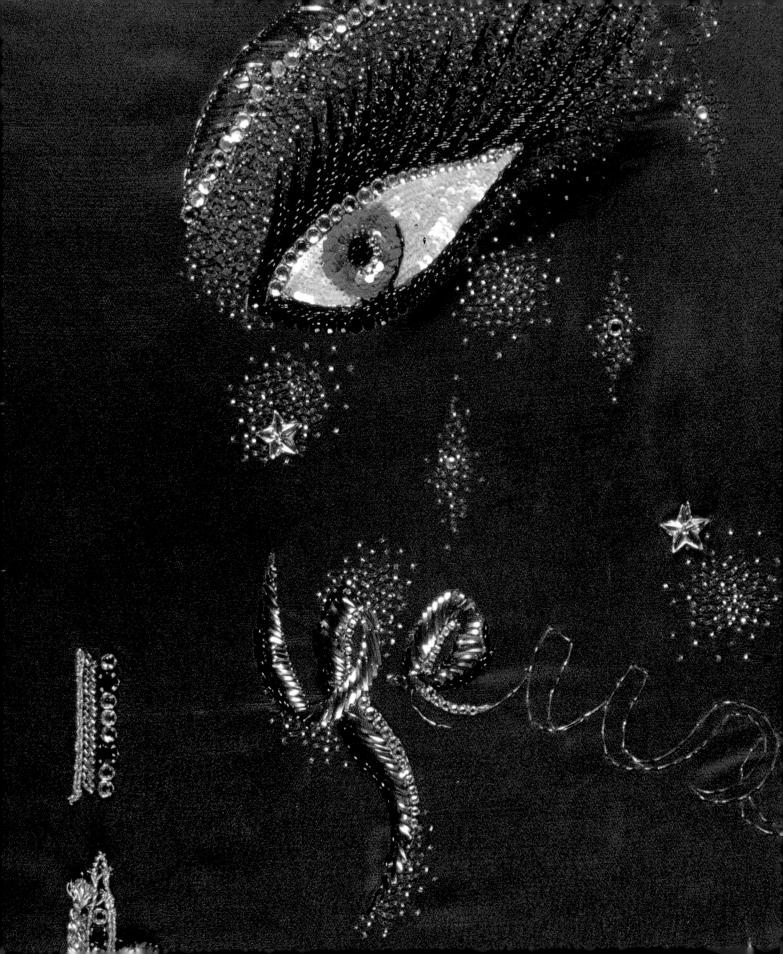

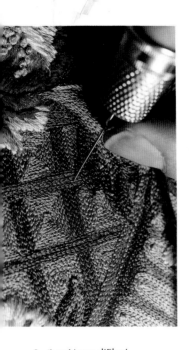

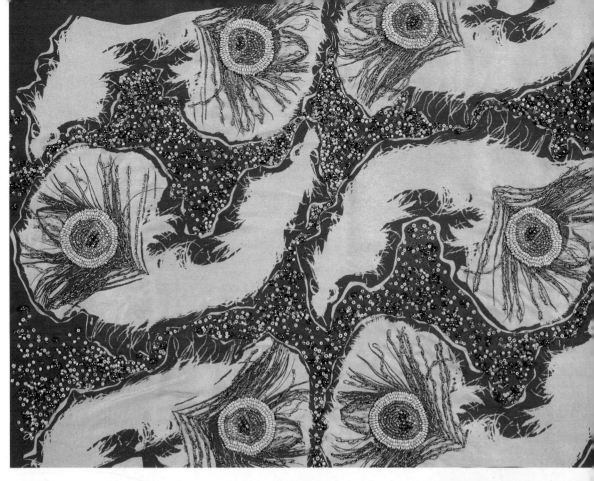

9 'Les Yeux d'Elsa'
 Embroidery
 Lesage S.A. for Yves
  Saint Laurent
 France, 1980/1

10 Embroidery
 Lesage S.A.
 France, 1990

11 Hand-embellished,
  screen printed crêpe-
  de-chine
 Luiven Rivas Sanchez
 UK, 1990

12 'Cosmic Cows'
 Hand-embellished
  rayon jersey
 Freddie Robbins
 UK, 1990

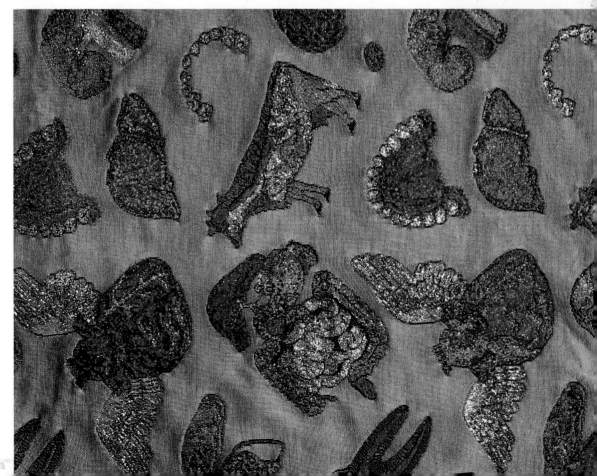

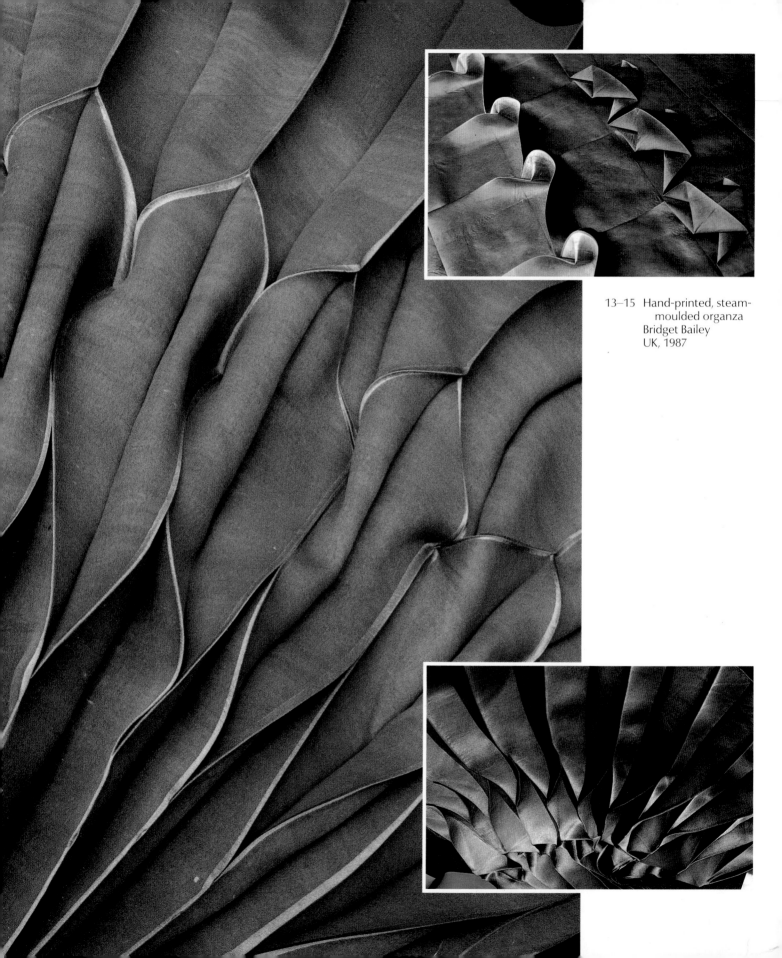

13–15 Hand-printed, steam-
moulded organza
Bridget Bailey
UK, 1987

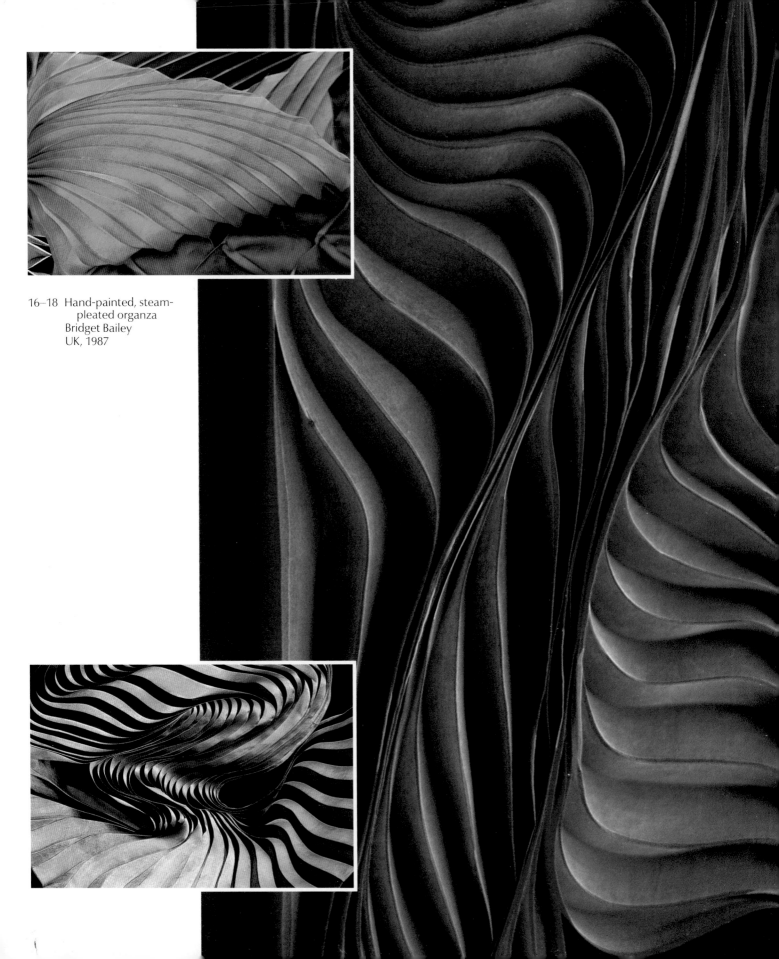

16–18 Hand-painted, steam-
pleated organza
Bridget Bailey
UK, 1987

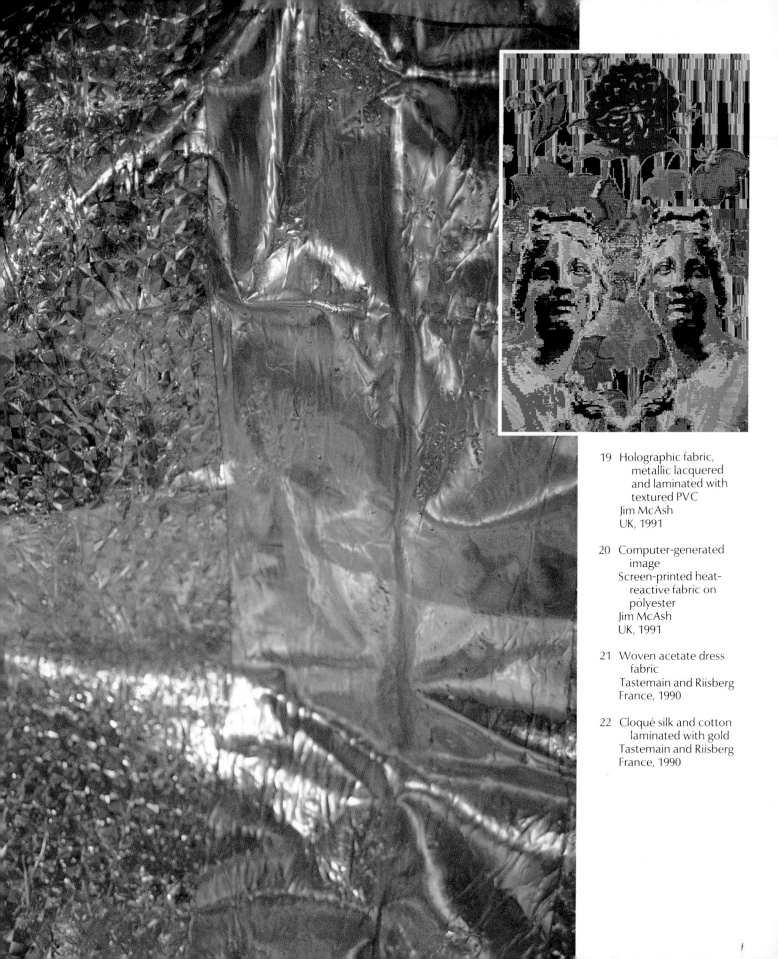

19 Holographic fabric,
    metallic lacquered
    and laminated with
    textured PVC
    Jim McAsh
    UK, 1991

20 Computer-generated
    image
    Screen-printed heat-
    reactive fabric on
    polyester
    Jim McAsh
    UK, 1991

21 Woven acetate dress
    fabric
    Tastemain and Riisberg
    France, 1990

22 Cloqué silk and cotton
    laminated with gold
    Tastemain and Riisberg
    France, 1990

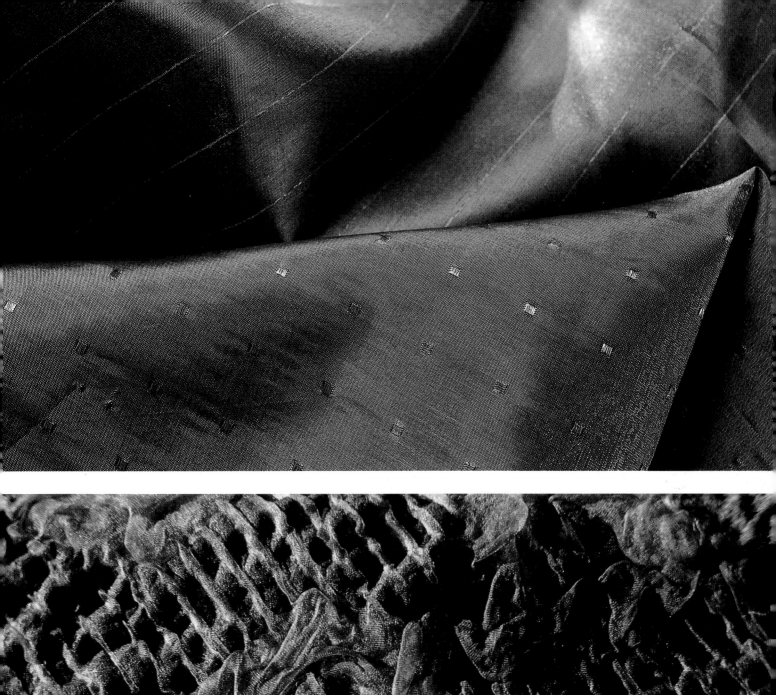
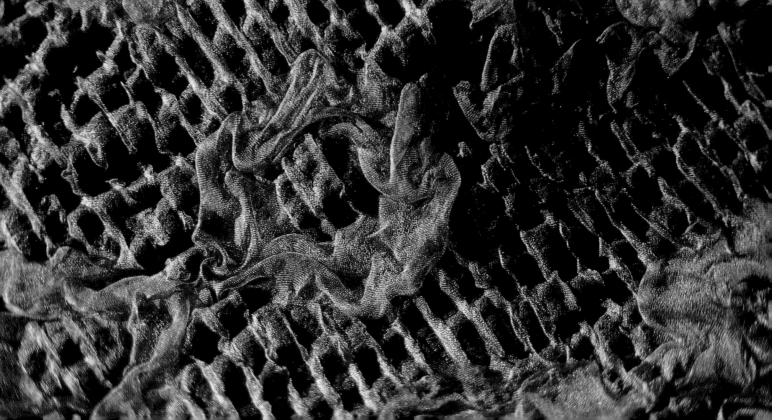

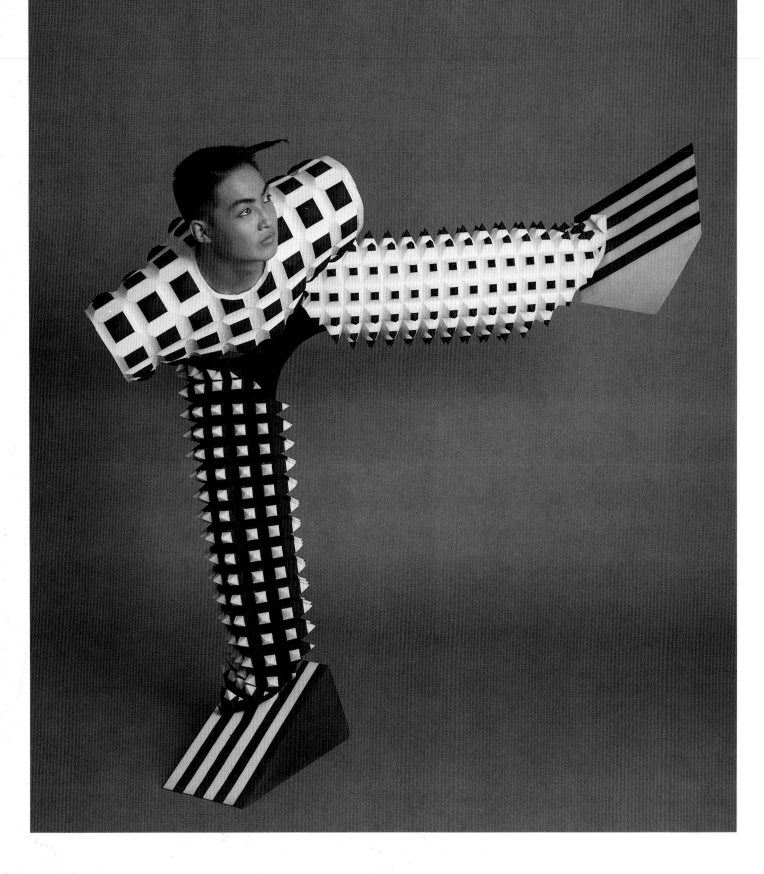

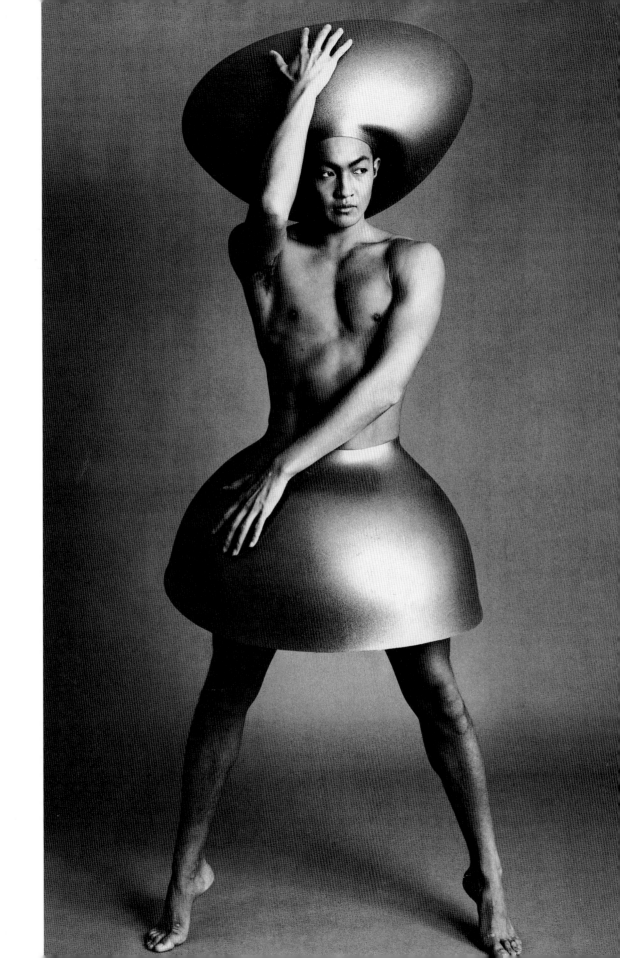

23 'Skater'
   Closed cell foam
   Laminated, profiling
      vacuum moulding
   Maria Blaisse Flexible
      Design
   Holland, 1990

24 'Spheres'
   Flexible foam
   Maria Blaisse Flexible
      Design
   Holland, 1989

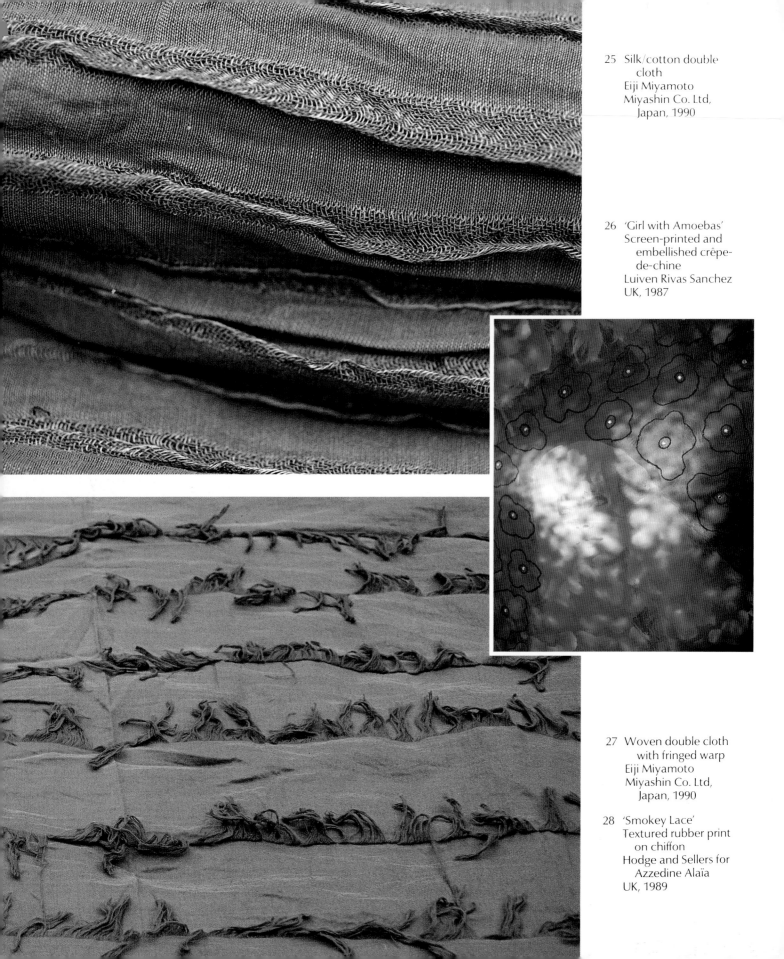

25 Silk/cotton double
 cloth
 Eiji Miyamoto
 Miyashin Co. Ltd,
 Japan, 1990

26 'Girl with Amoebas'
 Screen-printed and
 embellished crêpe-
 de-chine
 Luiven Rivas Sanchez
 UK, 1987

27 Woven double cloth
 with fringed warp
 Eiji Miyamoto
 Miyashin Co. Ltd,
 Japan, 1990

28 'Smokey Lace'
 Textured rubber print
 on chiffon
 Hodge and Sellers for
 Azzedine Alaïa
 UK, 1989

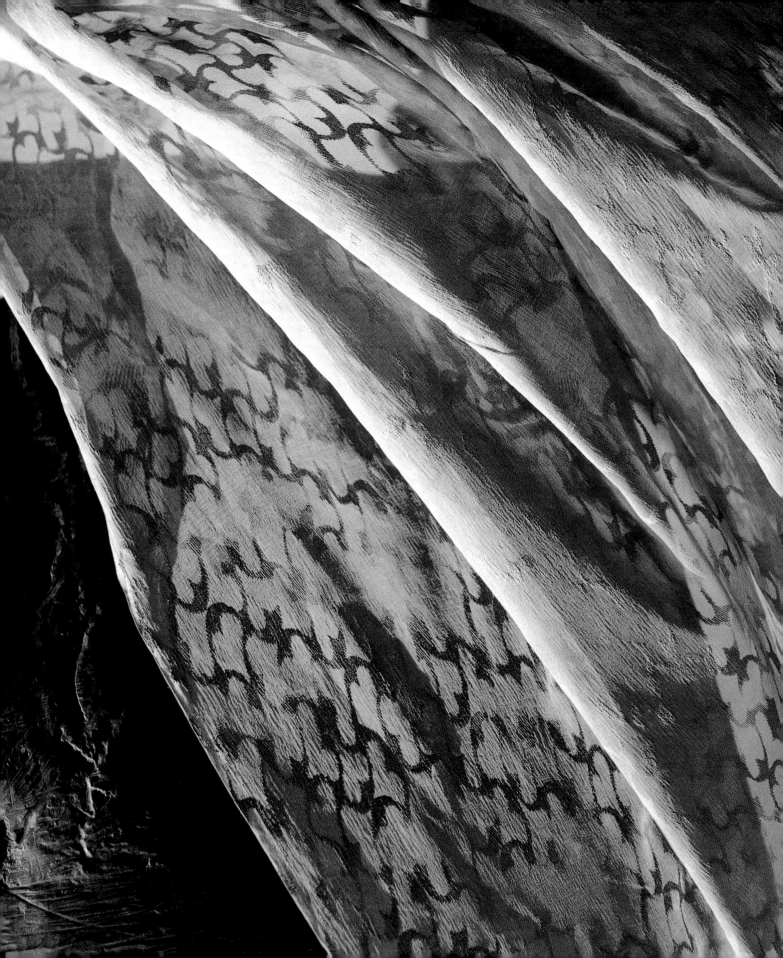

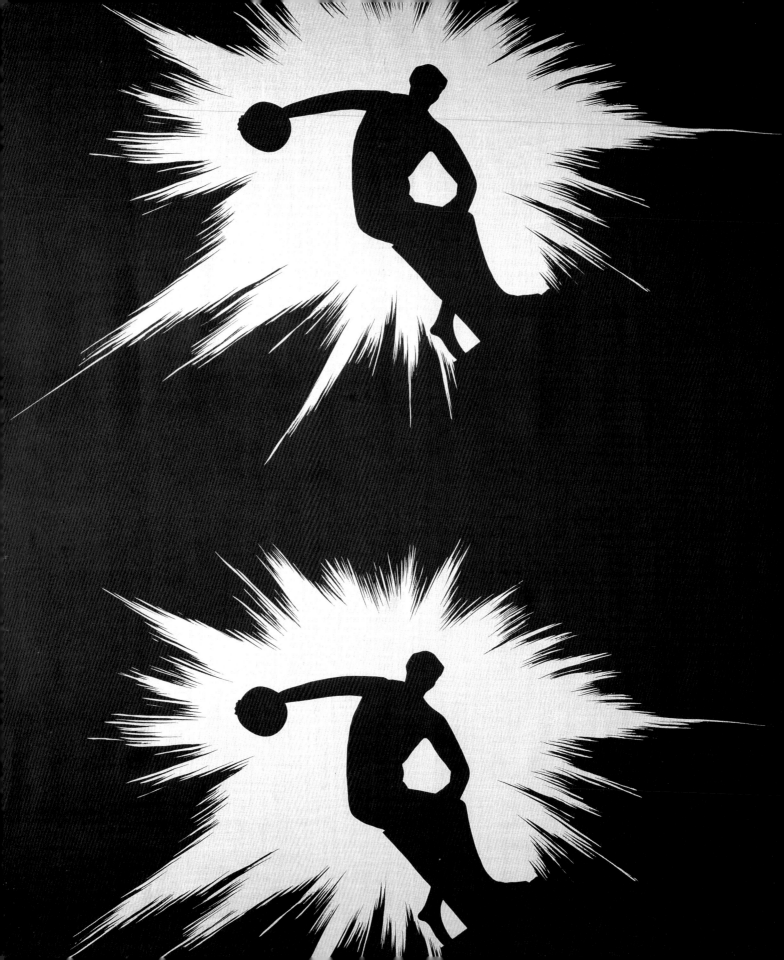

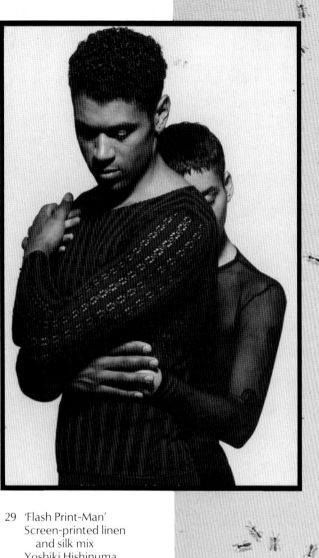

29 'Flash Print-Man'
Screen-printed linen
and silk mix
Yoshiki Hishinuma
Hishinuma Institute,
Japan, 1989

30 'Rayon stripe top'
'Swirl mesh top'
Do Modo, 1990

31 'Ant Fabric'
Screen-printed cotton
Karen Petrossian for
Claude Montana
France, 1990

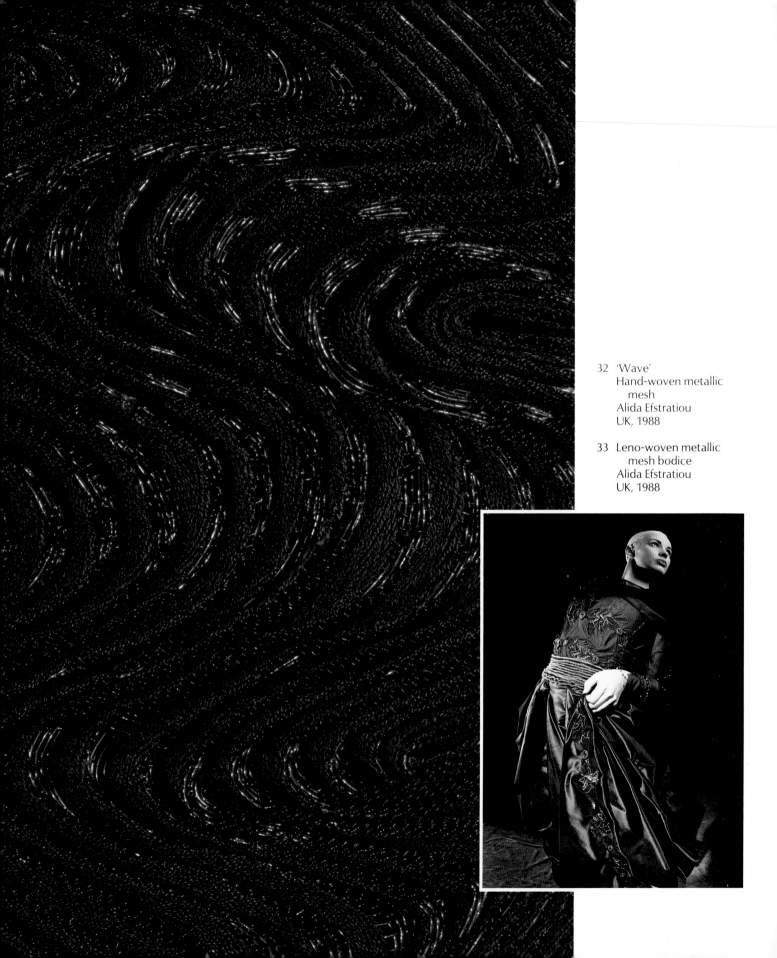

32 'Wave'
    Hand-woven metallic
    mesh
    Alida Efstratiou
    UK, 1988

33 Leno-woven metallic
    mesh bodice
    Alida Efstratiou
    UK, 1988

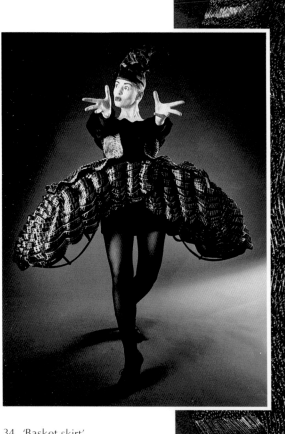

34 'Basket skirt'
Metallic mesh
Alida Efstratiou
UK, 1988

35 'Relief'
Metallic woven fabric
Alida Efstratiou
UK, 1988

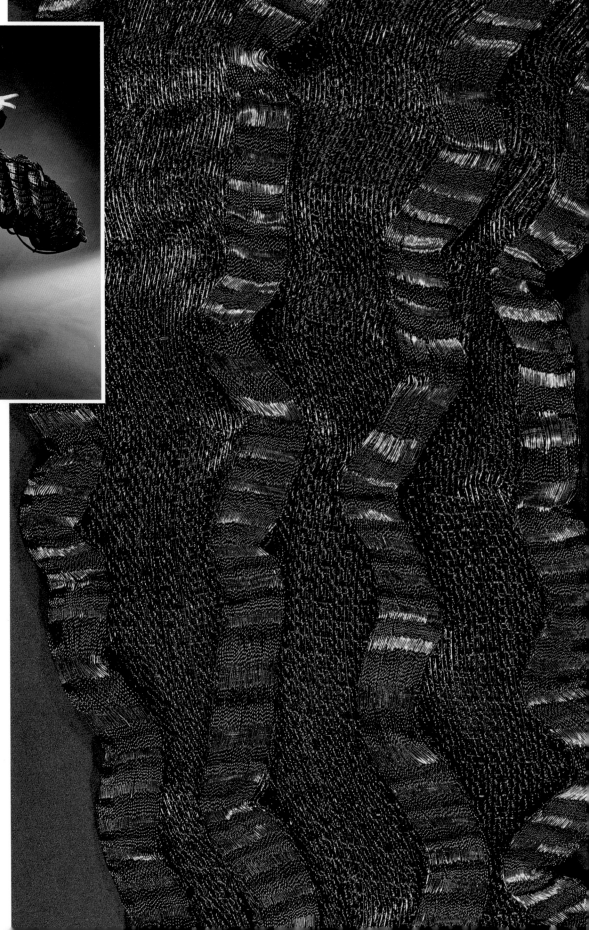

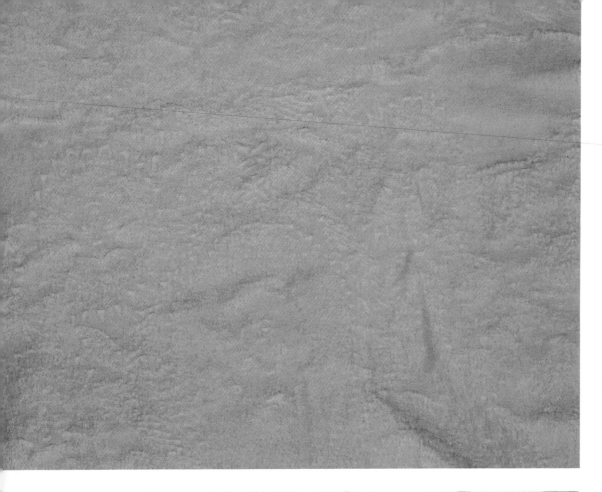

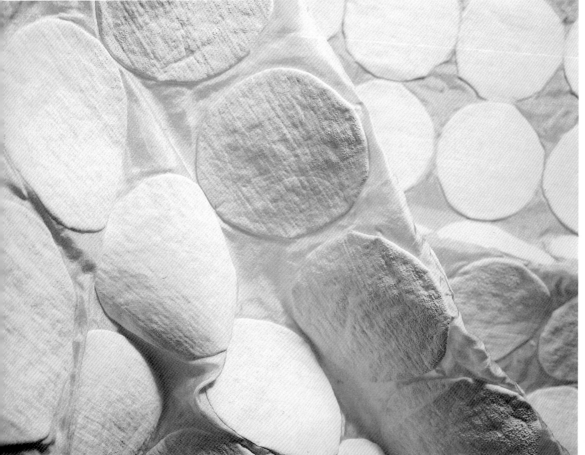

36 'Footprints in the sand'
    Double-knit core-spun
      lycra wool and cotton
      yarn
    Rosemary Moore
    Nittobo Seki,
      Japan, 1989

37 Rubber printed on
      cotton
    Nigel Atkinson
    UK, 1989

38 Scarf
    Synthetics and cotton
    Makiko Minagawa
    Miyake Design Studio,
      Japan, 1990

39 Scarf
    Spaced warp, linen
      and silk
    Makiko Minagawa
    Miyake Design Studio,
      Japan, 1990

40 'Hoola Hoop'
    Cotton double cloth
    Nuno Co., Japan, 1990

41 Asphalt pattern scarf
    Cotton jacquard
      double-cloth
    Reiko Sudo
    Nuno Co., Japan, 1990

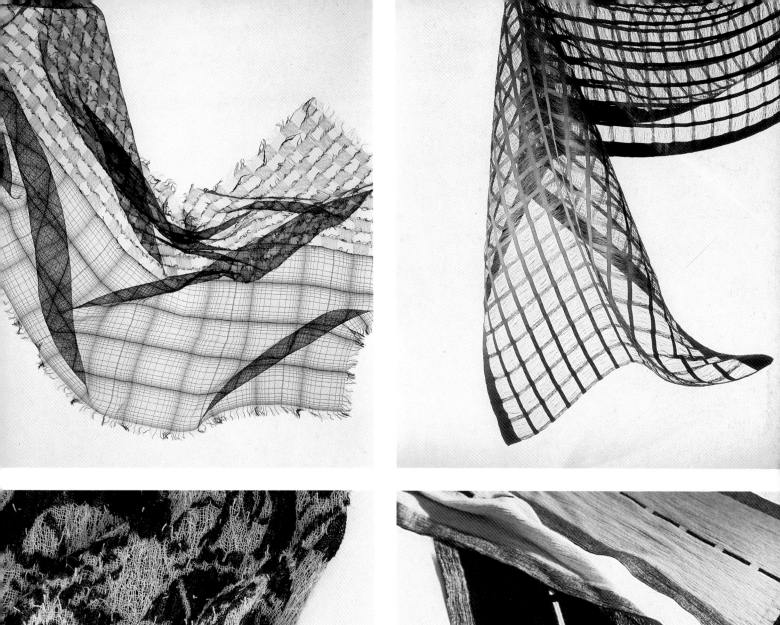

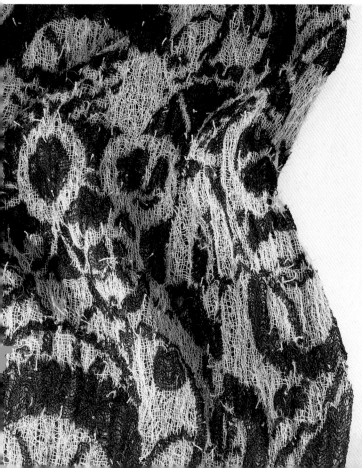

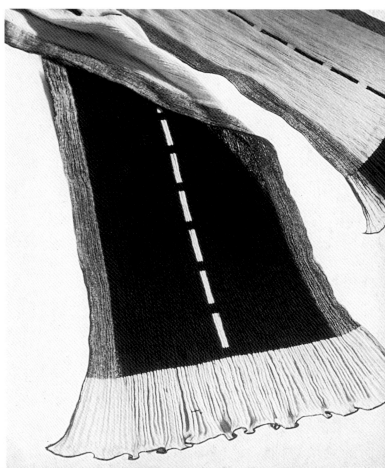

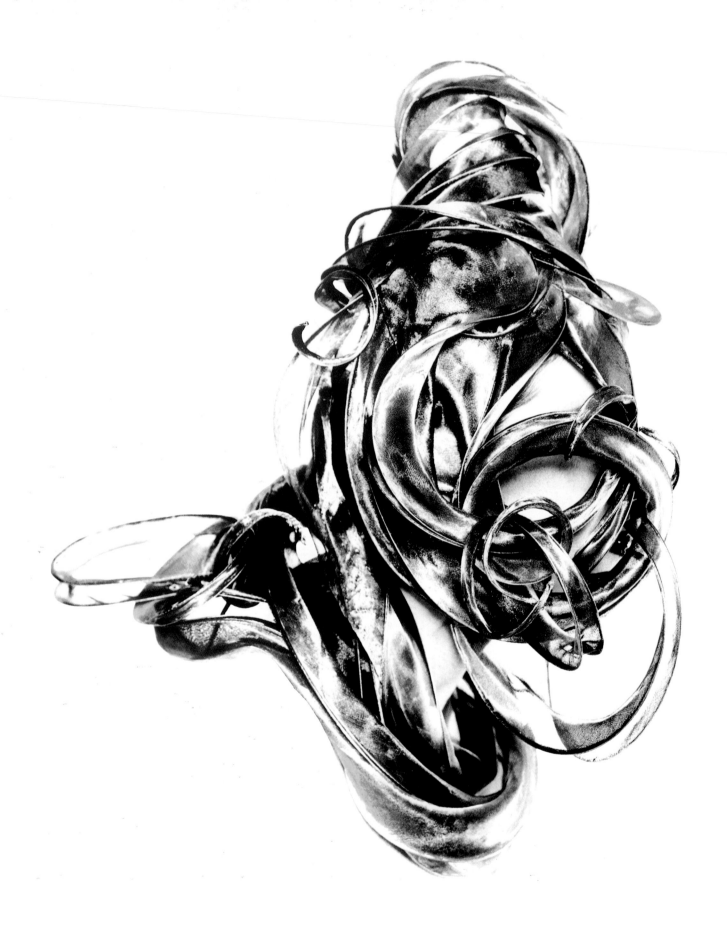

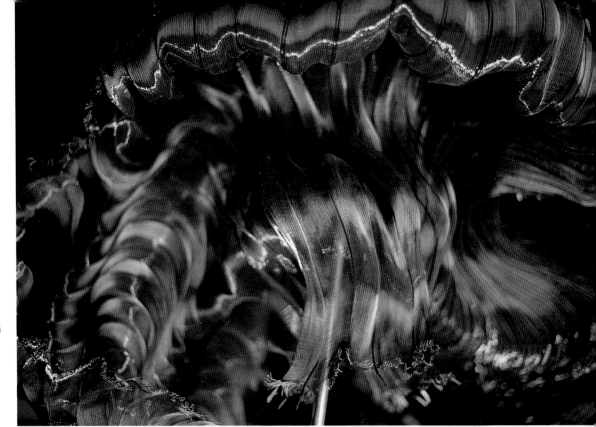

42 'The Medusa Hat'
Coiled metallic organza
Philip Treacy
Eire, 1990

43, 44 Hand-woven metallic
mesh
Alida Efstratiou
UK, 1990

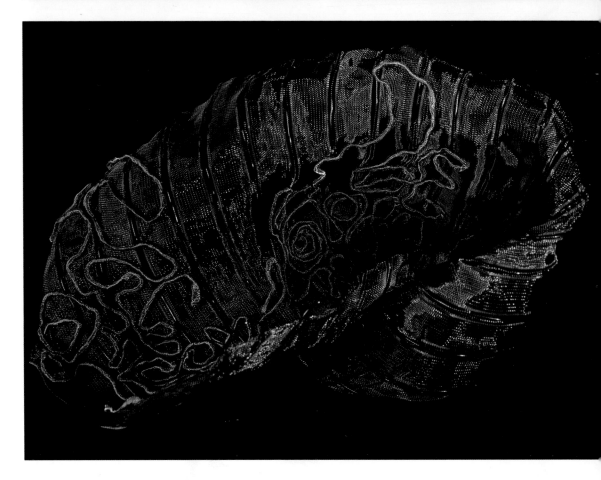

45 Speed-skater skinsuit
    Lycra/nylon mix
    Denni Vee Sports-
      clothing, UK, 1990

46 Rock-climbing tights
    Lycra
    Troll, UK, 1990/91
    Surfing top
    Neoprene and lycra
    O'Neill, UK, 1990/1

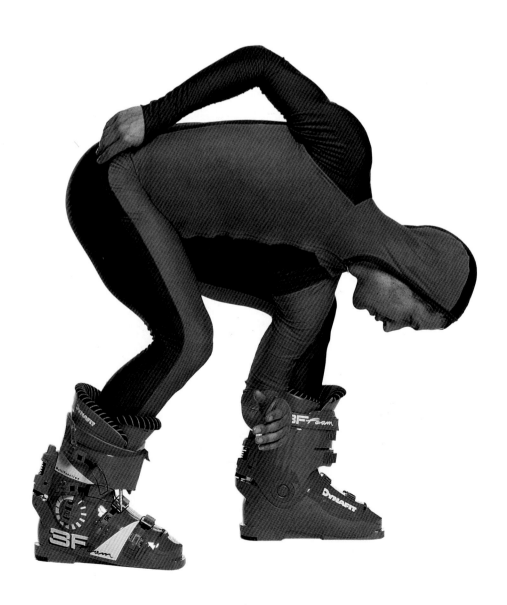

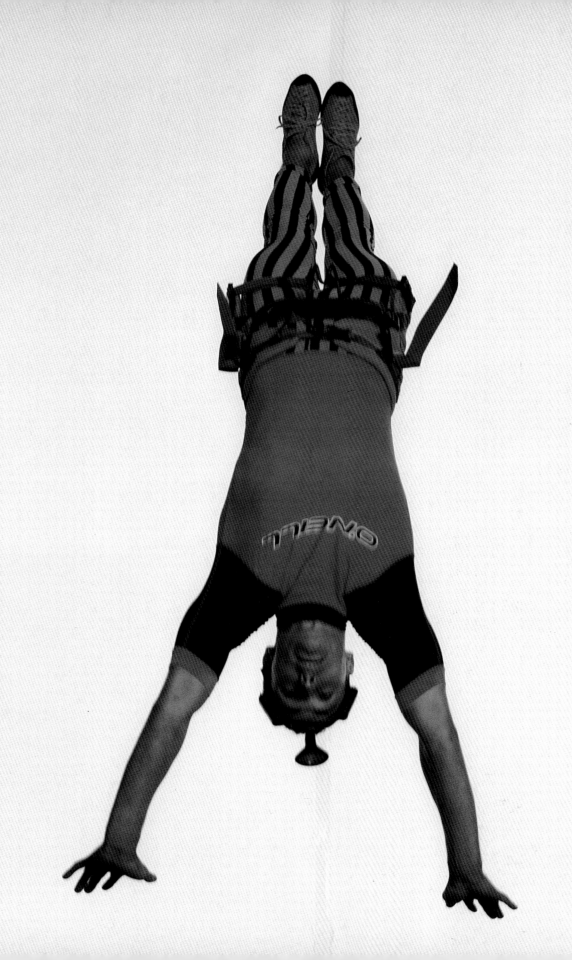

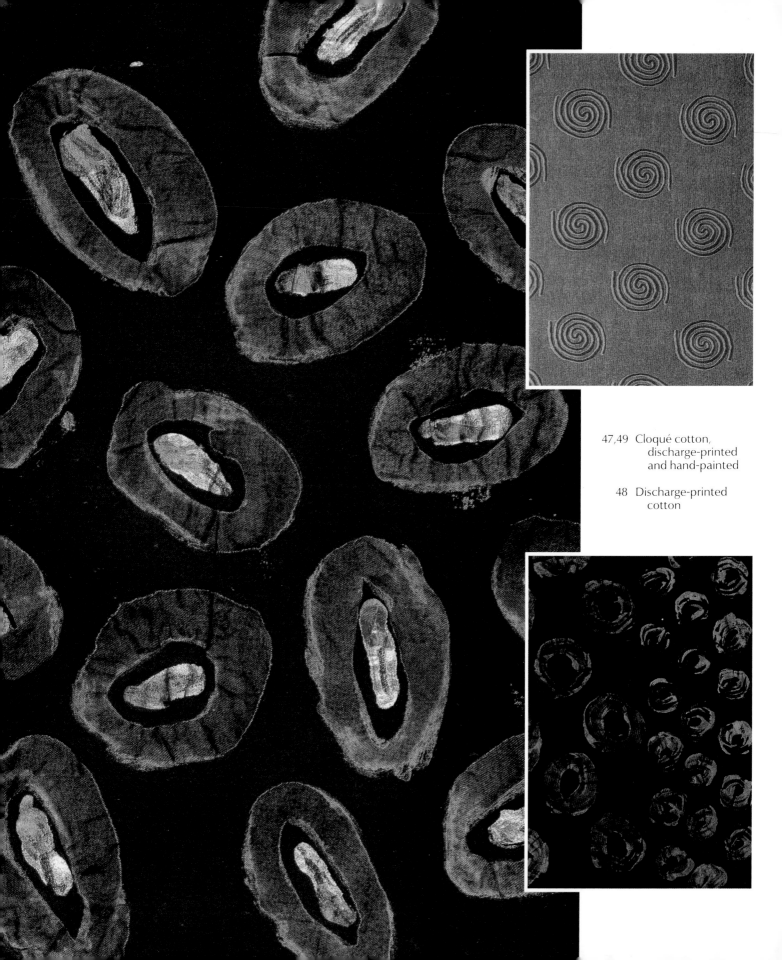

47,49 Cloqué cotton,
discharge-printed
and hand-painted

48 Discharge-printed
cotton

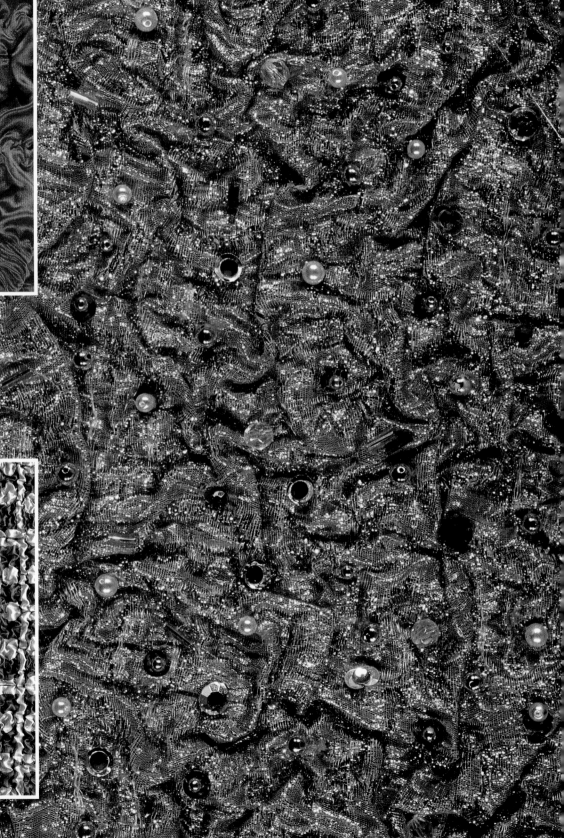

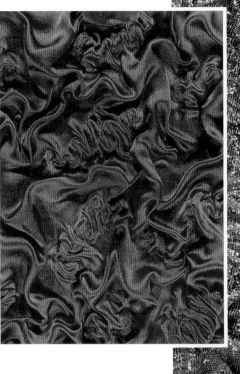

50,51 Hand-painted silk
laminated on to lycra

52 Printed cotton glued on
to lycra

All one-offs by Helle Abild
Denmark, 1990

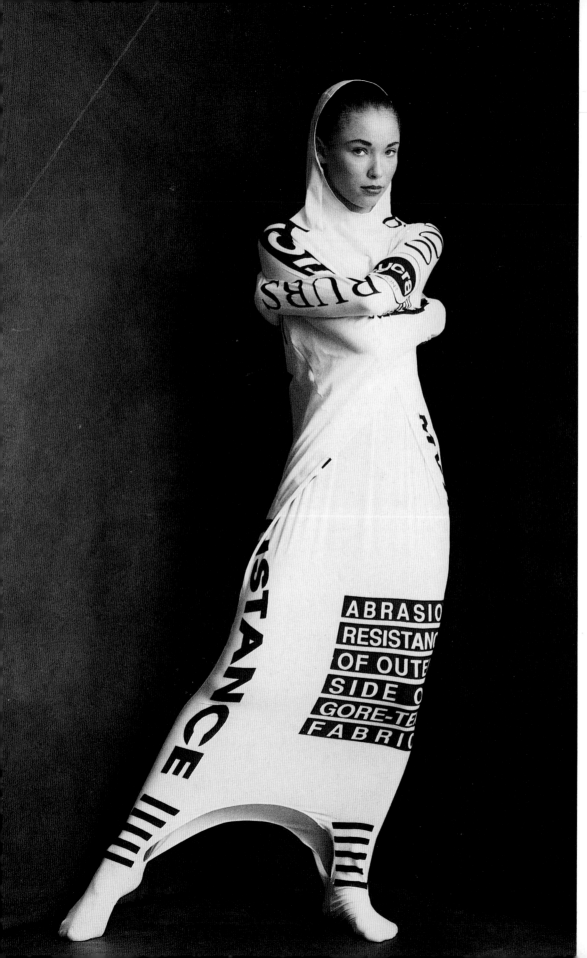

53 'Higher Graphics'
Screen-printed lycra
and chiffon mix
Georgina Godley
UK, 1990

54 'Clashing Cymbols'
Chiffon silk and lycra
mix, embellished with
neoprene rubber,
embroidery and
laminated Gore-tex
From the Sport '90
Collection
Georgina Godley
UK, 1990

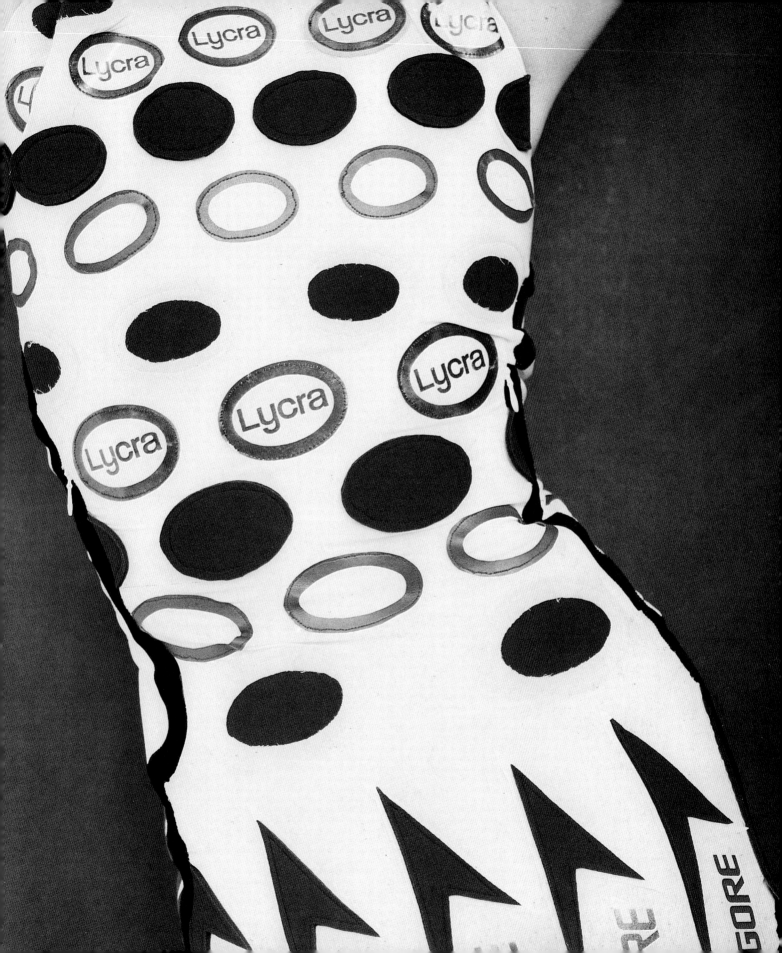

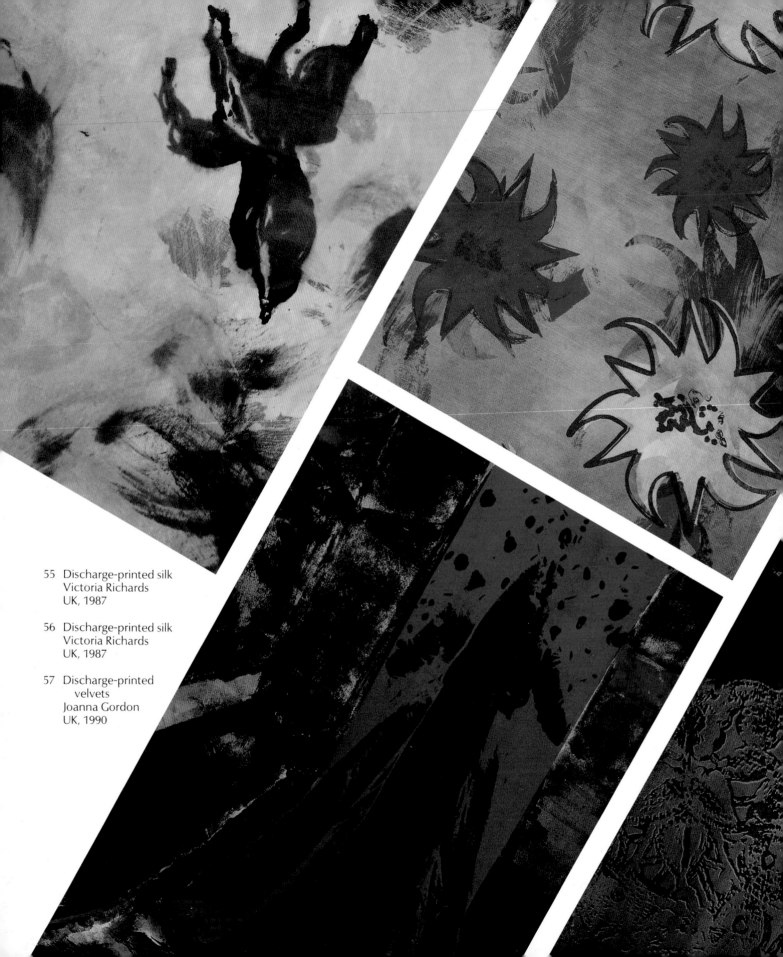

55 Discharge-printed silk
Victoria Richards
UK, 1987

56 Discharge-printed silk
Victoria Richards
UK, 1987

57 Discharge-printed
velvets
Joanna Gordon
UK, 1990

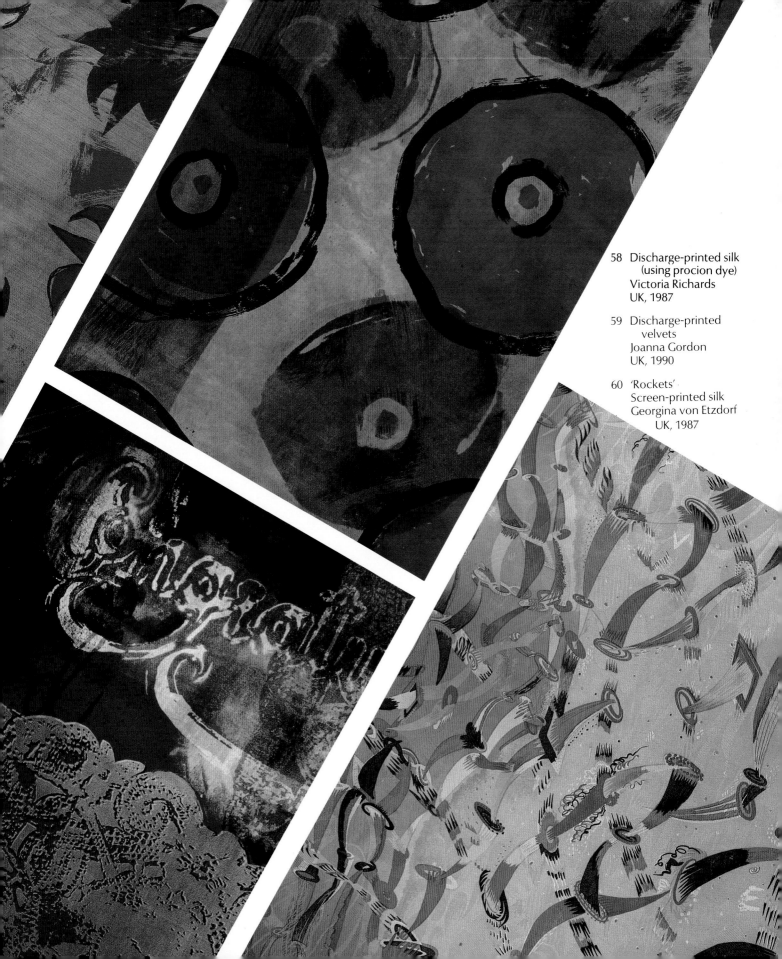

58 Discharge-printed silk
(using procion dye)
Victoria Richards
UK, 1987

59 Discharge-printed
velvets
Joanna Gordon
UK, 1990

60 'Rockets'
Screen-printed silk
Georgina von Etzdorf
UK, 1987

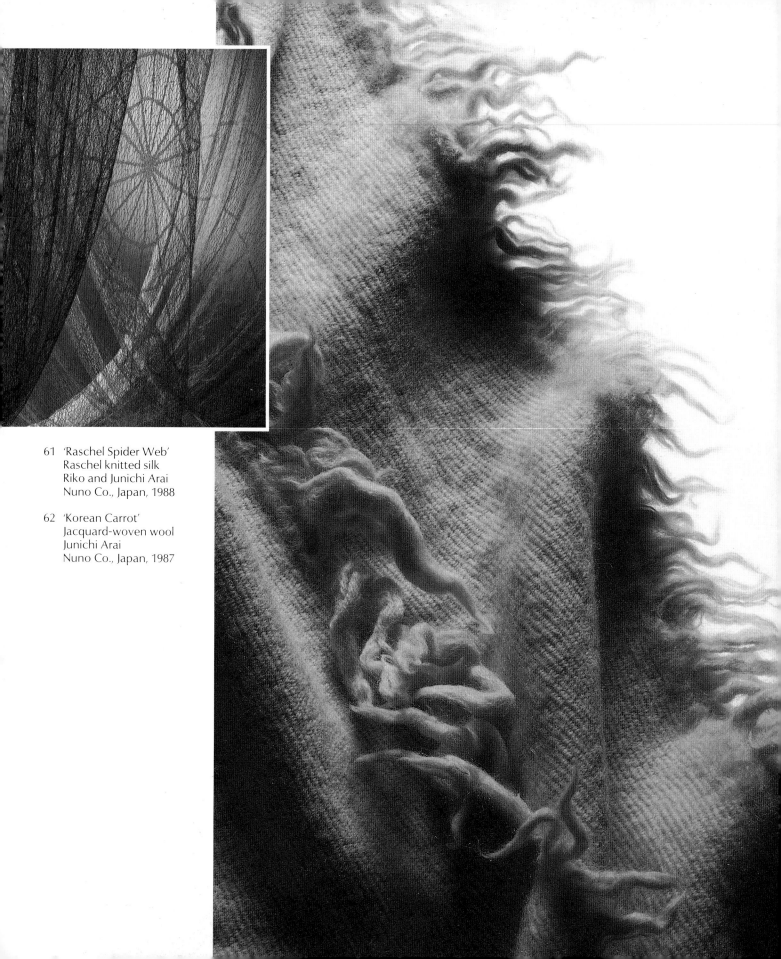

61 'Raschel Spider Web'
   Raschel knitted silk
   Riko and Junichi Arai
   Nuno Co., Japan, 1988

62 'Korean Carrot'
   Jacquard-woven wool
   Junichi Arai
   Nuno Co., Japan, 1987

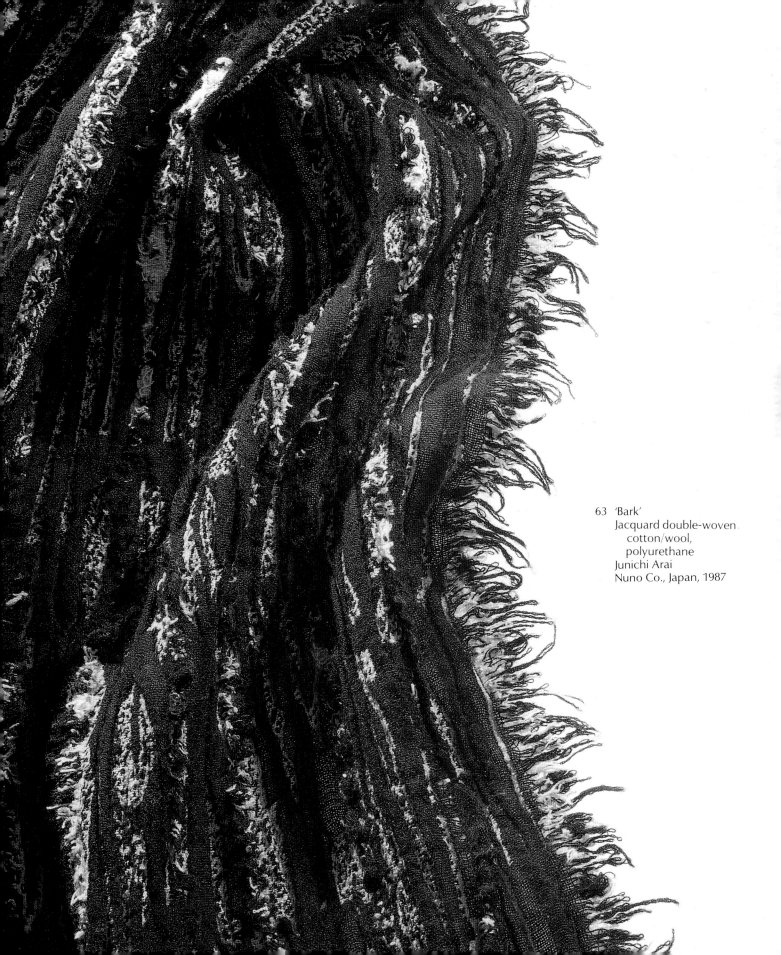

63 'Bark'
    Jacquard double-woven
      cotton/wool,
      polyurethane
    Junichi Arai
    Nuno Co., Japan, 1987

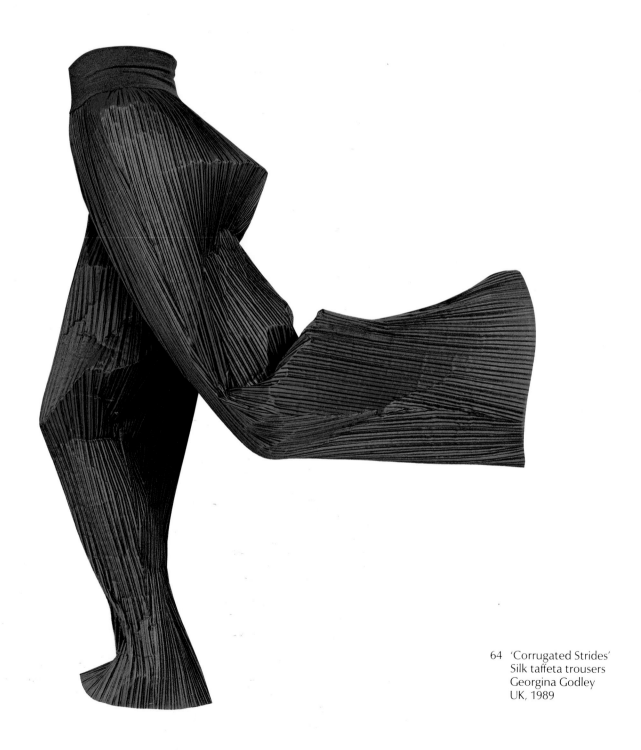

64 'Corrugated Strides'
Silk taffeta trousers
Georgina Godley
UK, 1989

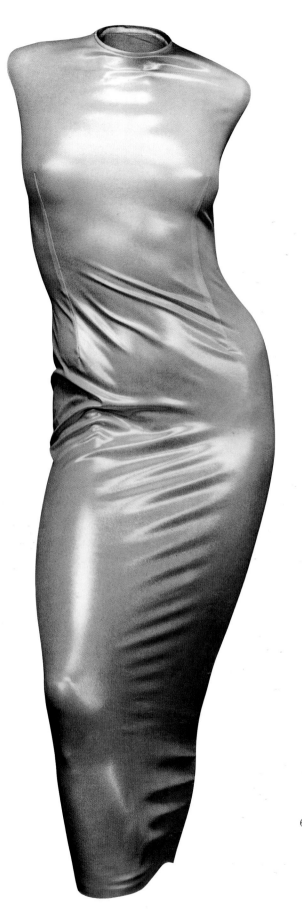

65 Dress
Plastic-coated polyester
Vivienne Westwood
UK, Spring/Summer 1988

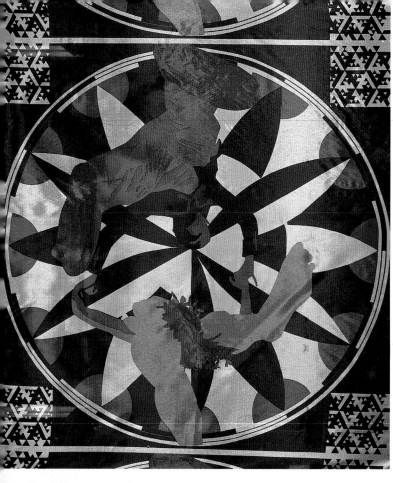

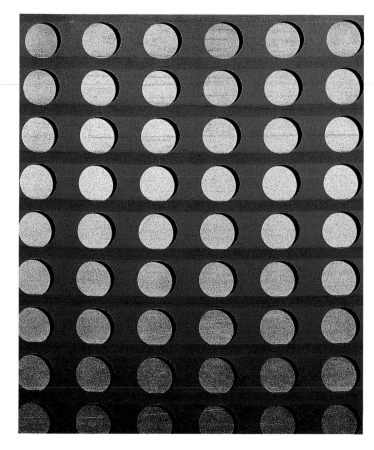

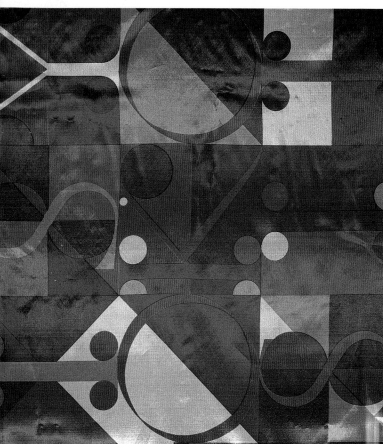

66 'Sorceress'
    95% rayon, 5% silk
    Yoshiki Hishinuma
    Hishinuma Institute,
    Japan, 1986/7

67 'Moon'
    Screen-printed
        polyester
    Yoshiki Hishinuma
    Hishinuma Institute,
    Japan, 1990

68 'Alphabet Print'
    Screen-printed
        polyester
    Yoshiki Hishinuma
    Hishinuma Institute,
    Japan, 1990

69 'Arabic Calligraphy'
    Screen-printed cotton

70 'Motifs Mosaic'
    Screen-printed fabric
    for Trend Union

71 'Environment'
    Fabric hanging

72 'Amphibians'
    Screen-printed cotton
    for Agnès B.

    All by Patrick Pinon
    France, 1988

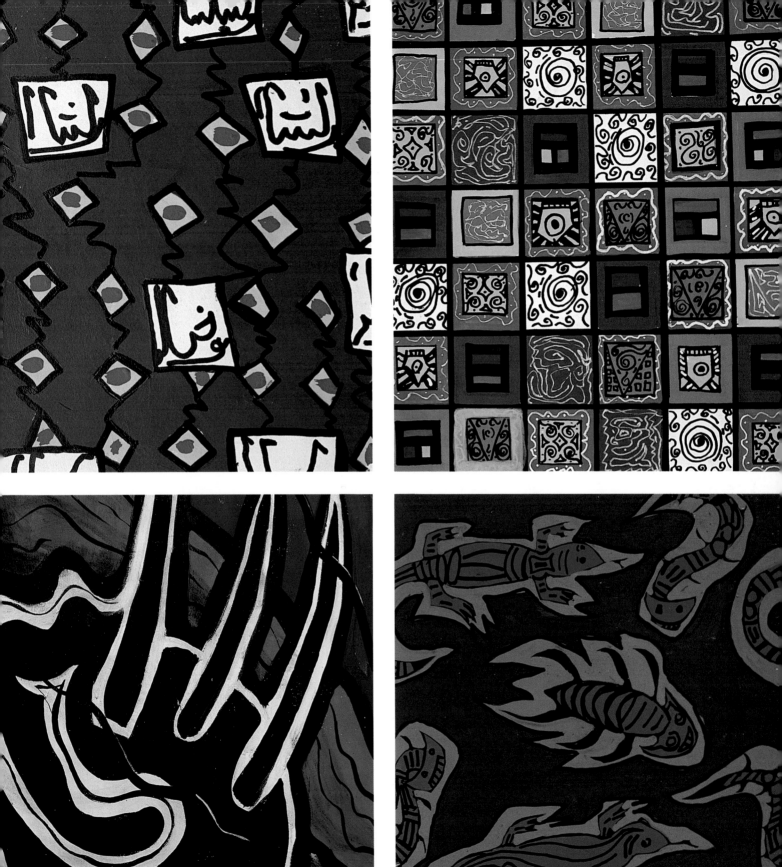

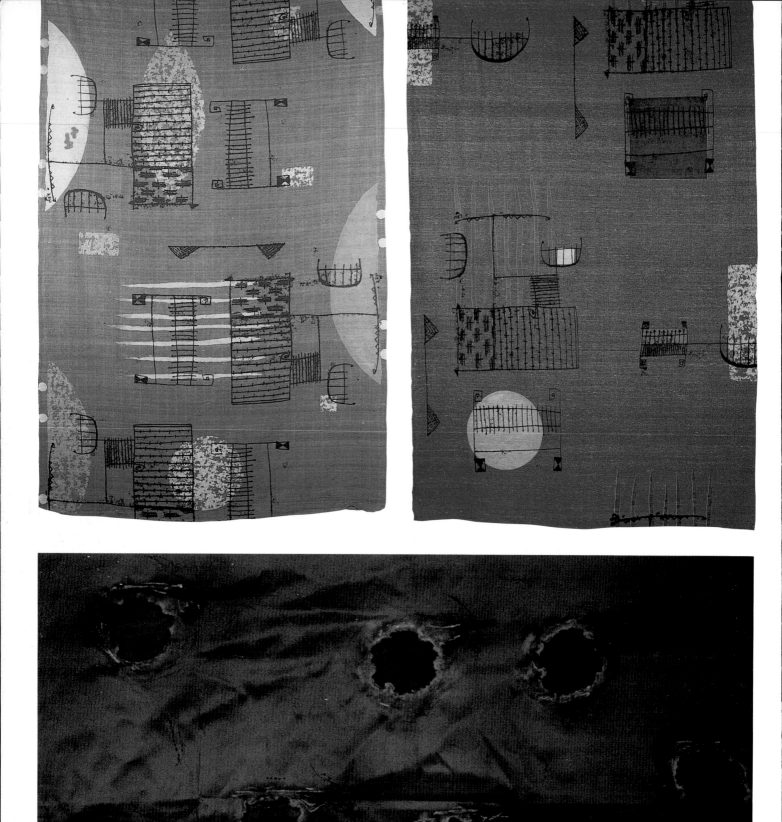

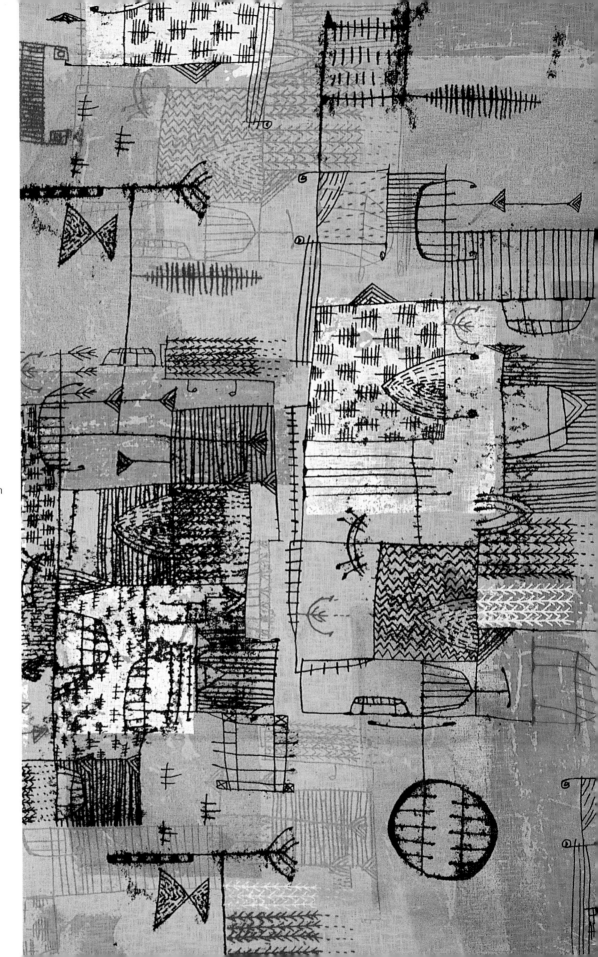

73,74,76 Wall hangings
          Screen-printed cotton
          and silk
          Jasia Szerszynska
          UK, 1988

     75 'Tissus Devorés'
          Hand-painted and
          devoré-printed
          fabric
          Eliakim, France, 1990

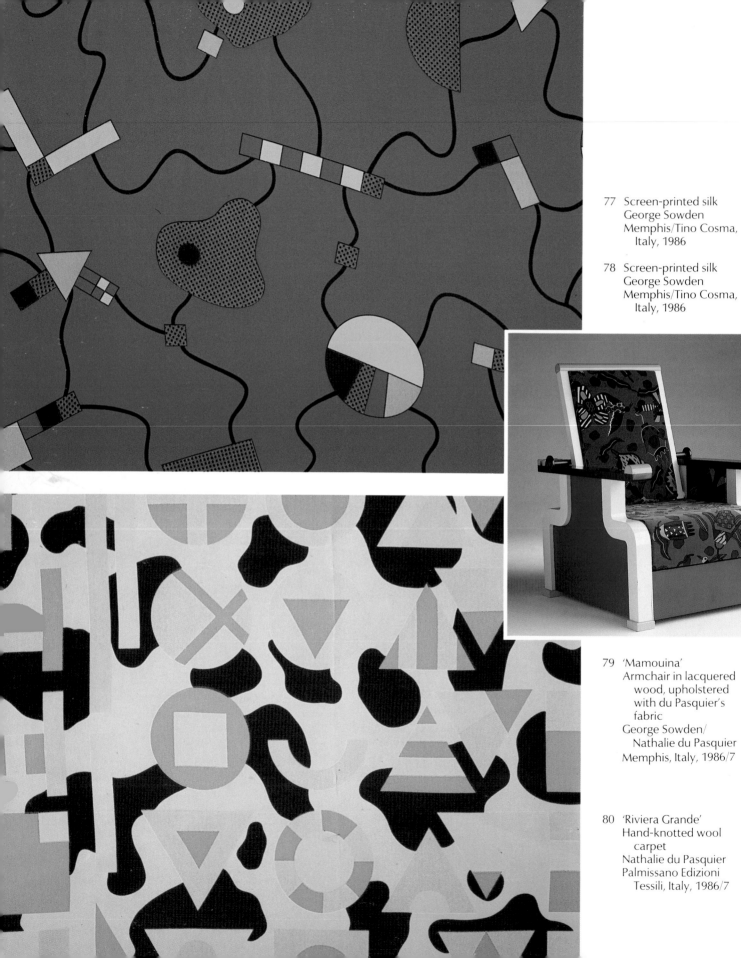

77 Screen-printed silk
    George Sowden
    Memphis/Tino Cosma,
    Italy, 1986

78 Screen-printed silk
    George Sowden
    Memphis/Tino Cosma,
    Italy, 1986

79 'Mamouina'
    Armchair in lacquered
    wood, upholstered
    with du Pasquier's
    fabric
    George Sowden/
    Nathalie du Pasquier
    Memphis, Italy, 1986/7

80 'Riviera Grande'
    Hand-knotted wool
    carpet
    Nathalie du Pasquier
    Palmissano Edizioni
    Tessili, Italy, 1986/7

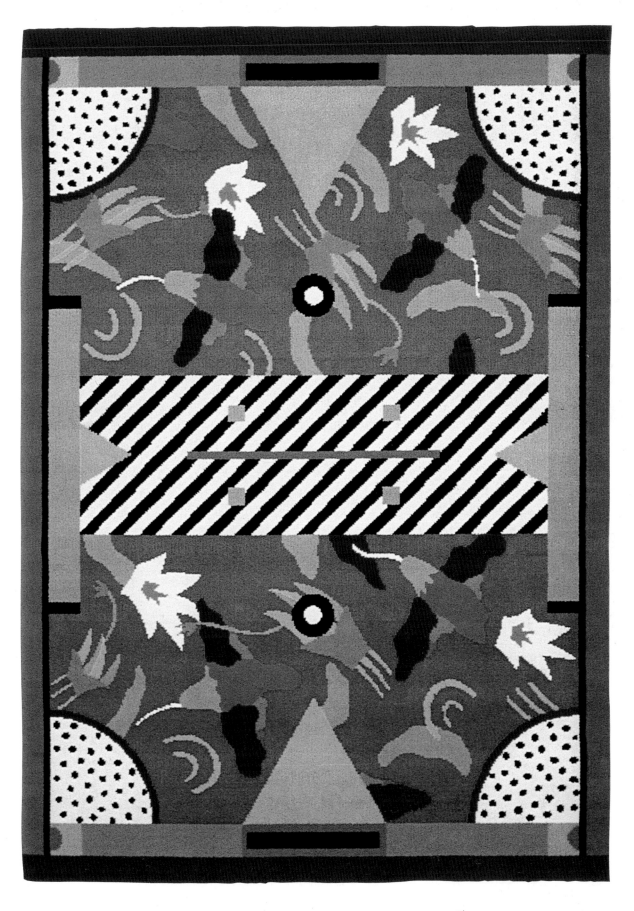

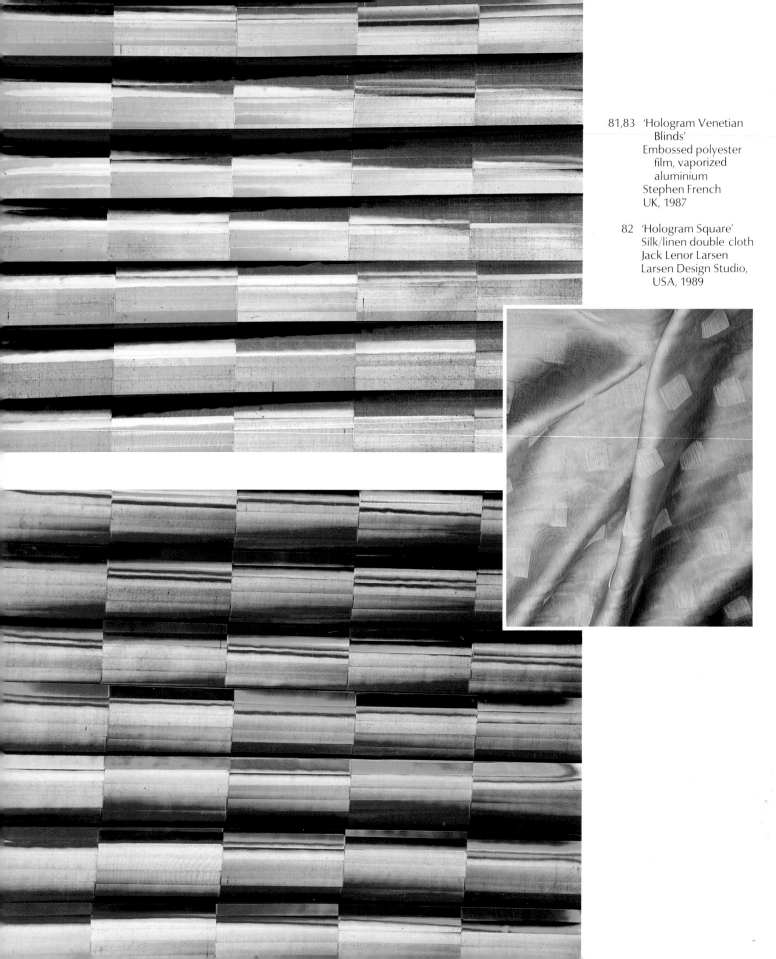

81,83 'Hologram Venetian
Blinds'
Embossed polyester
film, vaporized
aluminium
Stephen French
UK, 1987

82 'Hologram Square'
Silk/linen double cloth
Jack Lenor Larsen
Larsen Design Studio,
USA, 1989

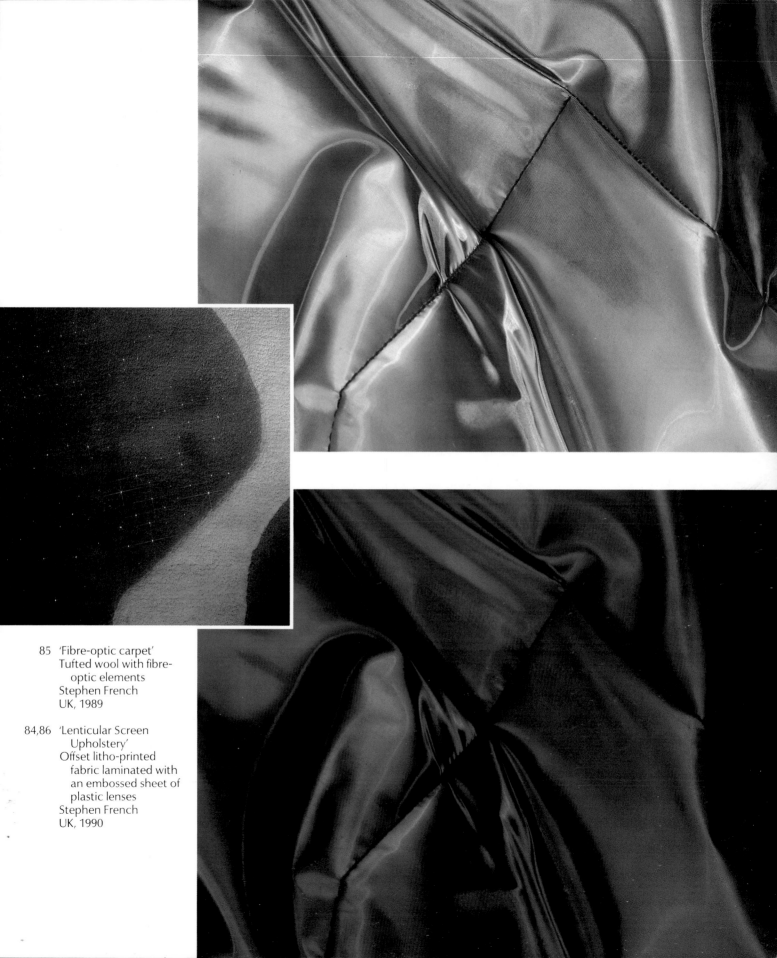

85 'Fibre-optic carpet'
   Tufted wool with fibre-
   optic elements
   Stephen French
   UK, 1989

84,86 'Lenticular Screen
      Upholstery'
      Offset litho-printed
      fabric laminated with
      an embossed sheet of
      plastic lenses
      Stephen French
      UK, 1990

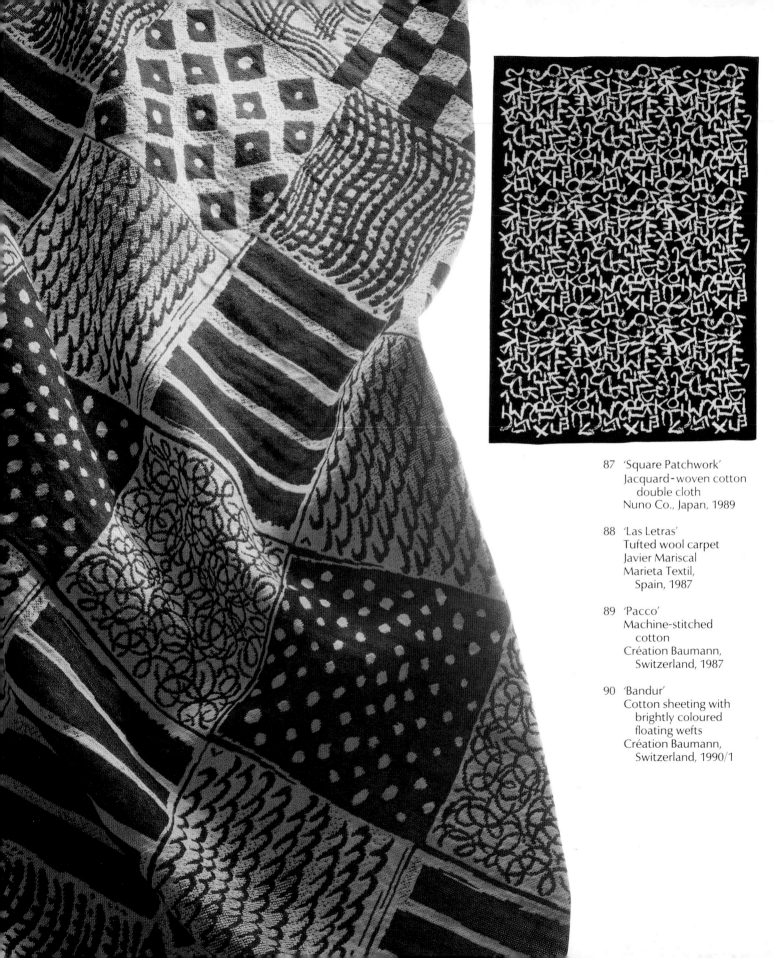

87 'Square Patchwork'
    Jacquard-woven cotton
    double cloth
    Nuno Co., Japan, 1989

88 'Las Letras'
    Tufted wool carpet
    Javier Mariscal
    Marieta Textil,
    Spain, 1987

89 'Pacco'
    Machine-stitched
    cotton
    Création Baumann,
    Switzerland, 1987

90 'Bandur'
    Cotton sheeting with
    brightly coloured
    floating wefts
    Création Baumann,
    Switzerland, 1990/1

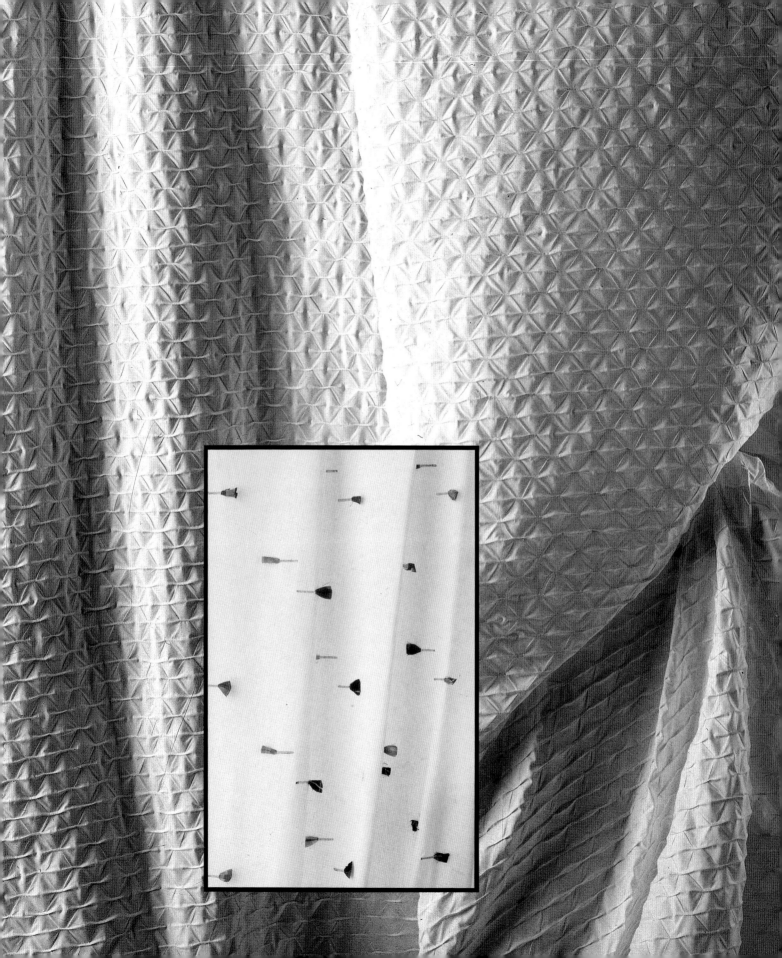

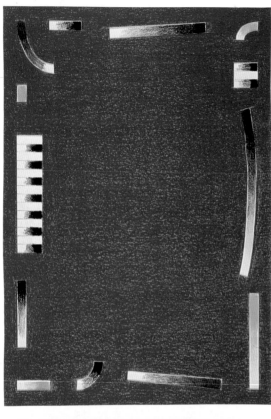

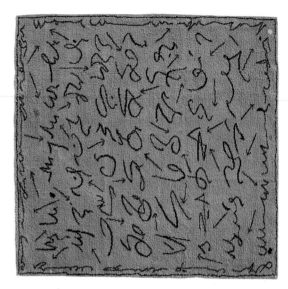

91 'Saez'
   Hand-woven cotton,
      wool and jute carpet
   Martine Bedin
   B. D. Ediciones de
      Diseño, France/Spain
   1988

92 'Yuyaka'
   Hand-knotted wool
      carpet
   Sergio Calatroni
   Sisal Collezione,
      Italy, 1990

93 Machine-woven wool
      carpet
   Christian Duc
   Toulemonde Bochard,
      Belgium, 1990

94 'Paoli et Paolo'
   Hand-knotted wool
      carpet
   From the General
      Dourking Collection
   Andrée Putman for
      Toulemonde Bochard
   France/Belgium, 1990

95 'Di Mano in Mani'
   Hand-knotted wool
      carpet
   Oxido
   Sisal Collezione,
      Italy, 1990

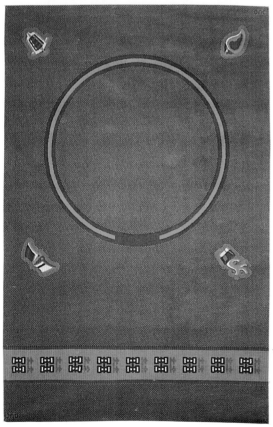

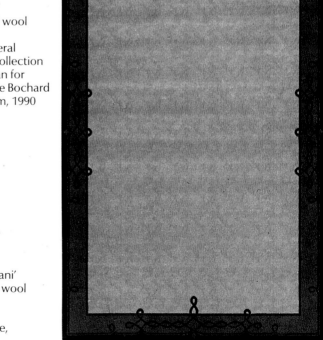

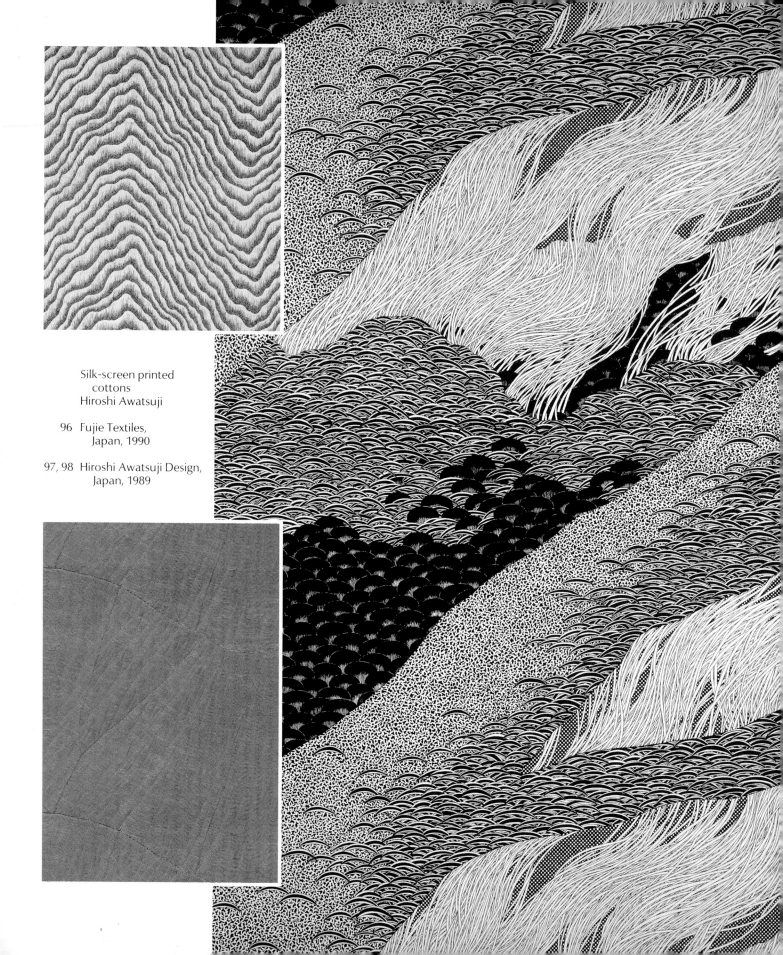

Silk-screen printed
cottons
Hiroshi Awatsuji

96   Fujie Textiles,
     Japan, 1990

97, 98 Hiroshi Awatsuji Design,
        Japan, 1989

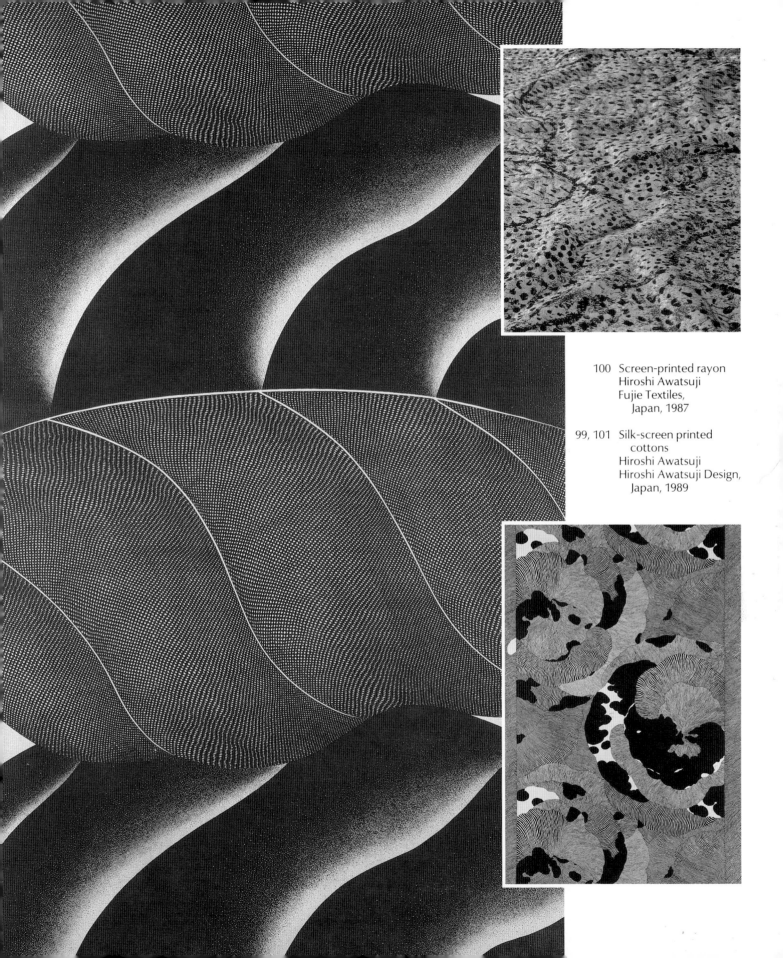

100 Screen-printed rayon
Hiroshi Awatsuji
Fujie Textiles,
Japan, 1987

99, 101 Silk-screen printed
cottons
Hiroshi Awatsuji
Hiroshi Awatsuji Design,
Japan, 1989

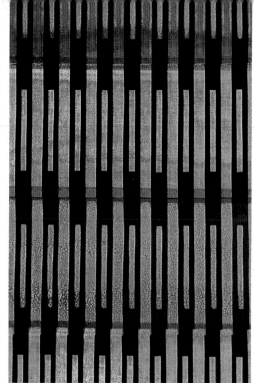

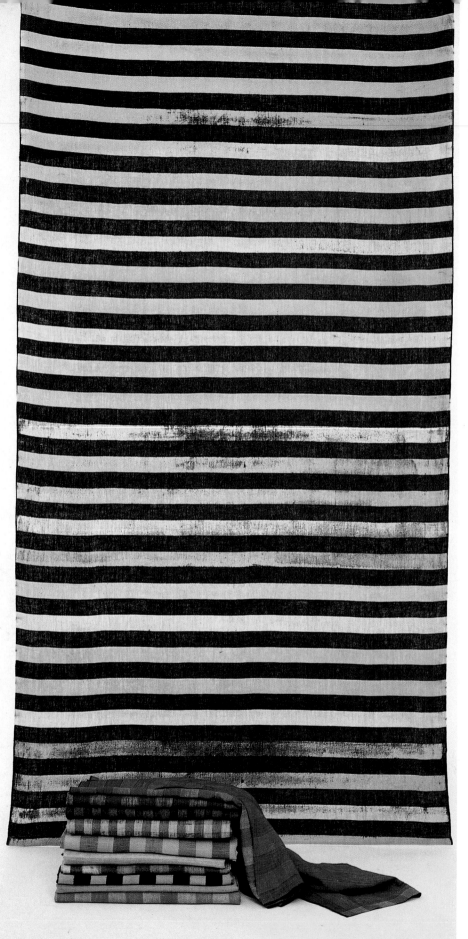

102　Banner
　　　Batik-dyed linen
　　　Anne Fabricius Møller
　　　Denmark, 1990

103,104　Banners
　　　Discharge-printed
　　　　cotton
　　　Bitten Hegelund
　　　　Sørensen
　　　Denmark, 1990

105　'Bruxelles I'
　　　Jacquard-woven lurex
　　　　polyester and rayon
　　　Reiko Sudo
　　　Nuno Co., Japan, 1990

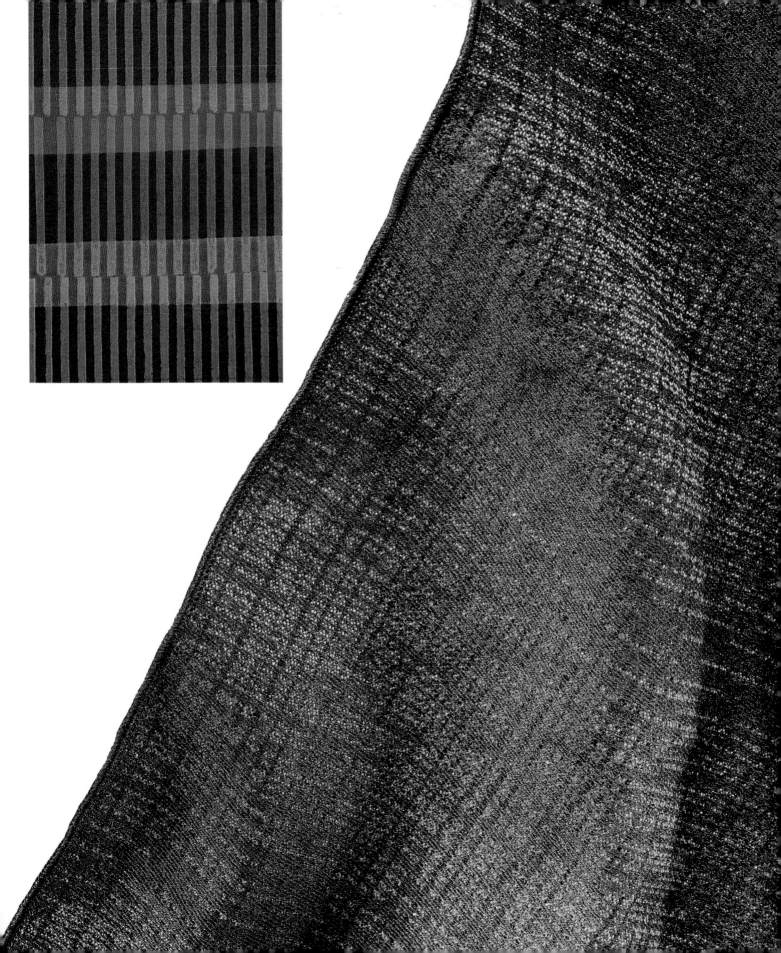

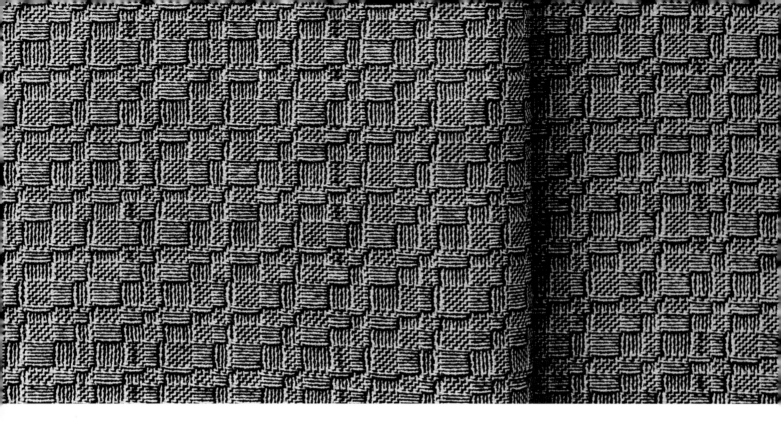

106 'Top Drawer'
Shadow-woven wool
Gretchen Bellinger
USA, 1986

107 'Isadora'
Pleated silk
Gretchen Bellinger
USA, 1986

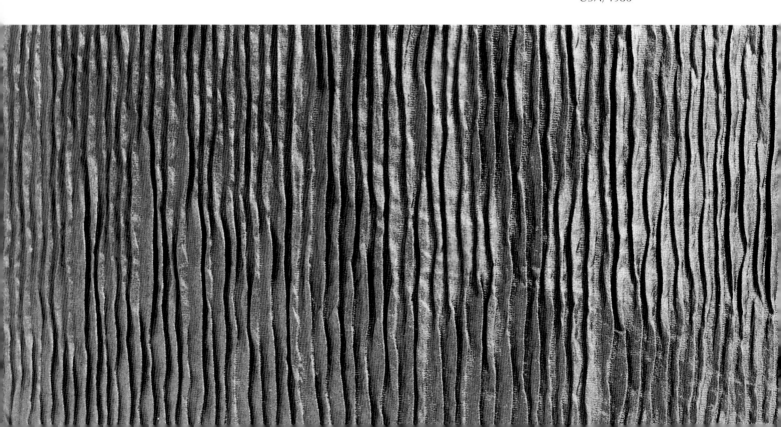

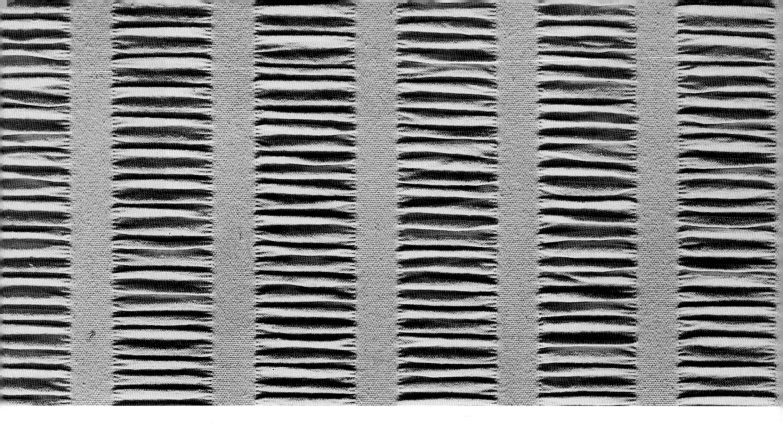

108 'Summerhouse'
      Seersucker-woven
      cotton
      Gretchen Bellinger
      USA, 1986

109 'Mazurka'
      Cloqué silk
      Gretchen Bellinger
      USA, 1986

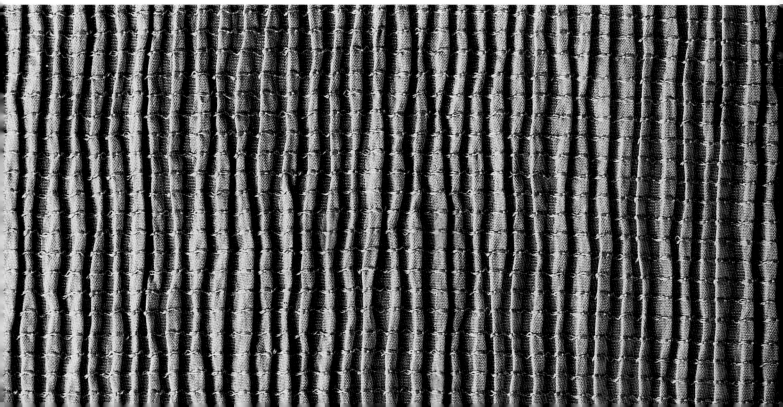

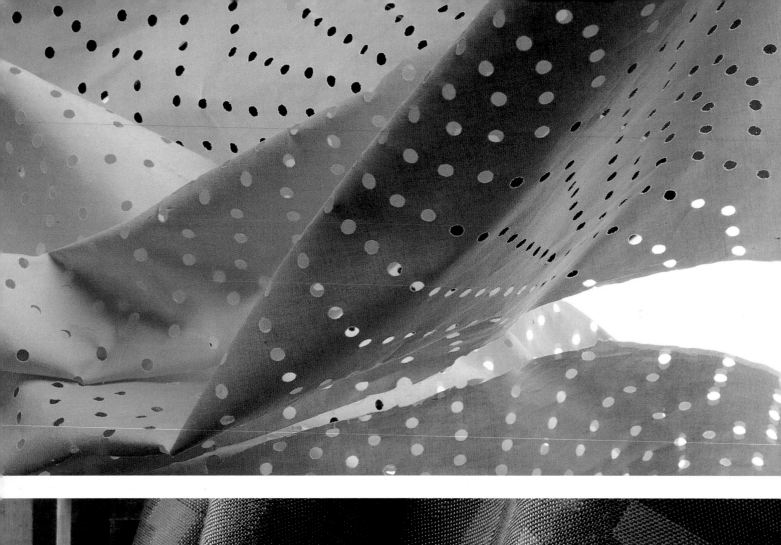
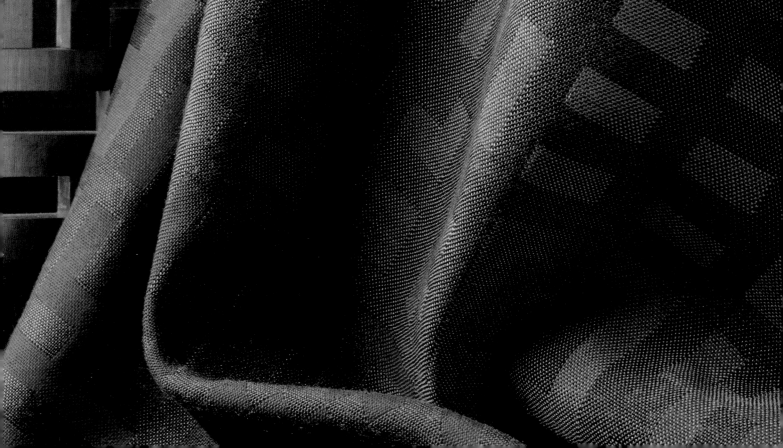

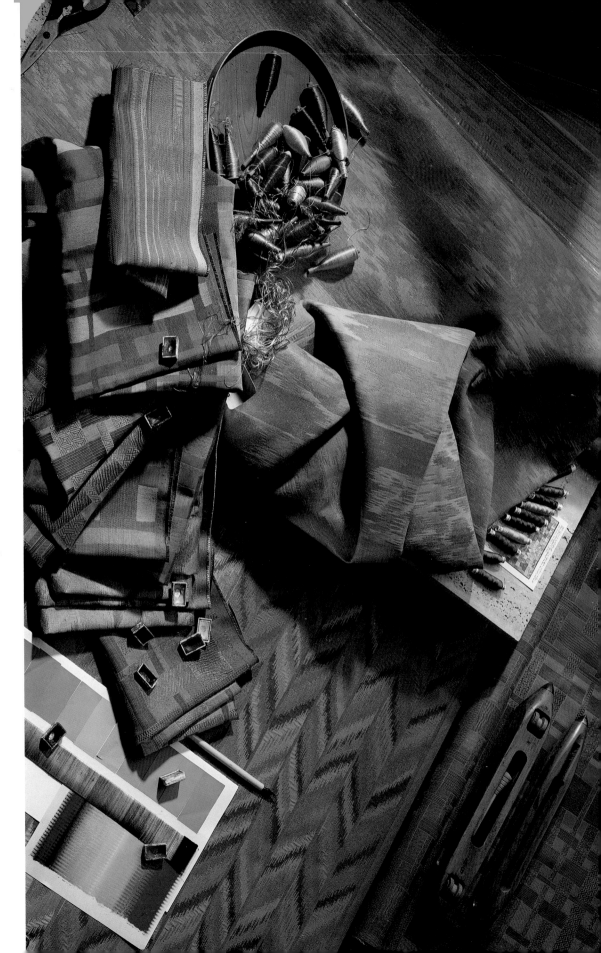

110 'Opticross'
Punched cotton curtain
Ross Littell
Kvadrat, Denmark, 1989

111 'Etruska'
Double-woven
polyester bedspread
Finn Sködt
Kvadrat, Denmark, 1989

112 Fabrics and yarns
Zimmer und Rohde,
West Germany, 1990

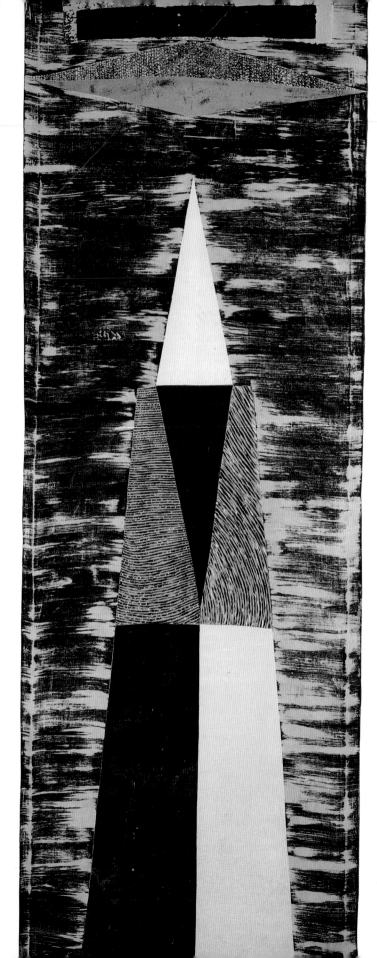

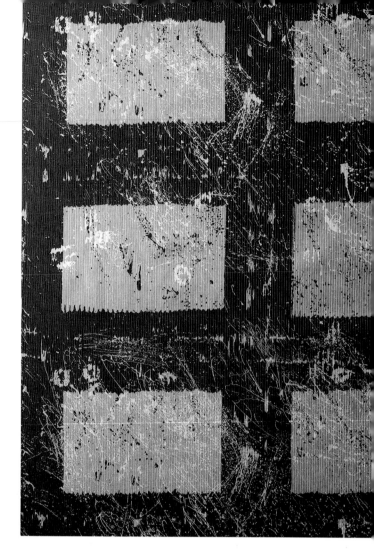

113 Banner
     Hand-painted and
        discharge-printed silk
        with bleach and
        process dyes
     Sally Greaves Lord
     UK, 1987

114 'Soft Sand'
     Screen-printed cotton
     From the Classic
        Contemporaries
        Collection
     Astrid Sampe
     Ljunbergs, Sweden, 1988

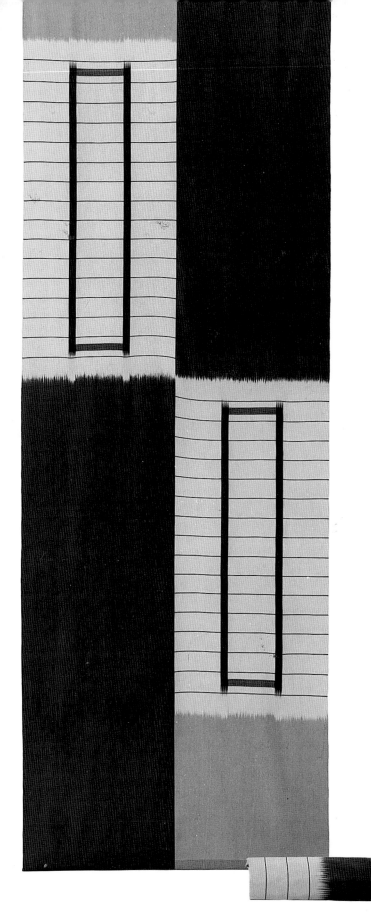

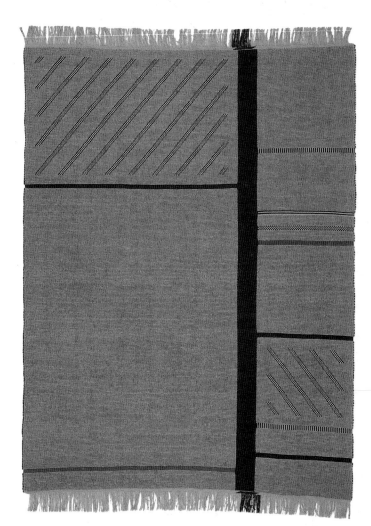

115 'Bauhaus'
Silk ikat banner
Sharon Fisher
Denmark, 1990

116 Carpet
Plain-woven cotton
Kristine Kjaerholm
Denmark, 1990

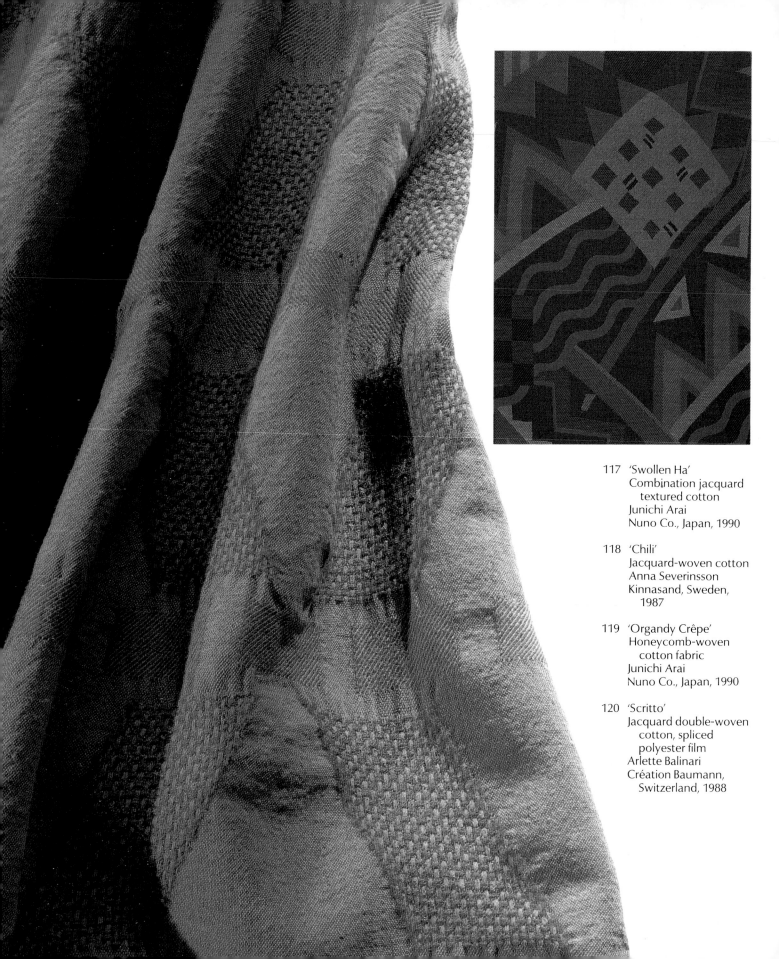

117 'Swollen Ha'
    Combination jacquard
      textured cotton
    Junichi Arai
    Nuno Co., Japan, 1990

118 'Chili'
    Jacquard-woven cotton
    Anna Severinsson
    Kinnasand, Sweden,
      1987

119 'Organdy Crêpe'
    Honeycomb-woven
      cotton fabric
    Junichi Arai
    Nuno Co., Japan, 1990

120 'Scritto'
    Jacquard double-woven
      cotton, spliced
      polyester film
    Arlette Balinari
    Création Baumann,
      Switzerland, 1988

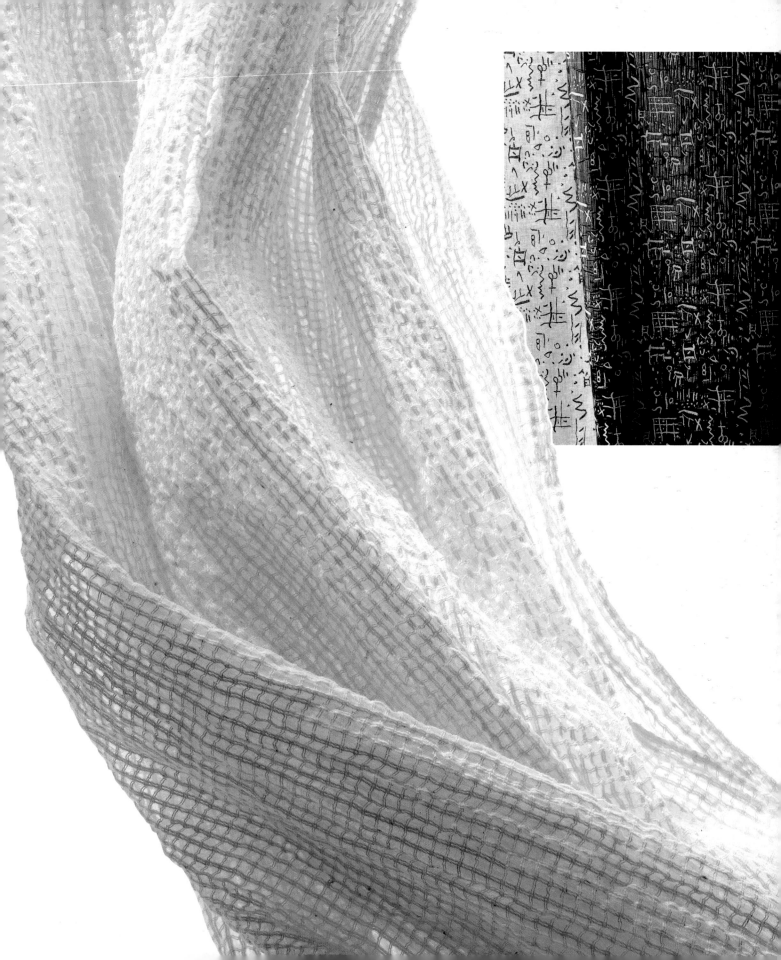

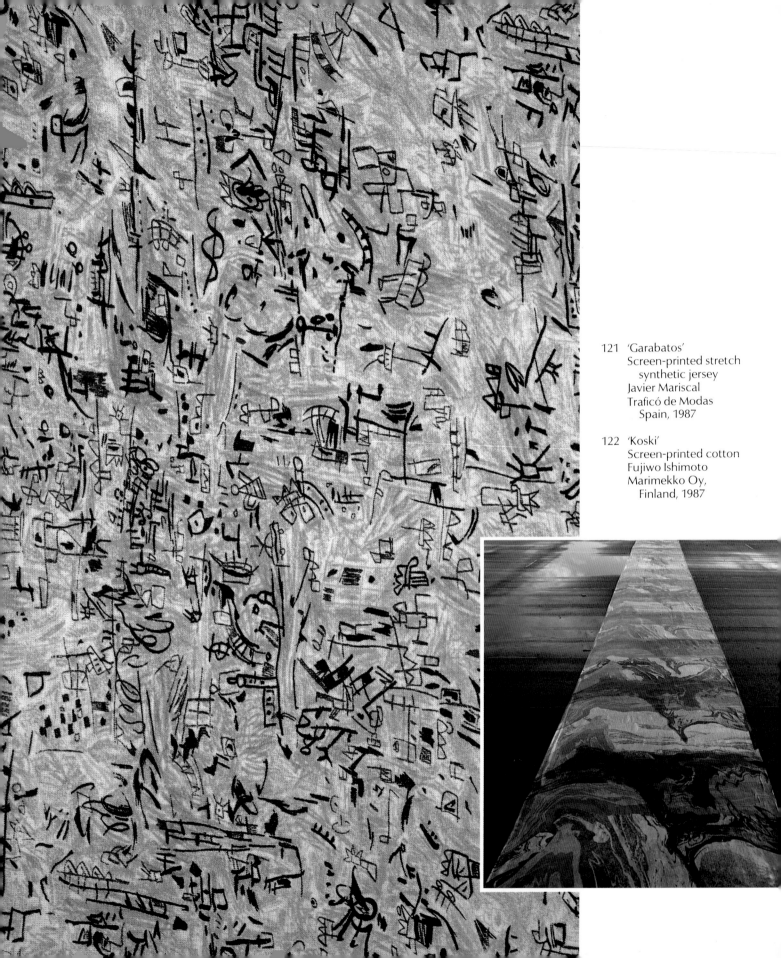

121 'Garabatos'
Screen-printed stretch
    synthetic jersey
Javier Mariscal
Traficó de Modas
    Spain, 1987

122 'Koski'
Screen-printed cotton
Fujiwo Ishimoto
Marimekko Oy,
    Finland, 1987

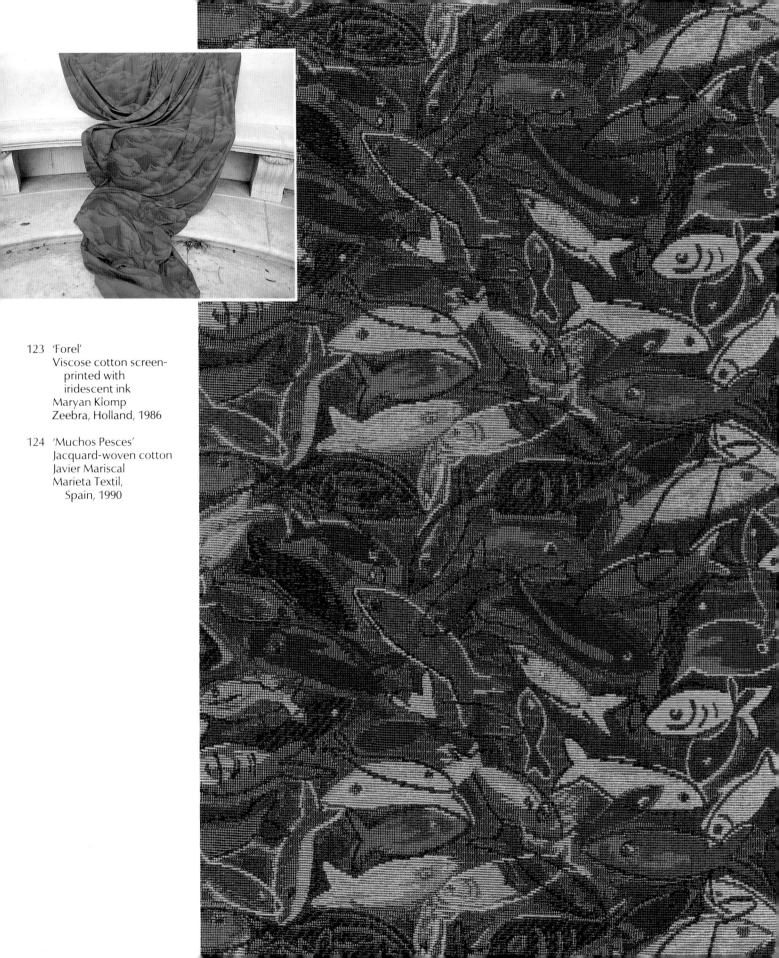

123 'Forel'
Viscose cotton screen-
printed with
iridescent ink
Maryan Klomp
Zeebra, Holland, 1986

124 'Muchos Pesces'
Jacquard-woven cotton
Javier Mariscal
Marieta Textil,
Spain, 1990

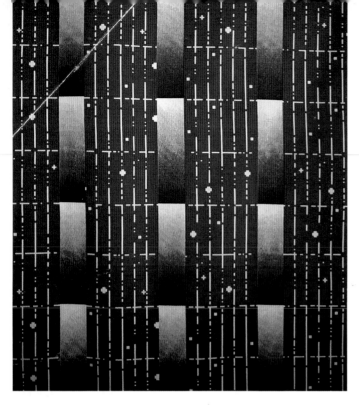

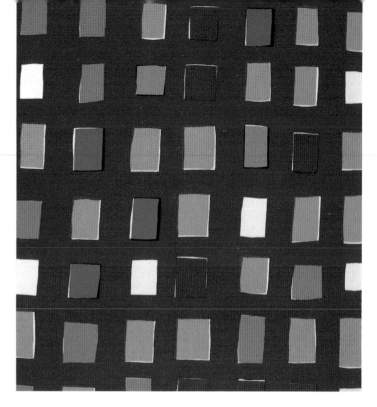

125, 127, 128 Computer-generated
images, screen-
printed on cotton
Vibeke Riisberg
Denmark, 1990

126 'Festivo'
Screen-printed cotton
From the Classic Contem-
poraries Collection
Viola Gråsten
Ljunbergs, Sweden, 1990

129 Screen-printed cotton
Else Kallesøe
Denmark, 1986

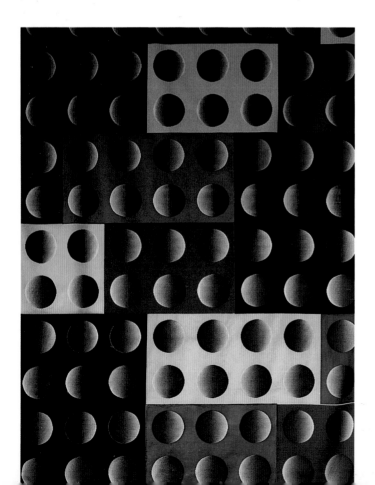

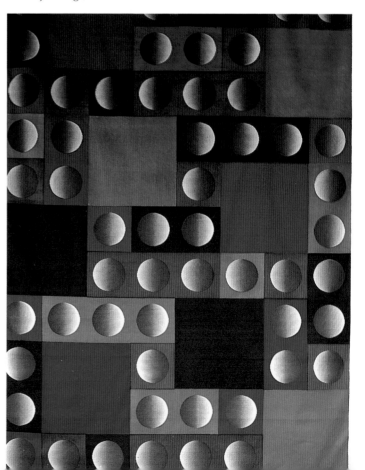

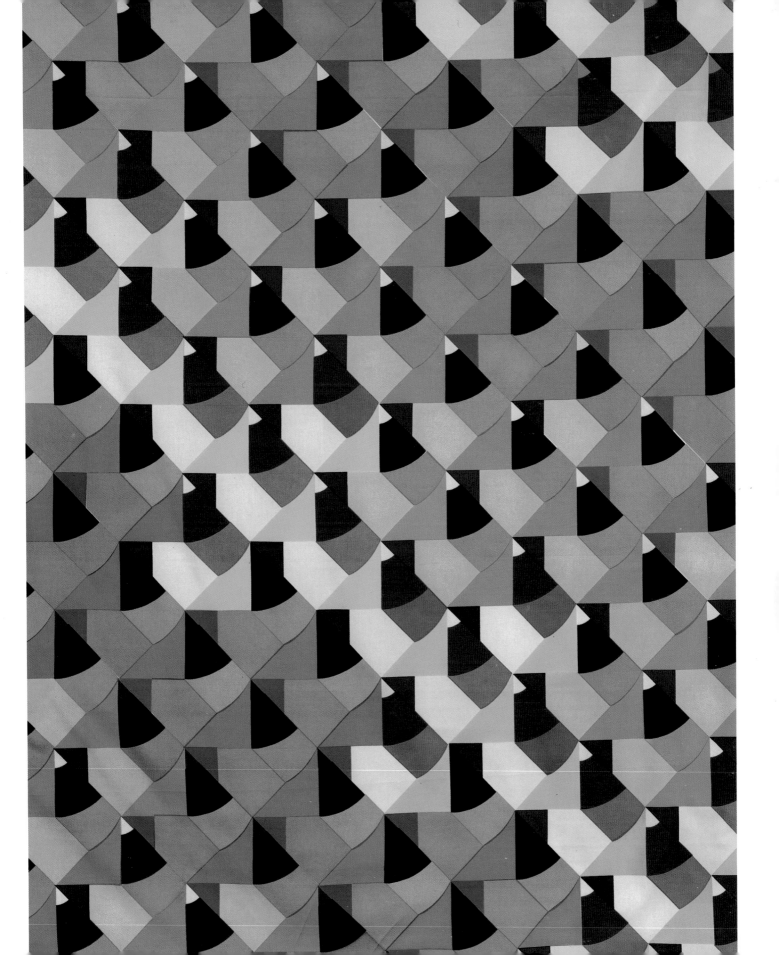

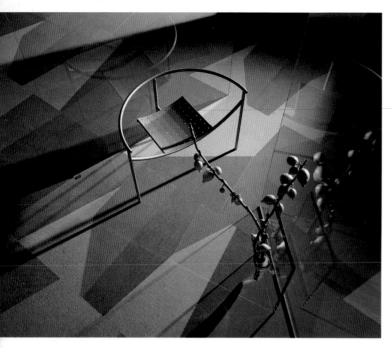

130 'Dialog 3'
   Sol LeWitt
   Royal Wilton woven
      polyamide carpet
   Vorwerk, West
      Germany, 1990/1

131 'Dialog' (first collection)
   Rotary screen-printed
      polyamide carpet
   Arata Isozaki
   Vorwerk, West
      Germany, 1988/9

132 'Dialog 2'
   Rotary screen-printed
      polyamide carpet
   Jean Nouvel
   Vorwerk, West
      Germany, 1989/90

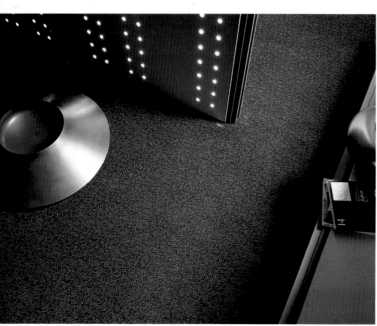

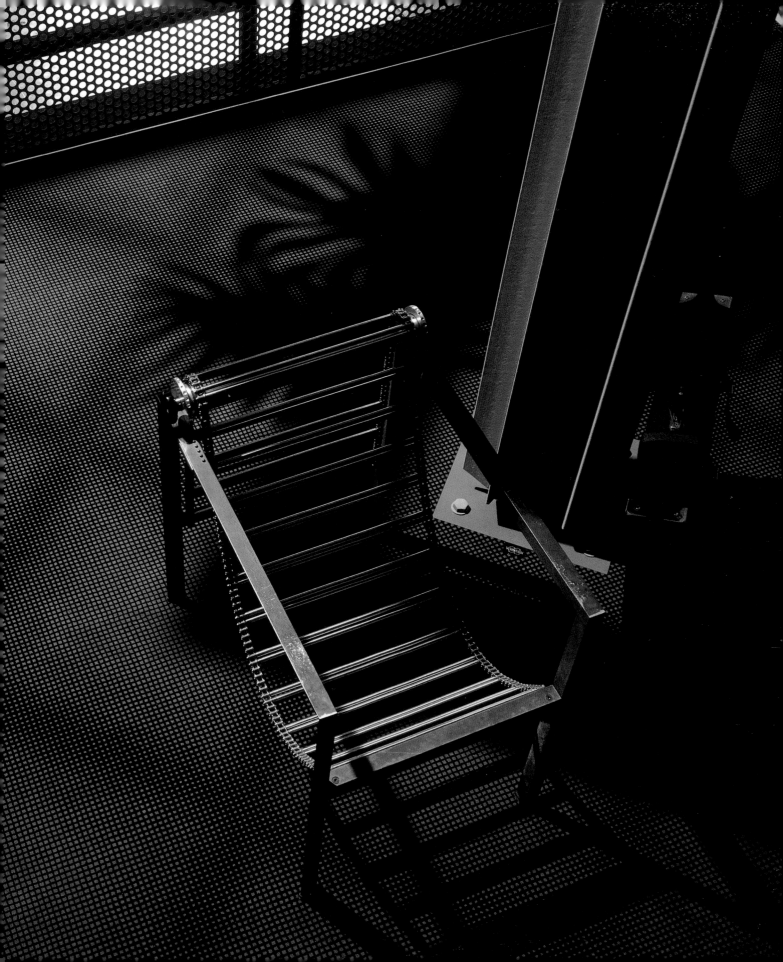

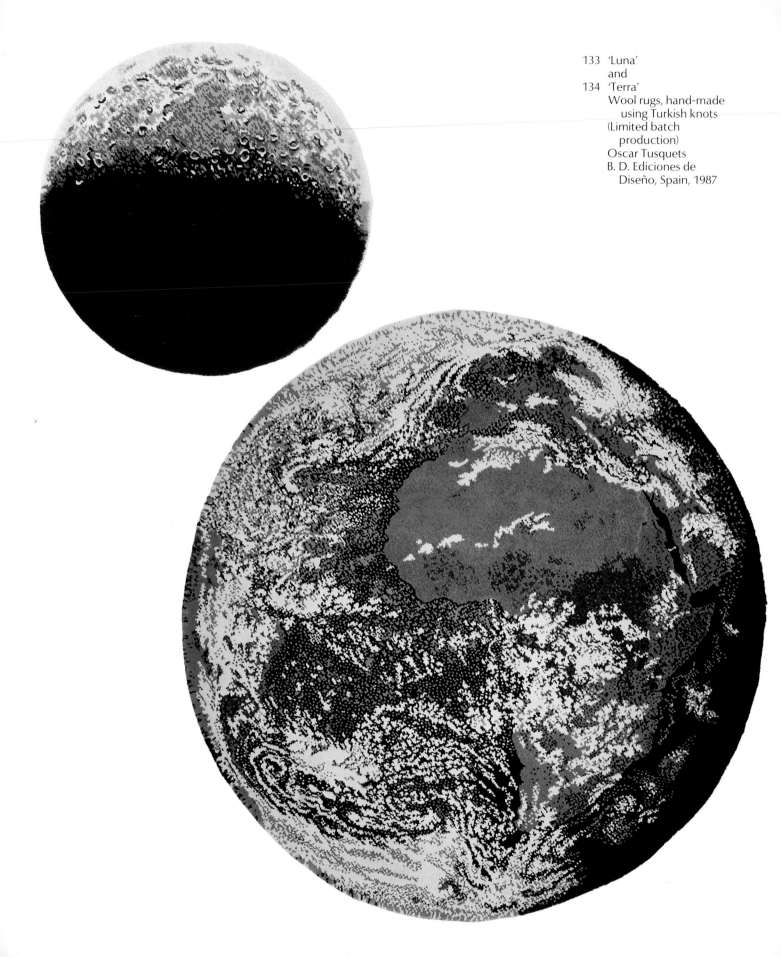

133 'Luna'
and
134 'Terra'
Wool rugs, hand-made
using Turkish knots
(Limited batch
production)
Oscar Tusquets
B. D. Ediciones de
Diseño, Spain, 1987

CRAFT TEXTILES

TEXTILES are amongst the most hybrid of contemporary crafts, spawning a broad variety of developments and techniques, including embroidery, felting and even basketry (which, because it concerns the interlacing of fibres, has been absorbed into the textile family). These techniques are practised by different kinds of craftspeople who display equally diverse attitudes to their separate disciplines. There are the environmentally conscious dyers, and printers, for example, who attempt to achieve self-sufficiency in the practice of their craft, and then at the other extreme there are the Parisian embellishers who decorate silk dresses for the couturiers, catering for the demand for perpetual innovation within a basically conservative idiom.

A principal function of the craft movement in industrial societies has been to provide an alternative aesthetic to that of mainstream mass-produced goods. Earlier this century, craft weavers reacted against the mechanical perfection and smooth finish of industrially produced cloth by creating rougher, 'wholesome' cloths that proclaimed the fact they were hand-made. It is possible that in its imitative tendencies and capabilities, industry drove the crafts towards the exaggeration of the hand-made aesthetic.

Today, flexible production technologies and the sophistication of manufacturing techniques have meant that there is increasing convergence between craft and design. In the past few years, industrially produced textiles have displayed a greater variety of printing and weaving techniques inspired by the traditional handicrafts than ever before. Interest in the contemporary crafts will continue to develop as it is realized that they offer resources, a 'bank' of styles and experimental approaches to technique, that can sensitize designers to the sensual and decorative potential of fabrics. The burgeoning numbers of designer-makers provide evidence that the cross-over between contemporary craft and design is in full flood.

The contemporary crafts have, however, developed at a tangent from – and also as an alternative to – the traditional crafts. It is noticeable that in countries such as Spain, Italy and France, where craftworkers (though rarely textile craftworkers) still exist and vestiges of the old systems of training and apprenticeship remain, the contemporary crafts have won little ground. They are essentially different from the traditional crafts which they set out to replace in that they are practised self-consciously, largely (though not exclusively) by art-school educated members of the middle class. On the whole they supply contemplational objects – objects that have been contemplated in the process of making, and whose main purpose is to evoke contemplation in the viewer.

During the 1960s and 1970s mounting dissatisfaction with the urban industrial environment led to a search for alternative ways of life, which had the effect of developing the range and popularity of the textile crafts considerably. A number of the alternative and counter-cultural movements that spread from California in the 1960s, such as hippies, back-to-naturists and folk revivalists, identified with the idea of craft as a way of life. Thanks to them the rather esoteric, art-school influenced studio craft movement changed and crafts became popularized. Crafts began to be sold at rural trade fairs all over America and, to a lesser extent, in Europe as well. The inevitable price for such popularity was a falling-off of standards: much work was criticized as being banal, and the craft textile movement became firmly associated with macramé plant-pot holders. The hippy image of crafts proved difficult to shake off; and indeed, it was from the naive, soft-headed reputation of hippyism that the younger generation of designer-makers of the style-conscious 1980s took such pains to distance themselves.

The counter-cultural trends of the 1960s and 1970s did, however, have other, positive results, leading to a reassessment of and revival in the domestic crafts of quilting and embroidery. The geometric patterning of quilts made them especially interesting to a generation raised on abstract art. In 1971 the Whitney Museum of American Art in New York staged a major exhibition of antique quilts entitled 'Abstract Design in American Quilts', which for the first time presented quilts as an art form. This shift, from home to art museum and from bed to gallery wall, signified a leap in status for this popular craft.

The point made by the Whitney show, that eighteenth-century quilts created by 'anonymous artists' predated abstract modernism by over one hundred years, glossed over several important issues. The differences between quilting and contemporary painting are significant, and have been highlighted by several feminist historians whose research has contributed much to our knowledge of quilting and other forms of needlework. They pointed out that quilts needed to be seen and valued as 'domestic art' rather than fine art, since they had been made at home, by women in the fulfilment of domestic duties. Quilt-making was also a communal and a social activity, and therefore contradicted the popular myth of the solitary male genius as contemporary artist on several counts. Quilts were also an important medium of communication between women. In the eighteenth and nineteenth centuries, quilters had developed an abstract language with specific social meanings that went beyond the purely formal concerns of abstract art and used quilts to commemorate rites of passage or other domestic events.

In the 1970s, quilting and embroidery came to be seen by some women as political media because both crafts were unsullied by men. Moreover, the environment and methods of production were themselves representational of salient issues. The skill-based techniques indicated the degree of care involved in these crafts, whilst the collaboration between women expressed a selflessness at odds with the competitive, egocentric individuality of male artists. For these ideological reasons, quilting and sewing were incorporated into the works of a number of feminist artists. One of the most famous mixed-media pieces in this genre was Judy Chicago's 'Dinner Party', completed in 1979. The 'Dinner Party' consisted of a banqueting table ornately laid with thirty-nine table settings for an imagined gathering of famous women from history and mythology, for which Chicago employed two hundred women and men to stitch the embroidered place mats and quilt the table cloth.

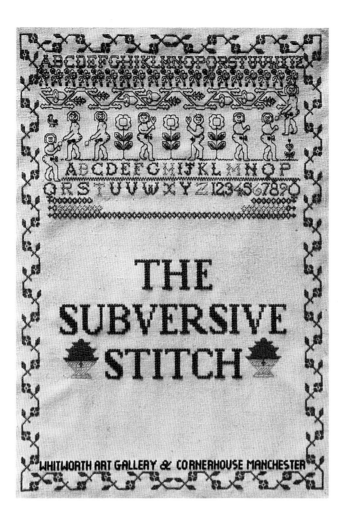

'The Subversive Stitch'
Linen sampler embroidered with cotton and wool thread
Lyn Malcolm
UK, 1988

Other artists have used quilting to indicate the position they spoke from within a certain culture. Afro-American mixed-media artist Faith Ringgold incorporated quilt-making in her art to express her commitment to feminism and her solidarity with her Afro-American roots. Her story-quilts combine quilting techniques with text, painted images of birth, marriage and death and, as in quilts such as 'Subway Graffiti # 2', her vision of life in New York. Ringgold's idea, central to much twentieth-century art, that the medium itself contains a message, was also used by another Afro-American artist, Joyce J. Scott, whose work is more overtly political.

In the 1970s and 1980s textiles were used by women to express their opposition to nuclear armaments. In Britain, the women encamped around the military air base at Greenham Common during the mid-1980s registered their feelings by playing on the traditional associations of needlework with homemaking and gentleness, weaving a web of wool strung with personal mementos, photographs and keepsakes into the barbed wire fence encircling the base. A similar tactical method was used in America in 1985. The Pentagon Peace Ribbon was a strip of fabric ten miles long made up of thousands of embroidered and appliquéd banners from all over the United States, which was tied round the Pentagon in a vast collaborative protest for peace.

Other women have also used needlework to express mixed feelings about the role that it has played in the history of their sex. The idea that domestic crafts may have been both a source of pleasure and a symptom of constraint is clearly expressed by Lyn Malcolm's piece 'Why Have We So Few Great Women Artists?', which stitches its question through an installation of carefully made samplers, rag rugs, knitting, embroidery and cakes. The device of stitched words is ingenious for a number of reasons, one being that it acts as a bridge between contemporary craft and modern art, which makes much use of text. It is a device that Malcolm also uses, very appropriately, in her sampler 'The Subversive Stitch', to highlight the ancient link that still exists between decoration and meaning whilst commenting upon the traditional function of samplers as repressive educational tools for women.

Of course not all quilts and embroideries express a political message. Three leading quilt artists, Nancy Crow and Pamella Studstill from the United States, and Pauline Burbidge from Great Britain, have bent the rules of piece-quilting in order to develop the quilt in different ways. All are art-school educated, all have developed a personal approach to quilting and all tackle the constraints imposed by patterning head-on.

Nancy Crow is an influential figure in the quilt art movement in America. Her quilts are a riot of colour and geometric patterning inspired by a long admiration of Mexican folk art and textiles, and they reveal that she is not only well versed in the grammar of ornament, but also highly skilled at inducing and controlling optical effects. Pauline Burbidge's quilts are ingenious in a similar way to Nancy Crow's. She is technically skilled at assembling figurative images into repetitive piece-patterns and playing with optical distortion in a manner reminiscent of the Dutch artist M. C. Escher. Her works are an exploration of colour inspired by pointillism. She arranges different colours of fabrics in various ways in order to examine the diverse relationships which emerge, and then heightens the effects she has achieved with still more colour.

Transgressing the conventions of patchwork is not, of course, an activity unique to the twentieth century, nor is the idea of creating quilts for visual effect rather than for use. Another contemporary American craftswoman, Jane Burch Cochran, has adopted an approach to patchwork that was considered extremely rebellious when it was introduced in the second half of the nineteenth century, but now has a tradition of its own. Christened 'crazy' because of their apparently random patterning, these quilts once stretched the very definition of quilt-making because they were embellished with beads, embroidery, silk flowers and, of particular interest to the contemporary artist, even paintings and photographs. The question raised by the nineteenth-century quilters – 'When does a quilt stop being a quilt?' – is still unanswered.

The issue of scale is in many ways central to the art/craft debate. During the 1960 and 1970s, large-scale art was in vogue, and this trend was naturally reflected in the fibre arts. For example, until very recently the minimum height and width of entries required by the Lausanne Contemporary Tapestry Biennale was 5 sq.m. (16 sq.ft.), a size that implied, almost by definition, state-funded work designed for civic spaces. To challenge these conventions concerning scale, the First International Exhibition of Miniature Textiles was staged by Ann Sutton at the British Crafts Council in 1974; in this case the maximum size of entry was 20 sq.cm. (8 sq.in.). The response to this exhibition was enthusiastic and prompted a trend of similar shows in Europe and America.

These exhibitions opened up the domestic market for the fibre arts as well as providing a forum for various media, such as embroidery, that were better suited to being shown on a smaller scale, and indeed it was found that pieces of this size provoked a more intimate, personal and playful

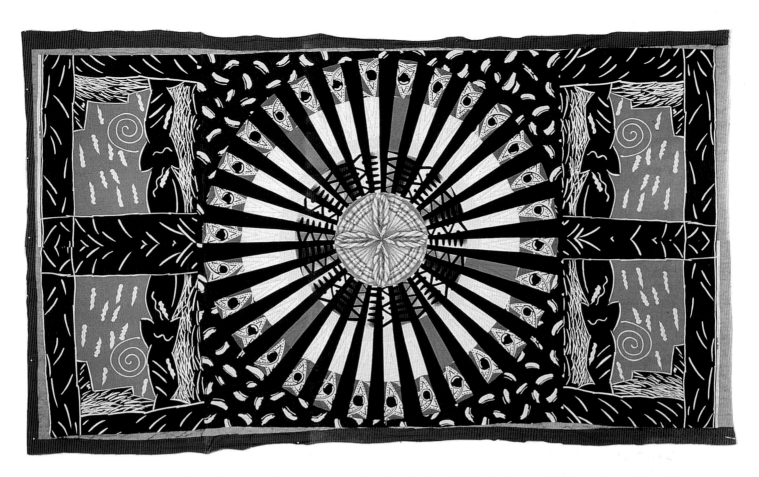

'Ratrace: The Treadmill', machine-pieced printed cotton. Hand-quilted by Kris Doyle, designed by Nancy Crow. USA, 1989

response in the public. The work of two American embroiderers in particular illustrates these qualities. Both Mary Brero and Tom Lundberg hand-embroider small, intense figurative images in different neo-primitive styles that serve to capitalize on the labour-intensive qualities of this medium. In this sense, their work marks a significant break with tradition. Because of the size of its stitches, and its connotations of a nineteenth-century vision of woman and home, embroidery has long been associated with painstaking and conservative dexterity. The traditional floral patterns and nineteenth-century rural genre scenes that are now sold as embroidery kits continue the image of embroidery as a conventional medium. Mary Brero's dazzling fractured images, however, challenge these conventions. Her style is 'raw' rather than genteel, influenced by a group of neo-primitive artists from Chicago called the 'Hairy Who', and her subject matter is contemporary and very urban.

Whereas Brero's embroideries are mosaics of isolated moments of intensity, Tom Lundberg's are more often about the spaces between events. His work seems to describe two states, one – such as in 'Mailman' – in which fragments of memory are brought together, the other in which the world refuses to be pulled into perspective and, like a bad snapshot, misses the subject and frames – as in 'Jogging' – a section of leg and the tail end of a dog. Brero and Lundberg's work questions our assumptions about embroidery and the sort of images that are suited to this medium. Their

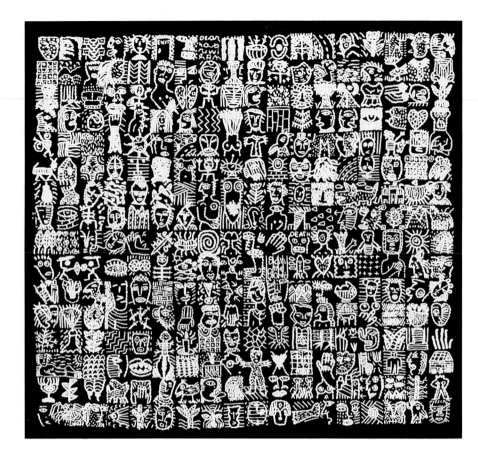

'Ideogram'
Cotton embroidered with dental floss
Mary Brero
USA, 1988

Opposite
Left:
'Permeance'
Crocheted, shellacked and painted
   cotton
Norma Minkowitz
USA, 1990

Right:
'Arrow'
Coiled and twined waxed linen thread
Ferne Jacobs
USA, 1986–88

painstaking work and unorthodox method of portrayal give their sometimes equally unorthodox subject matter added intensity.

By the early 1970s it was clear that in Europe as well as in the United States there was a wide constituency for the crafts. Craft galleries began to emerge and in turn they influenced the orientation of the works themselves. Gallery owners were careful to assert the quality and status of craftwork by promoting the names of certain individual craftspeople who, in response, began to produce more elitist, one-off objects. The strength of the contemporary art market in America also had its effect on crafts from the late 1970s onwards, and collecting became big business. As an American craft critic put it, the unique object fulfilled a growing need in the general public, especially amongst the up-and-coming, for a personalized identity, and indeed it was in America that the contemporary arts and crafts did particularly well.

One trend that began in America and highlighted the shift in craft towards an art form that was eminently suitable for the domestic market was basketry. The interest in basketry was prompted by the research into techniques – such as knotting, plaiting, felting and origami – that fibre artists were conducting during the 1970s as a means of exploring the sculptural possibilities of their medium; and so it followed that the new American baskets were conceived as small sculptural objects. One could hardly have anticipated that basketry would one day become a vehicle for wit and comment, but in fact several American artists have indeed created a number of works that cast an oblique and often humorously metaphorical view on the worlds of both masculine objects and domestic objects. The work of Californian basket-maker Ferne Jacobs is a case in point.

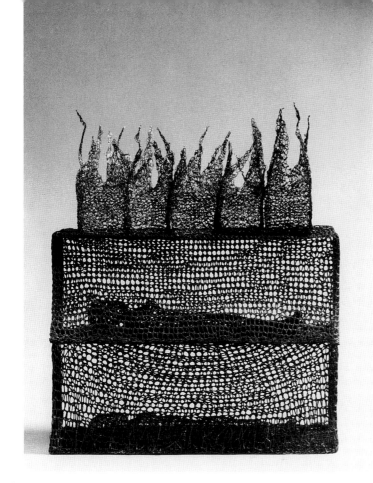

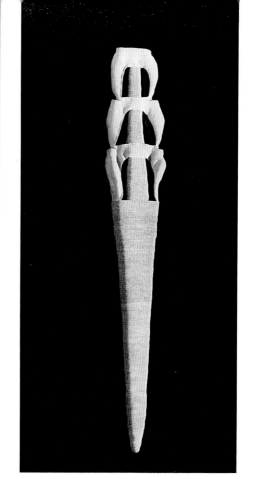

Jacobs uses a particularly painstaking basketry technique to remake conventionally hard, masculine objects such as daggers, giving them acceptable, sentient, organic and tactile qualities.

The idea of the 'tactile vessel', the fibre artist's answer to ceramics, is another important aspect of new basketry, and one of its leading exponents is Norma Minkowitz. Minkowitz creates 'vessels' from crochet, which she stiffens into shape with shellac. The delicate tracery-work is feminine without being trite, and her more recent figurative work features an analogy between the vessel and various parts of the female body to stimulate reaction and consequently to act as a gauge of attitudes. Here she plays on the lacy transparency of her material to explore different ideas to do with containment. A number of her vessels are 'pregnant': they reveal another element within them which may be a bird, a miniature body or simply an abstract form. The idea of the meshed cage is used in one of her most powerful works, 'The Jealous Eye'. This presents the frightening image of a spherical iris rolling backwards and forwards, forever trapped within its socket.

Karyl Sisson's vessels offer a very humorous perspective on domestic objects. Her work is about metamorphosis. She transforms everyday mass-produced objects – mainly zips and clothes' pegs of various sorts – into one-off creations that refer to domestic objects of a different sort: pots. Sisson's vessels are flexible; they are designed to be handled, or rather played with. They can be bent and twisted and made to adopt different postures or forms. They seem to be, as the titles of a number of pieces suggest, 'Living Things'. But despite their pliancy they contain a degree of menace: turned inside out, one pot transforms into a frightening orifice armed with teeth. One is acutely reminded that clothes' pegs can pinch and zips get stuck.

At the same time that the craft galleries have been promoting individual art-based craft, there has been a renewed interest in the traditional crafts. This is an indication of an important change of direction. For over twenty years the textile crafts had been predominantly influenced by contemporary art; in the last decade this process was reorientated as craft and, to a certain extent, art became focused on design.

The spread of computer-aided manufacture has done a lot to blur the divisions between art, craft and design: only this time the breaking down of boundaries has become less a question of ideology – as it was in the 1970s – but more one of tools. There are, however, a number of craftspeople working within a traditional craft idiom and striving to produce objects of quality and use who have made the deliberate and conscious decision to have nothing to do with industry. Such people are conservationists at heart, and the spread of the conservation movement has focused public attention upon them.

In Japan, Professor Itchiku Kubota's kimonos, which were exhibited in some leading cities in Europe at the end of the 1980s, are an extreme example of one tendency in the crafts towards displaying lavish intricacy and surplus skills. Professor Kubota has single-handedly revived the decorative art of Tsujigahana kimono-dyeing, a craft so elaborate and so time-consuming that it is alien to the contemporary economic and industrial 'realities' in Japan and the West. Tsujigahana kimono-dyeing is a craft based on multiple embellishment. Figurative images of the landscape are painstakingly assembled by immersing tied sections of silk in as many as thirty dye baths, and the finished result is further embellished with embroidery, hand-painting and gilding.

Hiroyuki Shindo has chosen to work in the folk tradition as a craftsperson rather than as a designer. He dyes kimonos using indigo and the traditional Japanese technique of resist dyeing, Shibori, following patterns that used to be worn by agricultural labourers. He is a follower of 'mingei', the craft philosophy put forward by Soetsu Yanagi in the 1930s which celebrated not only the look of Japanese folk crafts, but also the attitude: the selflessness and unself-consciousness of the anonymous artisans who made them. Shindo's customers are attracted by the way he practises his craft. He lives in a traditional Japanese cottage in the mountains near Kyoto and operates an ecological microcosm in which his indigo dyeing plays an integral part: the dregs from his indigo vats are used as fertilizer for his garden.

Shindo's attitude is similar to that of Susan Bosence, one of a small number of British block printers, who has fused her knowledge of traditional dye recipes with her views on conservation and progressive education. Bosence makes things of quality, value and individuality for personal use. Block printing, in her eyes, can be a very personal craft. It is one of the few areas of printing where the presence of the hand can be clearly felt in terms of the rhythm and shape of the repeat pattern cut into the block, the way in which dye is applied to it and the pressure with which it is applied to cloth. Block printing is a laborious and time-consuming activity: it requires an investment of self. Bosence's work is about personal integrity, a way of life; it has no captive market. Creating textiles in this way is no soft option. Bosence works hard, to provide a valid alternative to machine-made fabrics; she keeps her patterns simple and her prices low. She comes from an older generation and although her fabrics may be judged conservative in terms of style, her sacrifices of wealth and self are, in terms of the 1990s, deeply non-conformist. So far, they do not seem to be the sort of sacrifices that a younger generation of students is prepared to make.

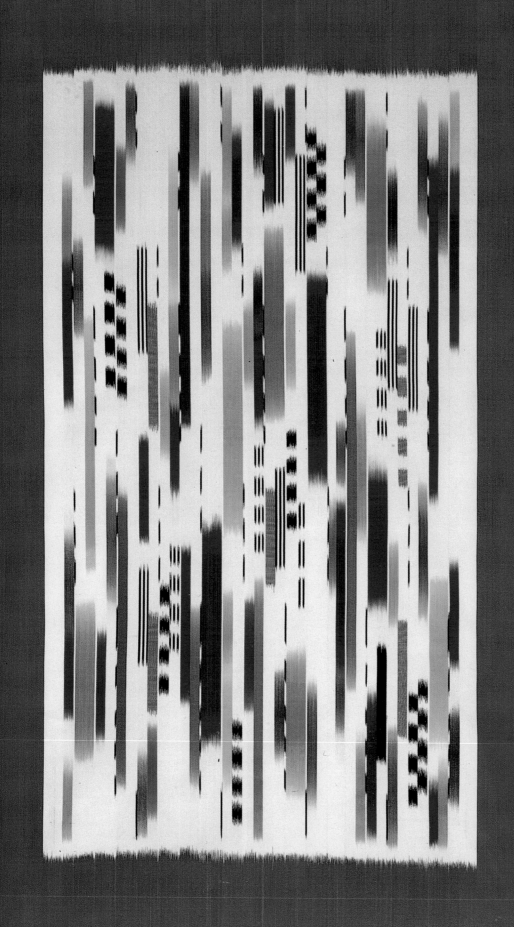

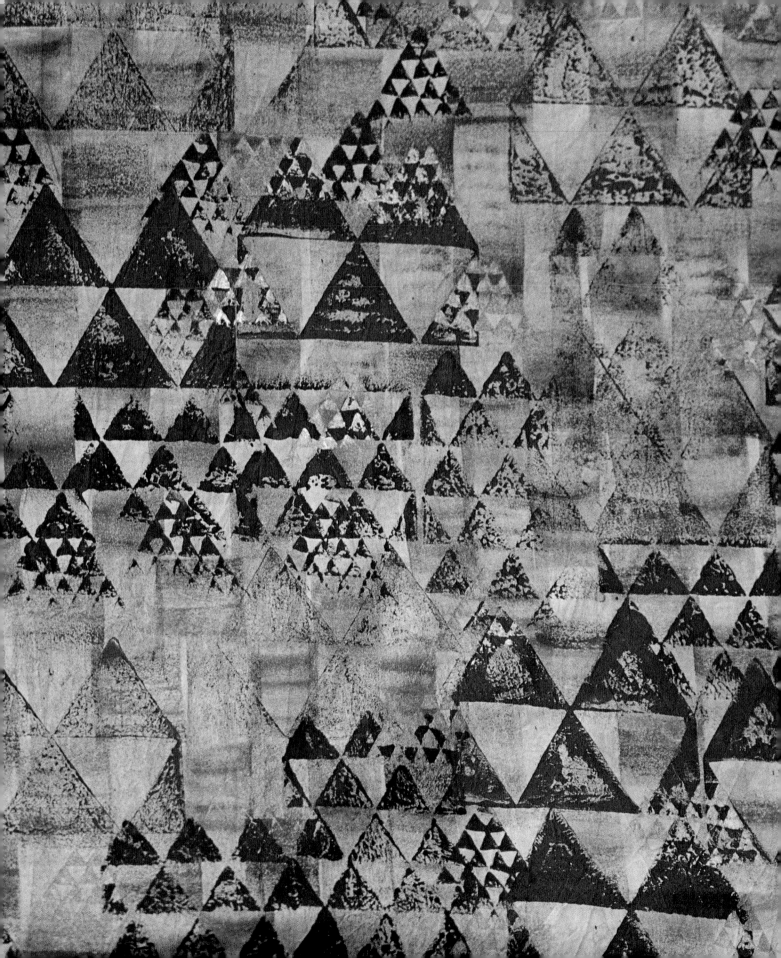

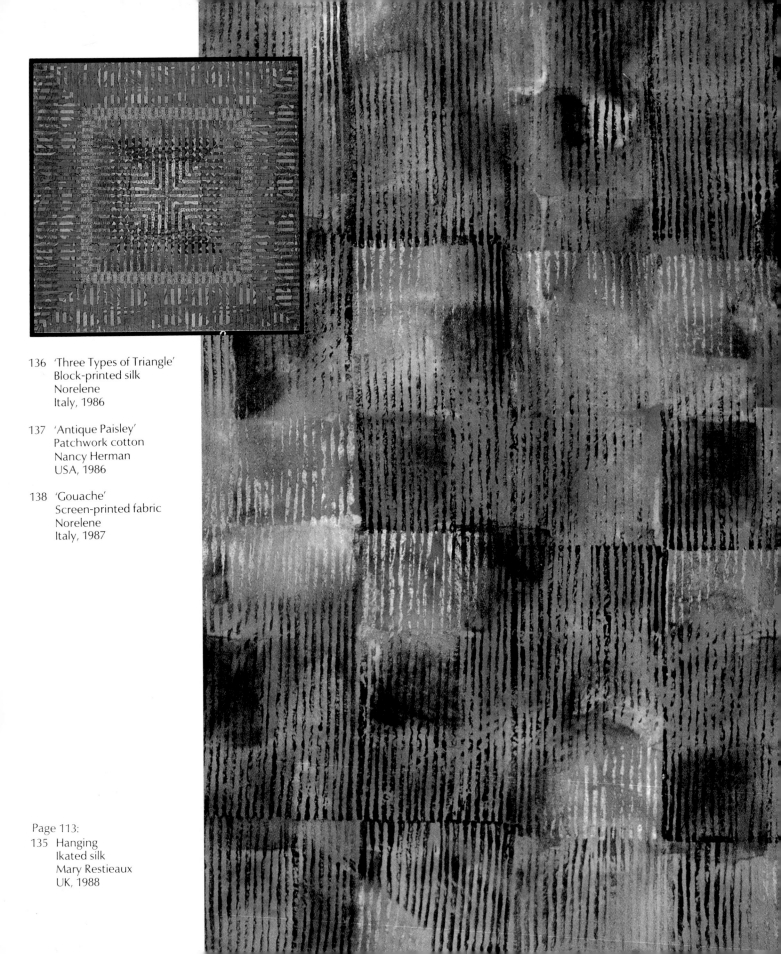

136 'Three Types of Triangle'
Block-printed silk
Norelene
Italy, 1986

137 'Antique Paisley'
Patchwork cotton
Nancy Herman
USA, 1986

138 'Gouache'
Screen-printed fabric
Norelene
Italy, 1987

Page 113:
135 Hanging
Ikated silk
Mary Restieaux
UK, 1988

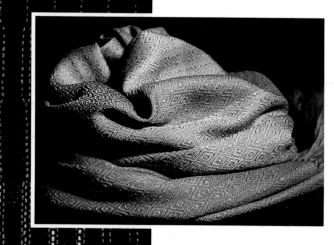

139 Woven wool
Eva Kandlbinder
West Germany, 1988

140 Sash
Dip-dyed woven silk
Renata Brink
West Germany, 1990

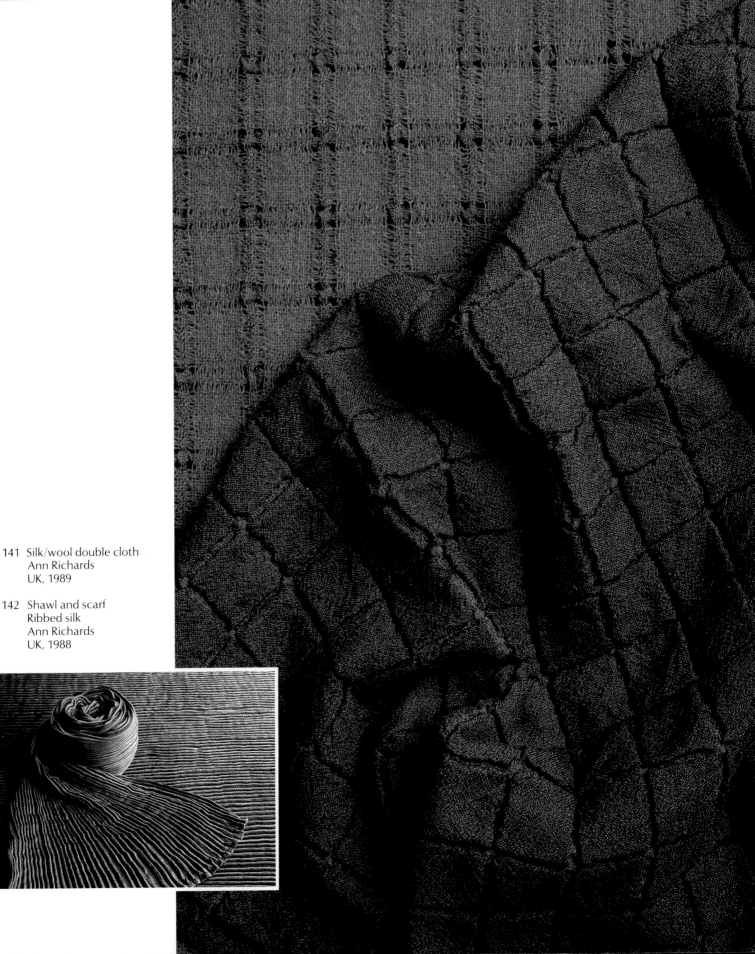

141 Silk/wool double cloth
Ann Richards
UK, 1989

142 Shawl and scarf
Ribbed silk
Ann Richards
UK, 1988

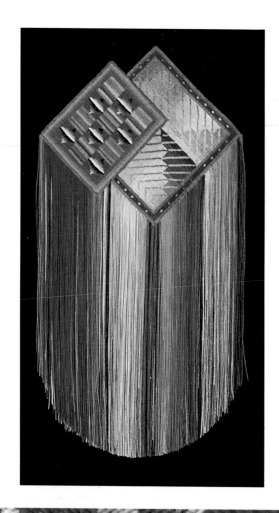

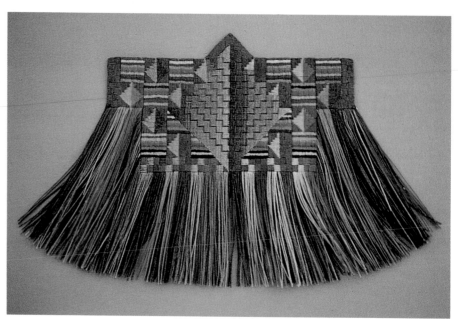

144 'Peruvian Leaf Tunic'
Knotted linen
Diane Itter
USA, 1987

143 'Carpet of Leaves'
Knotted linen
Diane Itter
USA, 1986
and
145 detail

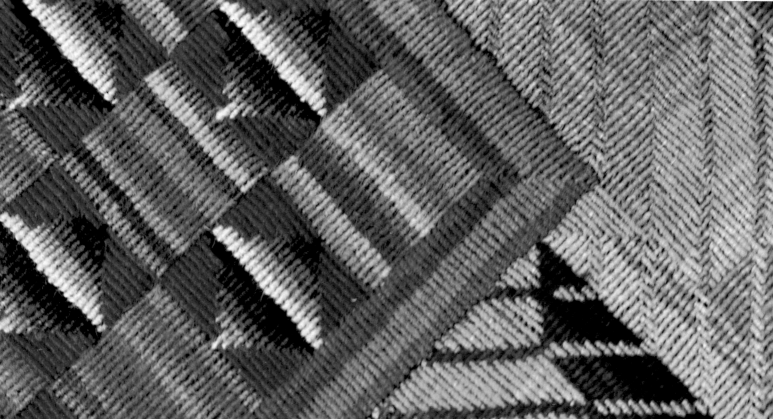

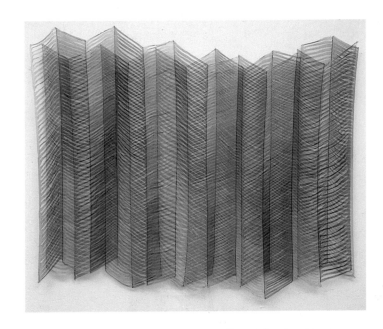

146 'Red, Blue and Yellow'
 Hanging
 Transparent organza
 Liesbeth Peeters
 Holland, 1989

147 'No. 26'
 Fibre painting
 Embroidery thread and
  wooden dowels with
  a canvas backing
 Scott Rothstein
 USA, 1989

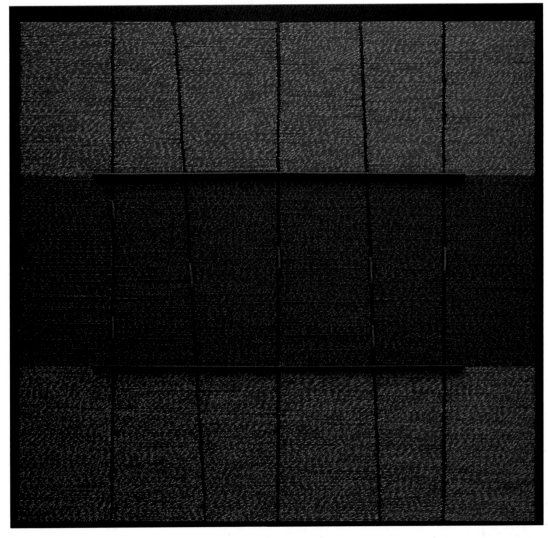

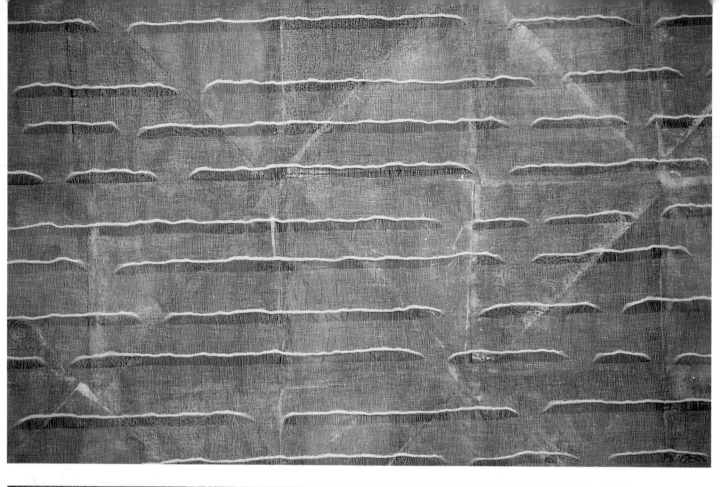

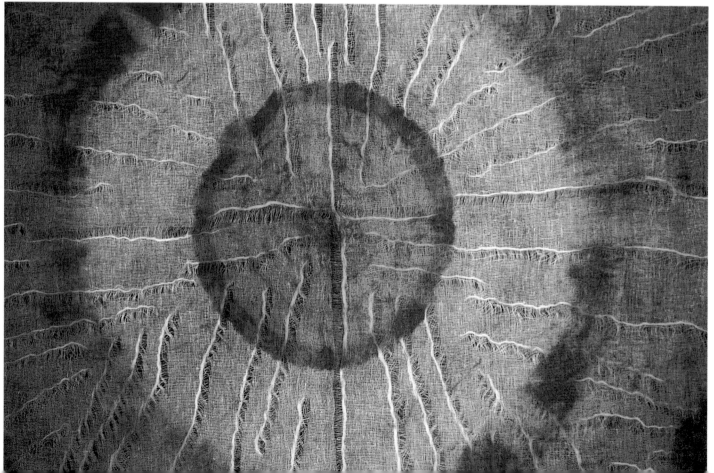

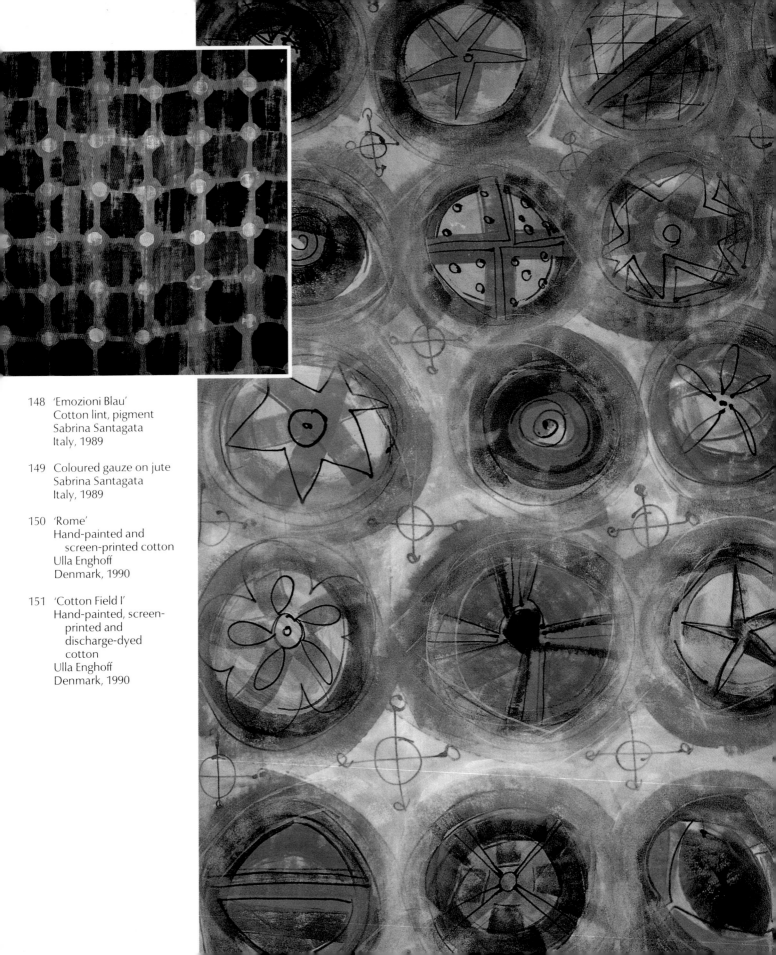

148 'Emozioni Blau'
Cotton lint, pigment
Sabrina Santagata
Italy, 1989

149 Coloured gauze on jute
Sabrina Santagata
Italy, 1989

150 'Rome'
Hand-painted and
    screen-printed cotton
Ulla Enghoff
Denmark, 1990

151 'Cotton Field I'
Hand-painted, screen-
    printed and
    discharge-dyed
    cotton
Ulla Enghoff
Denmark, 1990

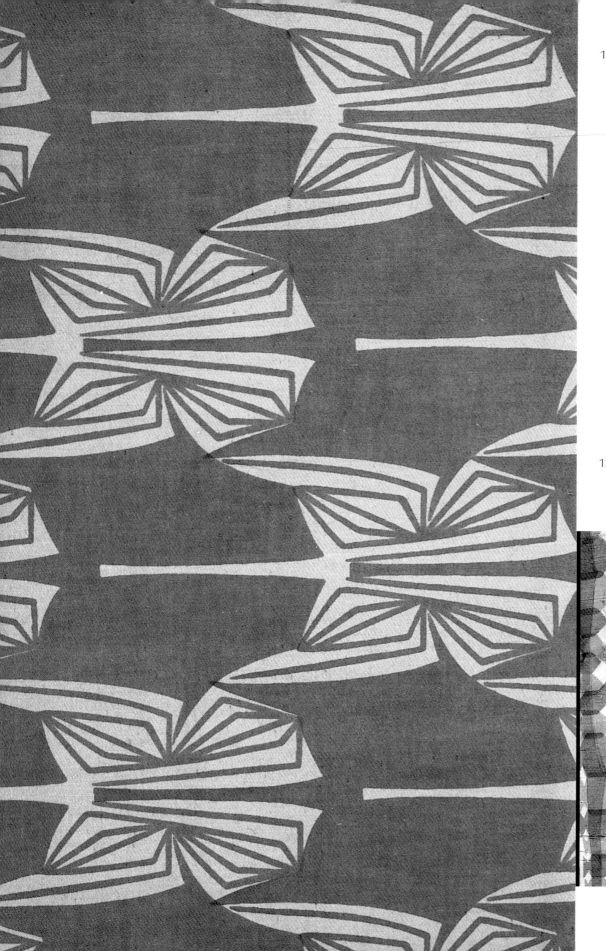

152 Curtain
Block-printed cotton
'Colil' C. Olesen
Denmark, 1962

153 Dress
Block-printed silk
'Colil' C. Olesen
Denmark, 1960

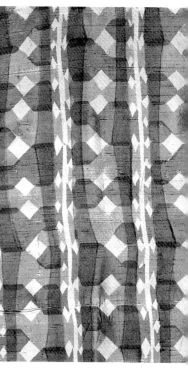

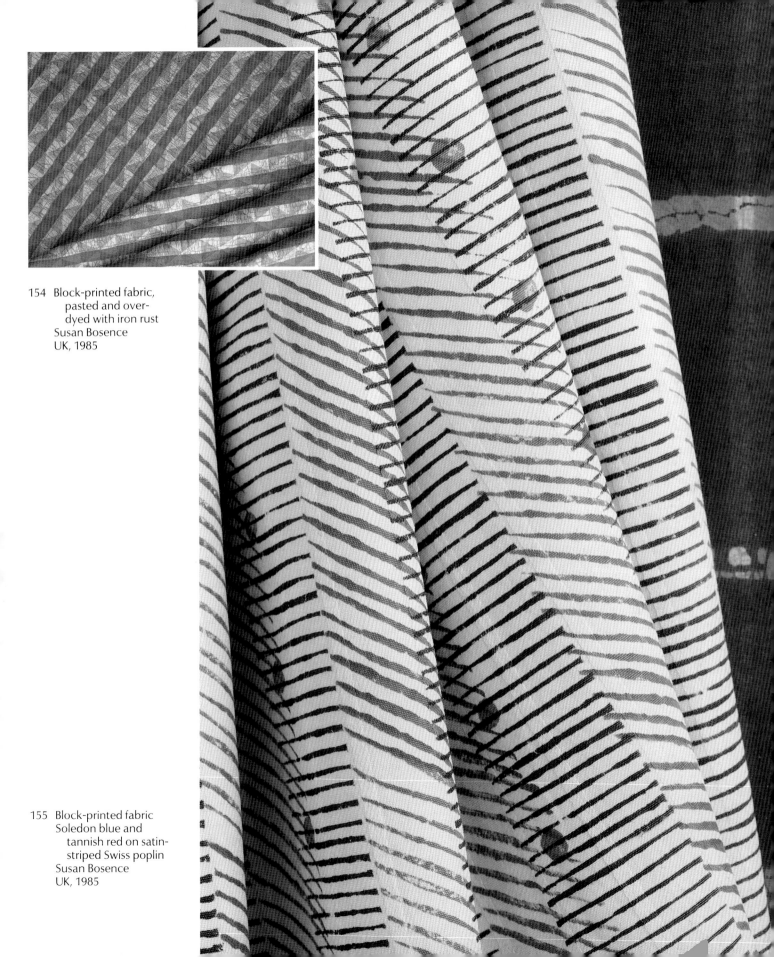

154 Block-printed fabric,
    pasted and over-
    dyed with iron rust
    Susan Bosence
    UK, 1985

155 Block-printed fabric
    Soledon blue and
    tannish red on satin-
    striped Swiss poplin
    Susan Bosence
    UK, 1985

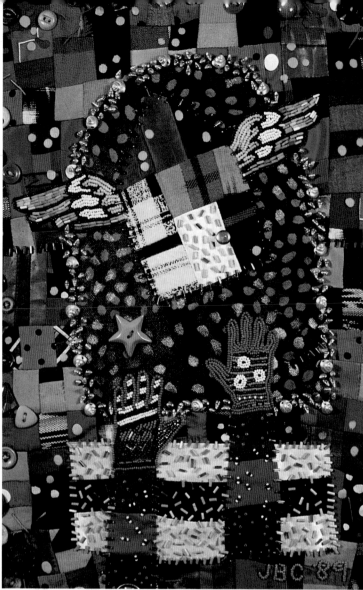

156 'Hospital'
Double-layered woven
mesh containing
objects
Susie Freeman
UK, 1986

157 'Reach' (detail)
Crazy quilt, with
embroidered and
appliquéd cottons
Jane Burch Cochran
USA, 1989

158 Quilt No. 14
Hand-quilted cottons
Pamella Studstill
USA, 1982

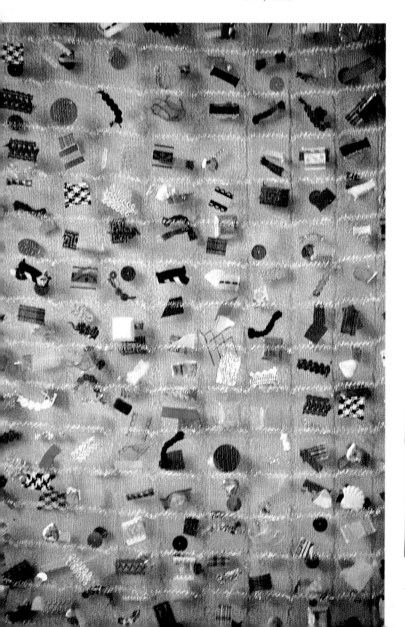

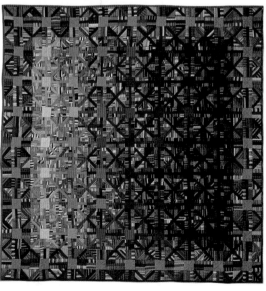

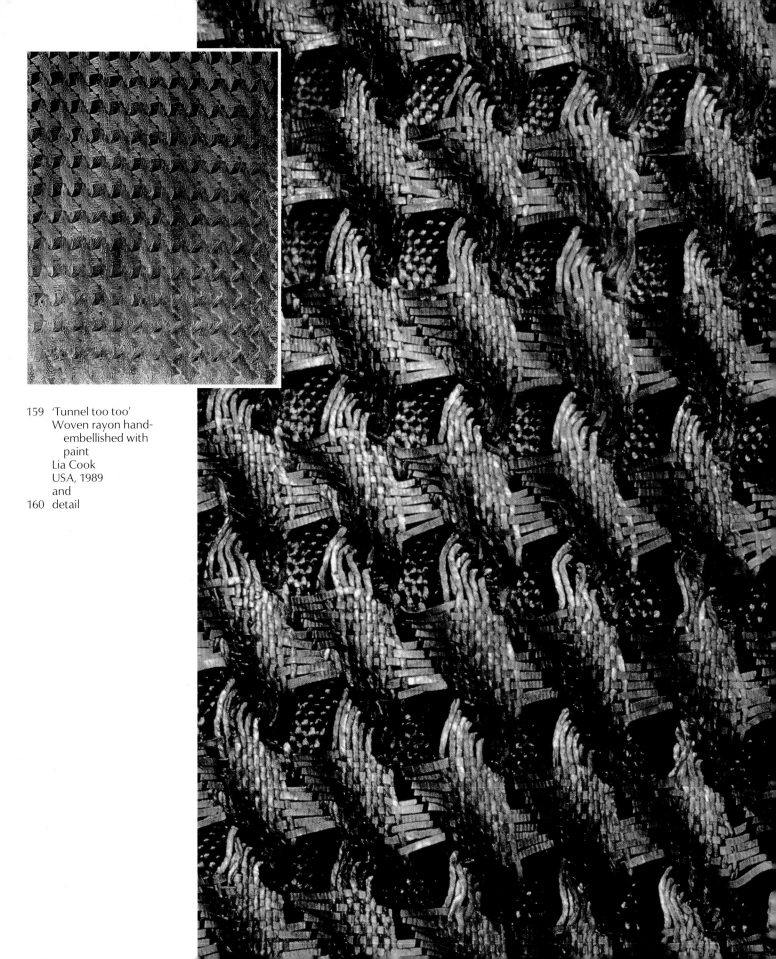

159 'Tunnel too too'
Woven rayon hand-
embellished with
paint
Lia Cook
USA, 1989
and
160 detail

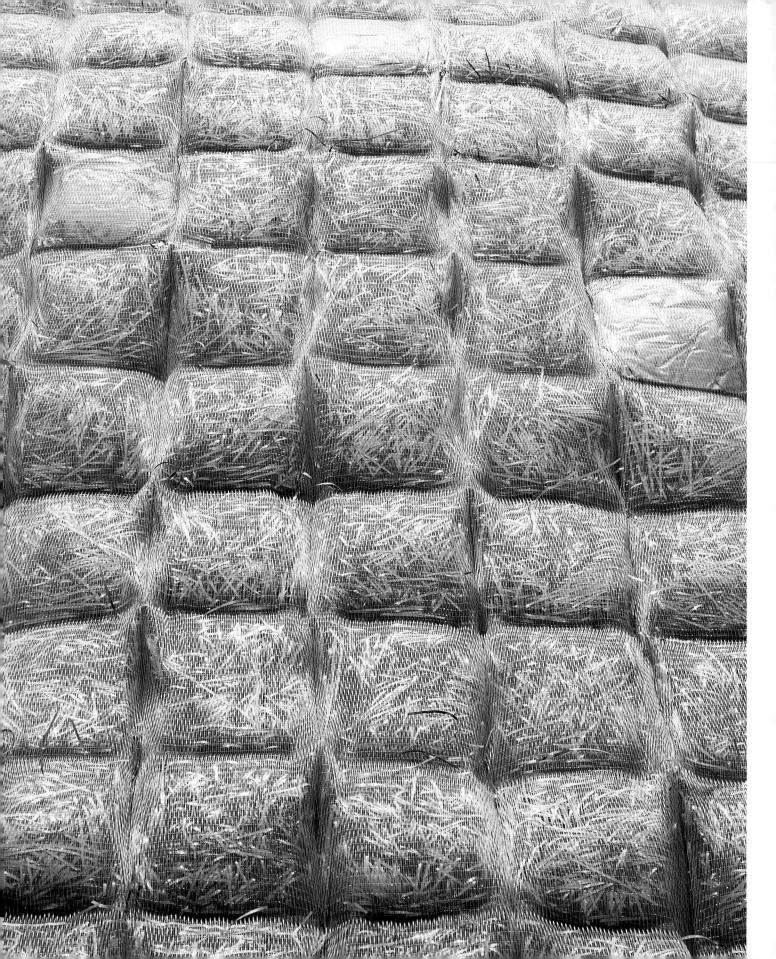

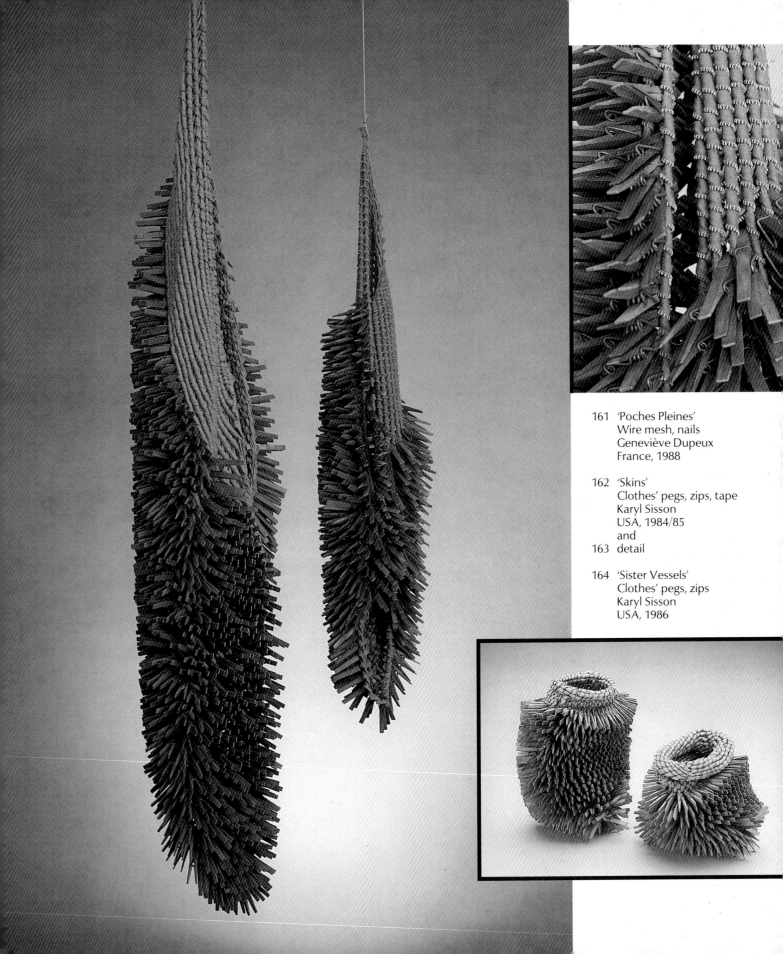

161 'Poches Pleines'
Wire mesh, nails
Geneviève Dupeux
France, 1988

162 'Skins'
Clothes' pegs, zips, tape
Karyl Sisson
USA, 1984/85
and
163 detail

164 'Sister Vessels'
Clothes' pegs, zips
Karyl Sisson
USA, 1986

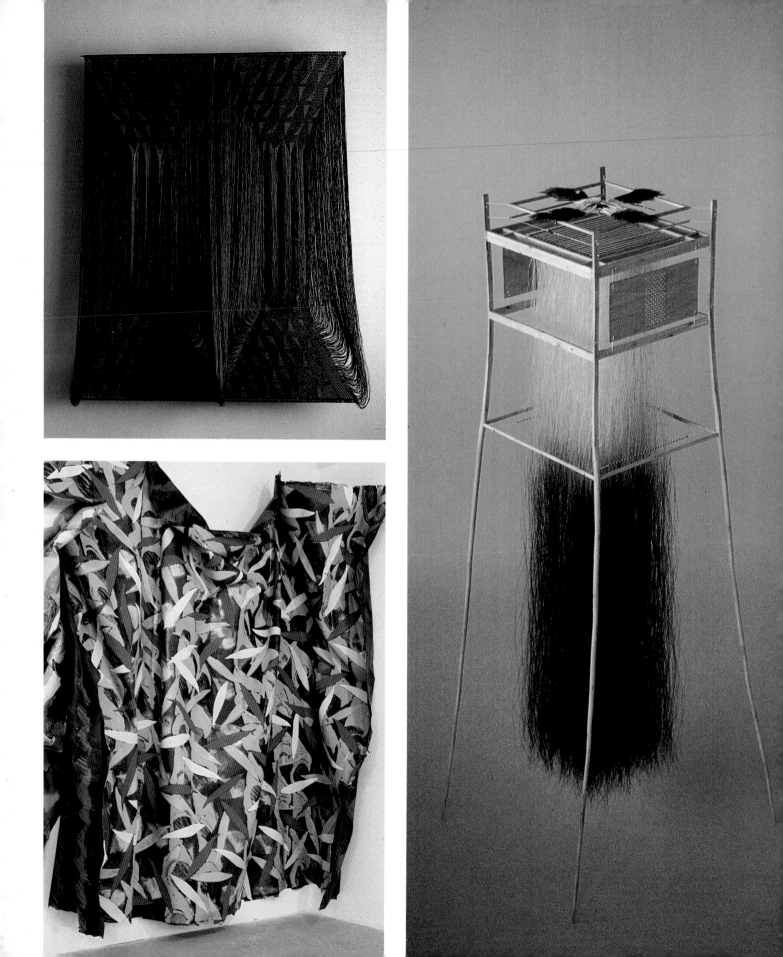

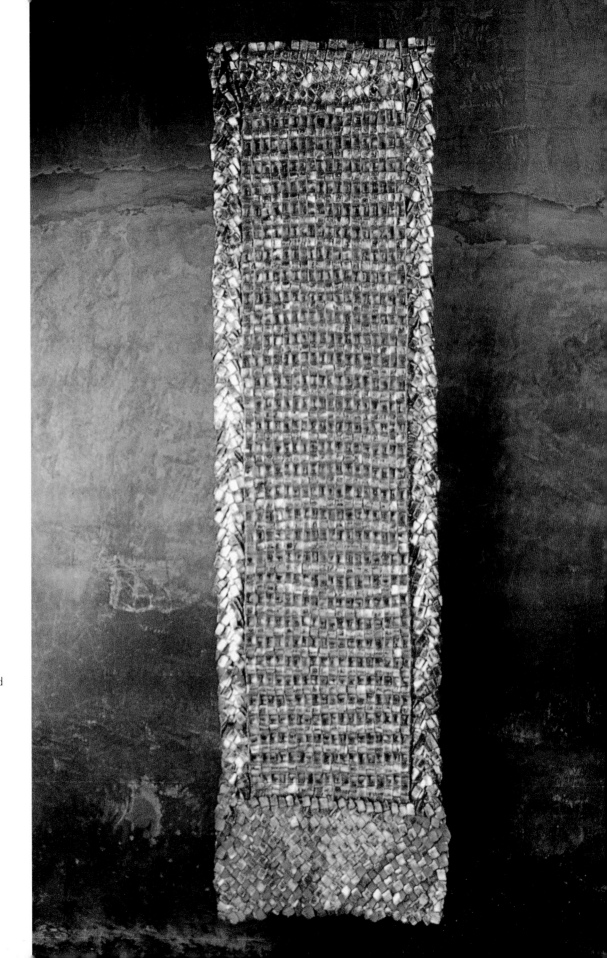

165 'Clouds'
Cotton sprang
Akiko Himanuki
Japan, 1987

166 'Fall Scene'
Painted on unstretched
    canvas
Neda Al-Hilali
USA, 1985

167 'Morning Station #7'
Mixed media
Dominic di Mare
USA, 1987

168 'Cesta Lunar 42'
Hanging
Printed linen with
    metallic pigment
Olga de Amaral
Colombia, 1990

169 'Soft Paddle'
    Coiled and twined
        waxed linen
    Ferne Jacobs
    USA, 1987

170 'White Figure Column'
    Coiled and twined
        waxed linen, thread
    Ferne Jacobs
    USA, 1986

171 'The Jealous Eye'
    Cotton, shellac, paint
    Norma Minkowitz
    USA, 1988

172 'Nadir'
    Cotton, shellac
    Norma Minkowitz
    USA, 1986

173 'Concavo e Convesso
        No. 2'
    Honeycomb-woven
        hemp
    Paola Bonfante
    Italy, 1988

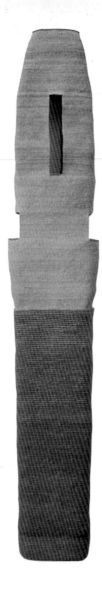

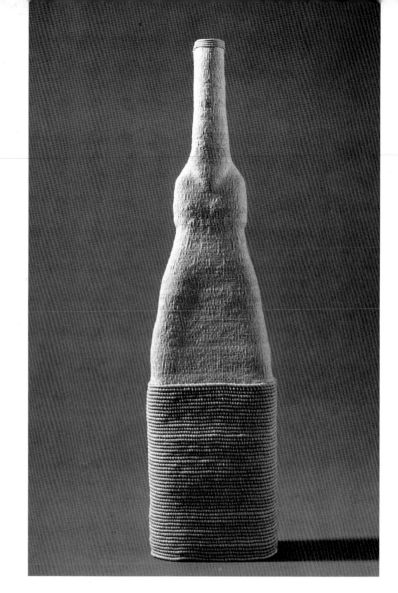

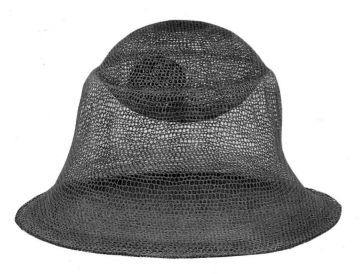

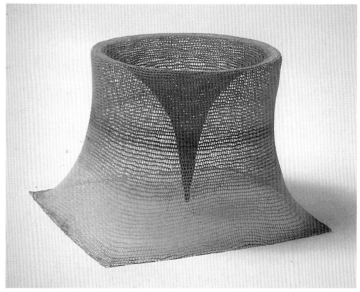

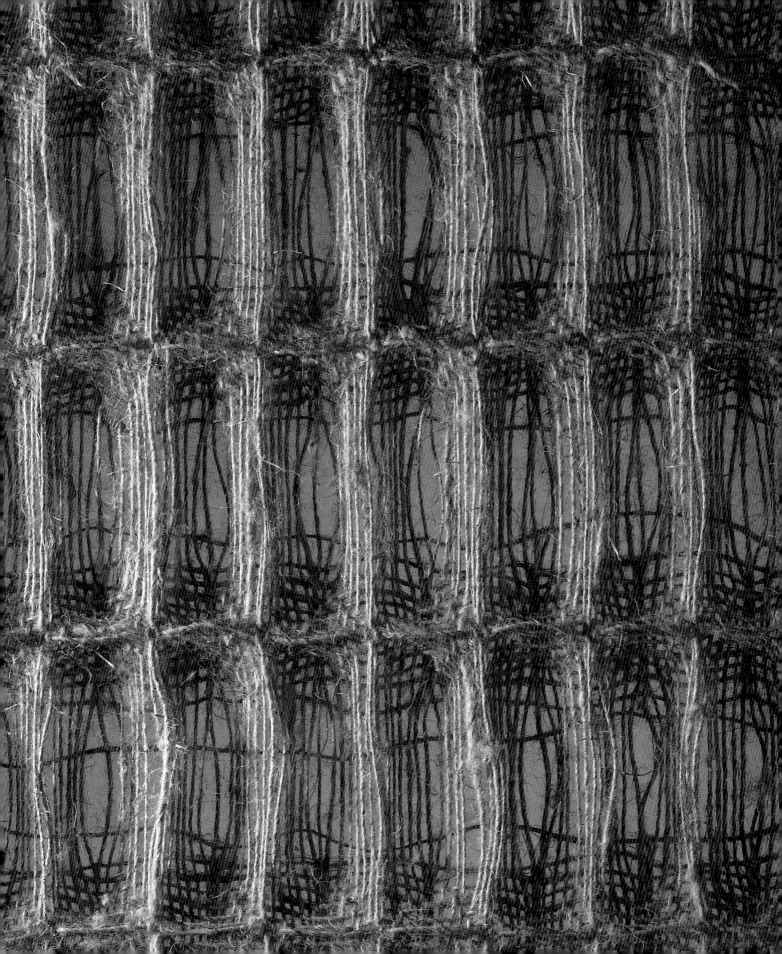

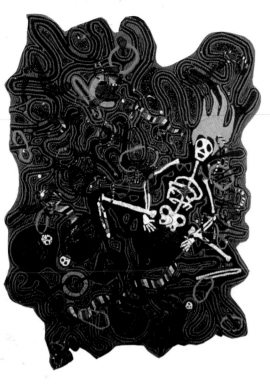

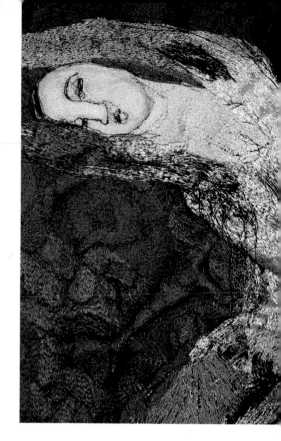

174 'Nuclear Nanny'
Appliqué and
needlework on
cotton
Joyce J. Scott
USA, 1984

175 'Blue Nymphs No. 4'
Machine embroidery on
cotton
Alice Kettle
UK, 1988

176 'Tar Beach Two'
Faith Ringgold
Printed by the Fabric
Workshop, USA, 1990

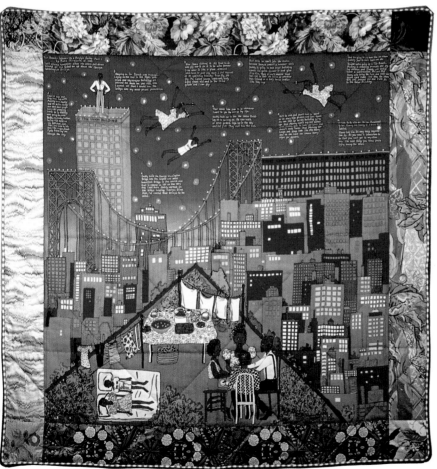

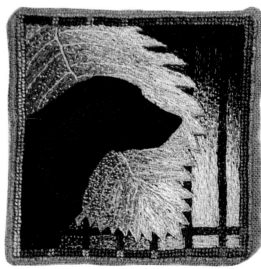

177 'Dog and Phone'
Cotton and silk
embroidery on linen
Tom Lundberg
USA, 1986

178 'Mind Spasms III'
Mary Brero
Embroidery and mixed
media
USA, 1987

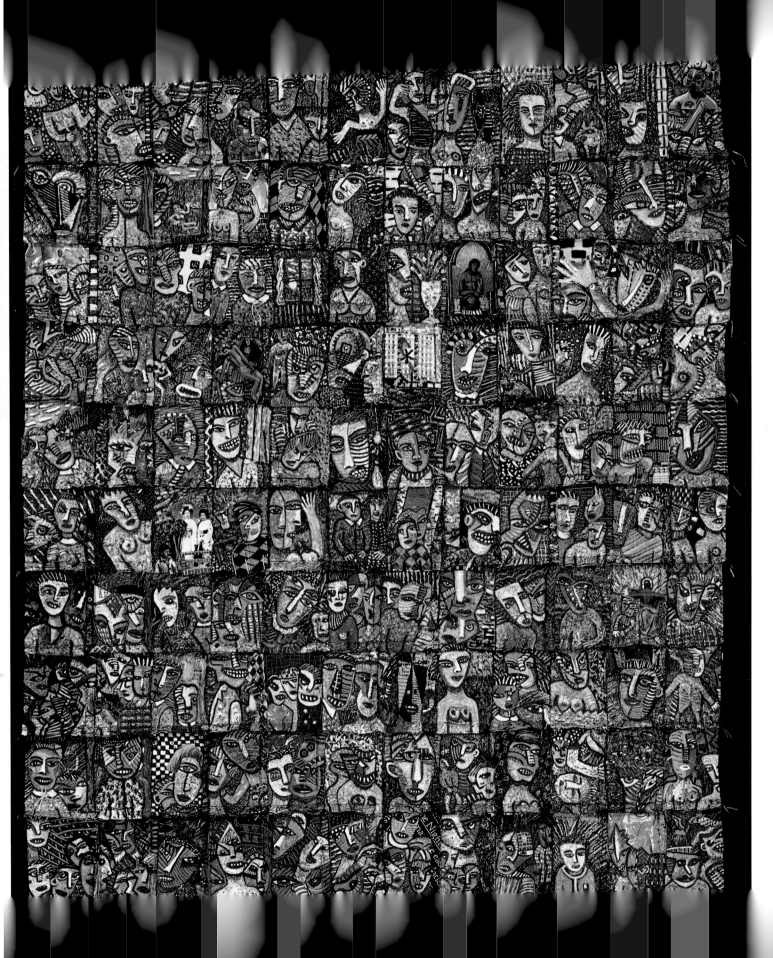

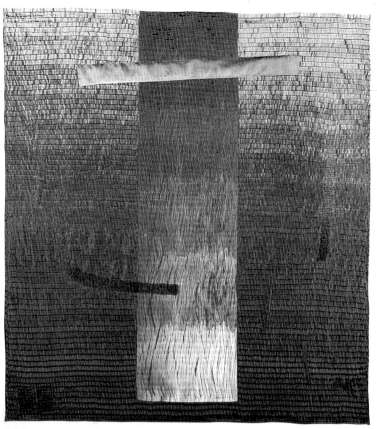

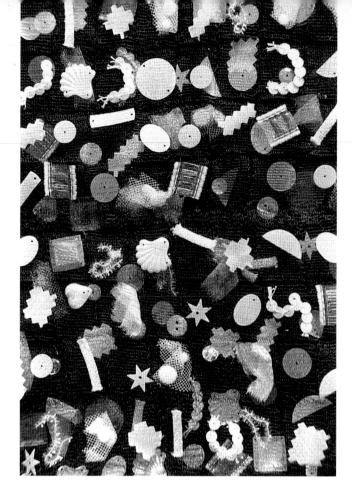

179 'Sorrow'
   Silk appliqué
   Michael Olzewski
   USA, 1990

180 Double-fabric mesh and
   objects
   Susie Freeman
   UK, 1987

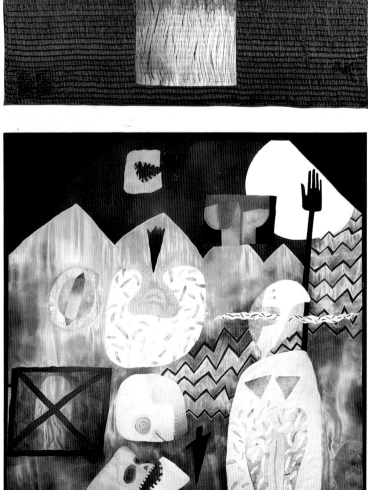

181 'Gate'
   Hanging
   Paint and appliqué on
     natural and synthetic
     fabrics
   Risë Nagin
   USA, 1989

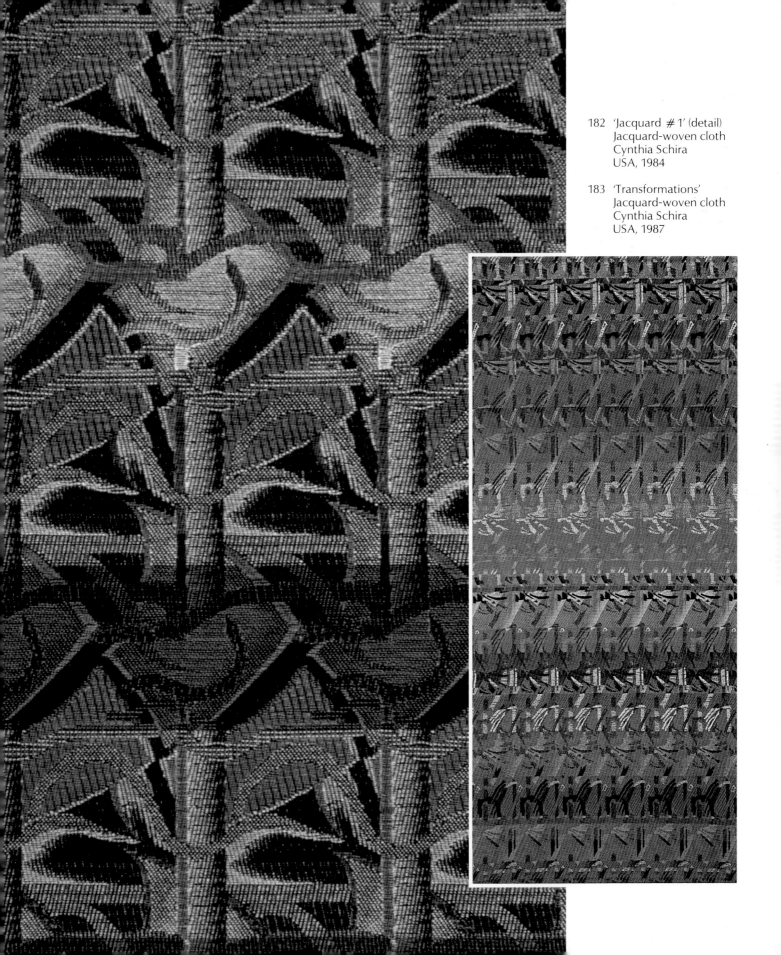

182 'Jacquard #1' (detail)
Jacquard-woven cloth
Cynthia Schira
USA, 1984

183 'Transformations'
Jacquard-woven cloth
Cynthia Schira
USA, 1987

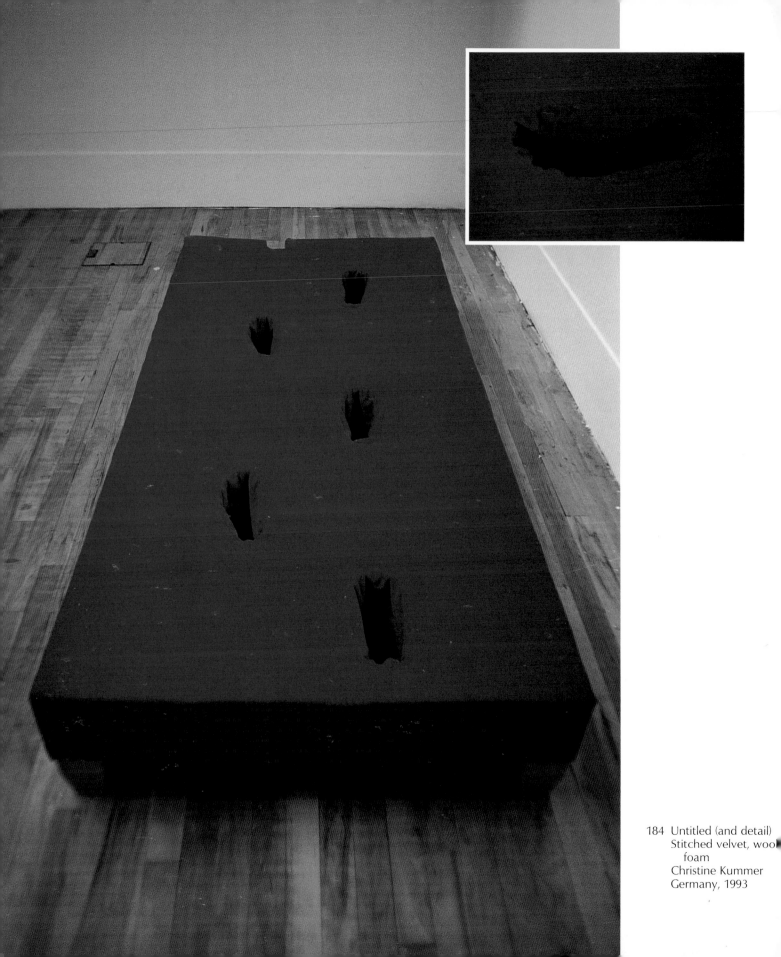

184 Untitled (and detail)
Stitched velvet, wool,
foam
Christine Kummer
Germany, 1993

TEXTILE ART

THE Second World War gave abundant confirmation to American politicians and intellectuals that their country was powerful. Hand-in-hand with this knowledge went an artistic revolt against the European aesthetics of beauty; in fact, one of the reasons why abstract expressionist painting became such an important feature of American culture was that it flaunted these traditional notions. Another was the quintessentially American sentiment that every citizen has the right to express him- or herself. These ideas had a profound effect on the new generation of art-school educated craftspeople who went on to become the founding members of the studio craft movement. On the West Coast the ceramicist Peter Voulkos took pots into the realm of sculpture. In textiles, tapestry was one area to benefit hugely from a post-war renaissance peopled by well-trained designers and artists, and Lenore Tawney and Claire Zeisler became the pioneers of the fibre art movement in their use of off-loom techniques.

Billed by Paul Smith, head of the American Craft Council, as one of the most talented weavers in the United States in the 1960s, Tawney explored in her early work the expressive potential of complex weave structures, inspired by Asian and American Indian textiles, which she rendered in totemic shapes. Her work progressed from distorting the selvages of fabric in the 1960s to abandoning the loom altogether in the 1970s. Tawney is most famous for her series of 'Clouds', started in 1978, which were fibre installations consisting of several thousand finely knotted linen threads suspended from the ceiling. The progressive dematerialization of her work was seen as evidence of its transformation from weaving into fibre art. Claire Zeisler also used knots, adapted from indigenous American Indian and Hawaiian knotting techniques, as a means of expanding into three-dimensional forms. Zeisler employed a team of assistants to work on her pieces using this painstaking technique. The result – sculptures of dazzling technical virtuosity. However, the monumental size of these pieces and, at least during the 1970s, their explicit sexual subject matter confounded many preconceptions, preconceptions of textiles as the domain of the homemaker, of what women's textile crafts should be about.

In 1963 the American Craft Council in New York staged the seminal exhibition 'Woven Forms', which, in the words of Paul Smith, its curator, 'introduced the work of five individuals whose different backgrounds as weavers have led them to a related basis of expression – the creation of sculptural shapes from interlaced threads'. This exhibition travelled round Europe, fuelling the growing interest in fibre arts on the Continent.

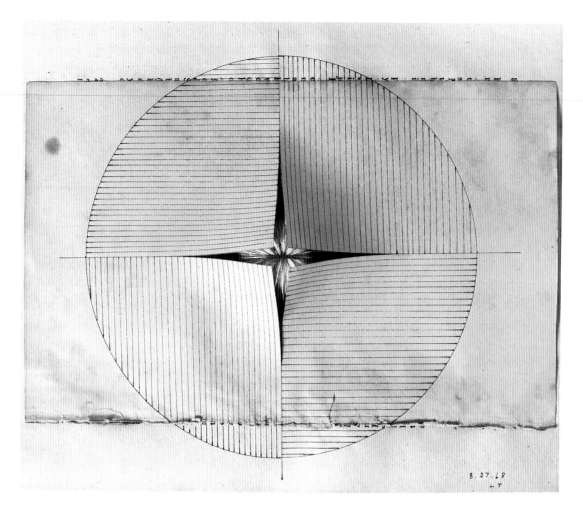

Was fibre art 'art'? The question became, and has remained, a moot point. In his introduction to the exhibition 'Craft Today: The Poetry of the Physical', of 1986, the critic Edward Lucie-Smith skirted round the issue by saying that any distinction between art and craft rested entirely on the intentions of the maker. An alternative theory, rather lugubriously entitled 'The Institutional Theory of Art', put forward a rather more cynical view, namely that an object could only be considered 'art' if the institutions – the art press, art galleries and museums, and so on – said that it was so. Unfortunately for the fibre artists, this was rarely the case, even with those institutions who had flirted with the idea for a short while. So, during the course of the 1960s and 1970s, an alternative infrastructure was created to support the fibre arts in the form of the crafts councils and museums.

At the same time, the widespread creation of new university buildings and the boom in civic architecture in general also helped the fibre art movement to develop rapidly. Textile hangings were amongst the few forms of decoration to have been approved by both the Bauhaus and Corbusier and were therefore popular with modernist architects. Jack Lenor Larsen, who with Mildred Constantine co-authored two major books on the subject, *Beyond Craft: the Art Fabric* and *The Art Fabric: Mainstream*, recalled that in the opinion of the Polish Minister for the Arts at that time, textiles, with their display of virtuoso, or at least recognizable, techniques, were seen to

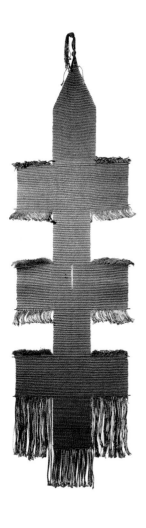

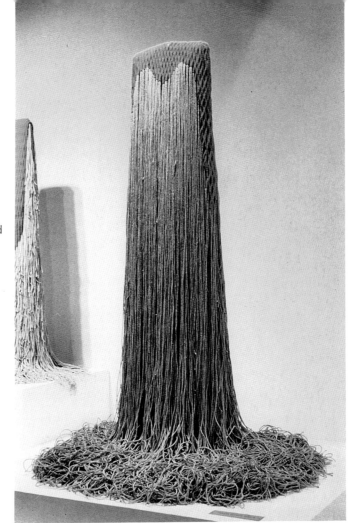

Opposite:
'In Silence'
Collage
Lenore Tawney
USA, 1968

Left:
'Lekythos'
Linen hanging
Lenore Tawney
USA, 1962

'Stella I'
Knotted sisal and
     cotton
Fibre form
Claire Zeisler
USA, 1977/8

be more populist and therefore ideologically suitable for the decoration of public places. Especially favoured were the intricate structural or modular pieces that evoked associations of order, calm and stasis, and the preservation of the status quo, of which the British weaver Peter Collingwood's macrogauzes, feats of structural engineering, were a supreme example. Such work was regarded, especially on the Continent, as vastly more suitable for civic display than the current fashions for expressionism and minimalism, which were considered decadent and disruptive of the social fabric.

The work of Sheila Hicks, one of the early stars of the American fibre art movement, provoked the French anthropologist Claude Levi-Strauss to comment that it 'provided the perfect antidote for the functional, utilitarian architecture in which we are sentenced to dwell, [which] it enlivens with the dense patient work of human hands'. Indeed, fibre art soon became the architects' standard solution for ennervating featureless rooms built in the modernist style. But, like much 1970s building, many of the pieces were rushed, and consequently badly made. One particular problem, overlooked at the outset, was the cleaning of these pieces. Unlike traditional Gobelin tapestries, which in any case are easy to maintain and can be rolled up when not in use, the coarse materials and textures of the new fibre art attracted much dust. Still worse, the sheer weight and scale of many pieces, combined with the difficulty of dismantling and reinstalling 'textile

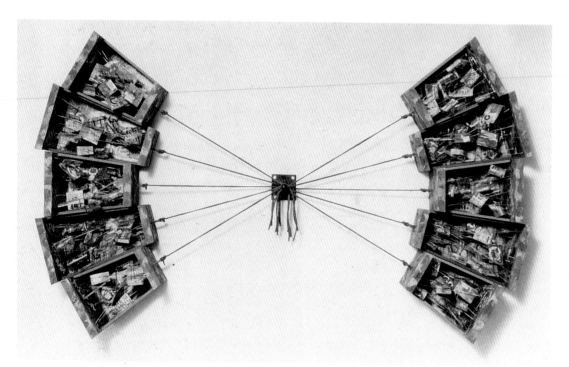

'Talk-talk'
Wall piece
Wire, wood, thread, paint and
    elements of text
Michael Brennand-Wood
UK, 1987/88

environments', made them difficult to move. The new fibre art was a cleaner's nightmare; thick
with filth, these grimy, hairy weavings eventually became a bête noire for the fibre art movement
in the 1990s.

In the late 1970s, at the same time that fibre artists such as Magdalena Abakanowicz and Olga
de Amaral were investigating the rustic, earthy side of fibre, another group began to explore the
relationship between textiles, lightness and wind using ultralight tension fabric structures. This
paralleled the development of light but strong fabric tension structures in architecture, used
beautifully by Studio Som to create the white tented rooves for the airport in Jedda. But whereas
architects saw tension structures as a development of the movement in modern architecture to
create ever lighter buildings, for which they used the latest man-made high resistance fabrics and
membranes, fibre artists contributed by researching and developing the traditions of tension
structures. Textile artists such as Daniel Graffin and Vera Svekely (France), Patricia Campbell and
Warren Seelig (USA), and Sally Freshwater (UK) explored the relationship between textiles and
wind in kites and sails and in fixed structures such as paper parasols and screens.

The interest in tension structures led to another development in fibre art, when the traditional
support for fine art painting, the stretched canvas, was recognized as a very basic sort of tension
structure itself. During the course of the 1980s a number of artists, including Neda Al-Hilali (USA),
Daniel Chompré (Finland) and Rushton Aust (UK) tried working on relaxed canvas as a way of
expressing the floppy material qualities of fibre. These works are gently provocative in that they
pose questions about the divisions between fine art and decorative art. In a similar vein textile
artists, among them Neda Al-Hilali, Théa Bernard and Maryan Geluk, also experimented with
different methods of treating, pulping, tearing and plaiting paper to reveal its material qualities.

One of Britain's leading textile artists, Michael Brennand Wood, investigated the relationship
between painting, textiles, and wood in a new way by making wooden grids invade the canvas.

Small fragments of paper, or patterned fabric, are lashed to these grids using coloured string. His constructions are intriguing objects that can be read as a comment on structure and narrative or pattern in fabric.

IN France Patrice Hugues has explored the role that patterns and motifs play in pictorial images. Hugues' technique is interesting; he 'deconstructs' photographs into several layers which he then prints on to lengths of net using a high-fidelity printing technique called heat-transfer printing. This approach is ingenious in that it gives Hugues the freedom of reassembling his images in different ways. It enables him to experiment with the depth of the field, and more importantly to analyse the effect that different textile patterns have upon the way one sees a picture.

Dress is an integral part of the way we view ourselves and project our personality, taste or simply our mood on a certain day. During the 1980s, at the same time that fashion designers and stylists in London, Paris and Milan were experimenting with style as a burlesque expression of culture, a group of artists started to investigate the meaning not of fashion but of clothing.

Caroline Broadhead is one of a group of artists who have started to comment on clothing and the way in which it is perceived. She is interested in the intimate aspects of clothing, the idea that they have been shaped not just by fashion but by somebody's life. 'Clothing holds a visual memory of a person', she says, 'and it is this closeness to a human being that I am interested in.' In her series of 'skeleton' clothes she uses the seams to create three-dimensional line drawings which express emotional states, movement, gesture, aspirations and dilemmas. By exhibiting colourless clothes of indeterminate style, she avoids the anecdotal, but the emotional states and dilemmas she describes – as in the elongated shirt in 'Stretch' – are specific.

The idea that clothing is a projection of the self has also been taken up by the Paris-based American artist Marian Schoettle, who has created a series of double shirts, linked by continuous sleeves. These shirts demonstrate our readiness to read posture into clothes: they come alive in performance. Another British artist, Rose Garrard, comments on a related idea of clothing as a cultural envelope. In her installation 'La Pittura, the Spirit of Painting Reclaimed' (1986), two nylon dresses printed with a medley of French Impressionist and Old Master paintings 'pose' as model and artist. This work, as its title suggests, has a specific meaning – it is about a female artist attempting to find her bearings within the male tradition of fine art.

The idea developed by the surrealists in the 1930s, that the world of manufactured goods can be an alien, hostile force with a life of its own, is the subject of Mitsuo Toyazaki's piece 'Over the Rainbow', which features an army of multicoloured gym shoes 'marching' across a cultivated landscape under a clear blue sky. Toyazaki is a young Japanese fibre artist whose works hang in the balance between fetishization and social comment, bland optimism and concern. His art is based on bulk-buying. By filling rooms with identical objects, such as paper tissues, respiratory masks and nylon tights, brightly dyed, he transforms them into an alien presence. Recurrent themes are fungus and disease: in 'Social Plants' (1988) upended nylons dyed lurid shades of green create an unnatural forest of stalacmites. Mitsuo Toyazaki's work is important in that it expresses the side of Japanese culture that revels in pop culture, plastic and day-glo colours. Using man-made materials and objects to ape the natural, he subverts the long tradition in textile art, especially in Japan, of expressing concern for nature.

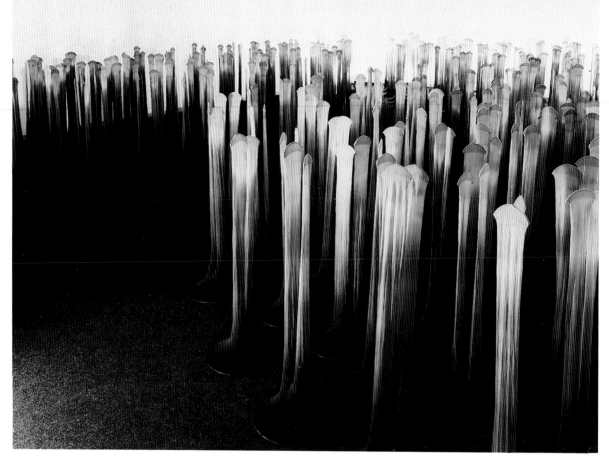

'Social Plants', installation of dyed tights. Mitsuo Toyazaki. Japan, 1988

Japan is fast becoming the world centre for fibre sculpture, and Mitsuo Toyazaki and Hideho Tanaka are prominent among the new generation of Japanese sculptors who have turned to fibre as a vehicle for expression. The link between textiles and nature and the natural cycle of change was dramatically demonstrated by Hideho Tanaka's performance piece 'Scorched Earth' (1984) which involved stitching vast sheets of fabric to a beach with cotton rope before setting them alight. Together with Akio Hamatani, and Kyoko Kumai, Tanaka and Toyazaki illustrate the tension between two opposing tendencies in Japanese culture – respect for nature and interest in new manufacturing technologies. Their work will call for an overall reassessment of the relationship between textiles and the natural world.

Such a relationship established firm foundations within the new Polish tapestry movement when shortages of conventional materials resulting from the Second World War necessitated the use of agricultural materials such as hemp, sisal and rope in tapestry-making, and the works themselves came to be seen as ideologically suitable for a largely agrarian people. The leading figures in the Polish tapestry movement were women, who for the first time started to weave tapestries of their own design rather than translating an existing painting on to cloth.

Tapestries are durable, they can easily last at least five hundred years and they reveal the quality of their manufacture: a client can see how much work he or she is buying, how much manual skill, time and effort. Astute marketing has also been used to make tapestry attractive to architects and designers. Indeed, in France, the entrepreneur François Pinton set up the International Center for Woven Architecture. Among the tapestry collection marketed by Pinton are designs by Sonia Delaunay made in 1970 and woven by the company. Artists and designers are employed by Pinton to produce contemporary themes and the results are just what a high bourgoise clientele wants: meretricious, rich and easy on the eye.

France is known, of course, as a centre for well-crafted tapestry because of its world-famous tapestry workshops – Les Manufactures Nationales des Gobelins. These comprise a state-owned tapestry 'factory' run by an institution called the Mobilier National. Among its remits is the lending out to French embassies and other government buildings furniture and tapestries acquired by the state during the French Revolution. Interestingly – because it focuses on the artist/craftsperson split with a vengeance – there is apparently no love lost between the Mobilier National and the Gobelin tapestry studios. For the Mobilier National has decreed recently that the weavers are no longer to put their initials beneath the artist's signature (the artist designs, the weavers weave) – and yet a tapestry can take up to twelve years to weave.

At the Edinburgh Tapestry Company in Scotland the relationship between 'artist' and 'weaver' is more democratic. The company is seventy-five years old and it has in recent years worked in collaboration with many artists including Britain's David Hockney and America's Frank Stella. The company's managers insist that the work they do with artists is a true collaboration and that weavers and artists discuss how a work should be treated and interpreted. Many of the most consequential tapestry artists are American; among the best-known tapestry weavers are Warren Seelig, Ruth Scheuer, Cynthia Schira, Gerhardt Knodel, and Peter and Ritzi Jacobi. To which one might add the astonishing artist from Poland, Magdalena Abakanowicz, who is working in the USA and whose textile works took weaving into profound art. Freed, however, from the restrictions of Communist censorship, she has since flowered yet more – as a sculptor working in metal.

Tapestry may even be viewed as 'subversive' in its own right, for one may argue that its most important attribute in the context of late twentieth-century art and craft is the skill, care and time it takes to create a work. The demands made on the tapestry artist's stamina and on his or her concentration can vastly exceed those endured by other contemporary artists working in other media. One of America's leading younger tapestry artists, Ruth Scheuer, claims that 'tapestry is a subversive activity for a world that is in a hurry'. Her work is figurative and shows fragmented snapshot scenes of American urban life – fragmented in the way we have become used to seeing in the graphic arts of modern video and thirty-second television advertising. She runs a large studio and she sometimes works collaboratively with other artists.

Scheuer often uses photography as a starting point in her designs. The use of photographic images as a basis for figurative works is not uncommon and results in very clear, rather formal imagery. The danger of the photograph, however, lies in its stiltedness. And this is an acute danger in tapestry which, because it is a medium of deliberation rather than accident, is prone to stiltedness anyway, and the use of photography can exacerbate this effect.

One of Scheuer's American peers, Cynthia Schira, is noted for her tapestries, drawn from themes in landscape and water, wherein the colours and shapes seem almost to dissolve into one another. Schira's work uses the special qualities of weaving and tapestry to create effects that other media cannot. Just as in good conté drawing or aquatint printing one is enamoured of the medium's textures, so too with Schira's work – the woven medium is also the message, not merely a vehicle.

The interest in the woven structure as an expressive form in its own right has been a most important characteristic of art textile work since the Second World War and has resulted in a succession of exhibitions and commissions in which woven forms have been used to create abstract sculptures and environments. In the late 1960s and early 1970s, especially in Europe, and most especially in Eastern Europe, public buildings such as 'People's Palaces of Culture' would have huge walls covered in woven textile forms that hung, clung and emerged like fungus or the internal landscapes of the human gut. A frequent, if covert image in such work was that of the vulva.

Ady Comou's work, generally untitled, is characterized by another fashion that grew strong in the 1980s – the fashion for giving work the aura of the totemic or the ritualistic. Not that specific rituals are referred to, or indeed indicated. However, the allusion to another sort of meaning – a meaning that cannot be put into words or figuration – has become an important aspect of the work of many artist/craftspeople throughout the industrialized world, and it pervades the media of ceramics, clothing and jewelry as well as tapestry and art textiles.

Organic work, although interesting in its own right, is of limited appeal to contemporary architects – and that is important. For it is architecture and the people who use buildings, especially public or corporate buildings, that provide a major context for defining the shape, content and purpose of tapestry. Tapestry, partly because of its usually grand scale, is a naturally public art. It is not only too big, it is also too expensive in the time and money committed to it to be hidden away in private homes.

And what the market for tapestry demands is imagery that either can be understood by a lot of people, or that does not demand any understanding at all but which works, like the building itself, in terms of colour, form and texture. In this regard, work of the German tapestry weaver Professor Elfi Knoche Wendel is of interest. She works with traditional weaving techniques but has eschewed all figurative content. She says: 'I make use of the thread and of woven structures as a means of expression, not merely as an instrument to translate a picture.' And about the content of her work, she adds: 'My structures are elements I took out of nature, not to describe a lost paradise but to find a new sensibility for myself and the viewer in a period that tries to escape all primitivism. But my work is not about nostalgia.'

Another notable German tapestry artist is Martha Kreutzer Temming. Her work shows a great gentleness. In her simple abstract compositions she creates the delicate emotion of solace – the rectitude of her tapestries provides a welcome relief after the more strident images of contemporary tapestry design.

But ultimately what characterizes the renaissance in tapestry production is variety. The reviving art of tapestry has not fallen prey to dogmatism and thus the contemporary movement is tolerant of all kinds of content. But the problem for women artists working in tapestry is that they still fall foul of the male hegemony operating throughout the fine art world. Not enough of the tapestry art that deserves to be in major public collections has yet appeared in them.

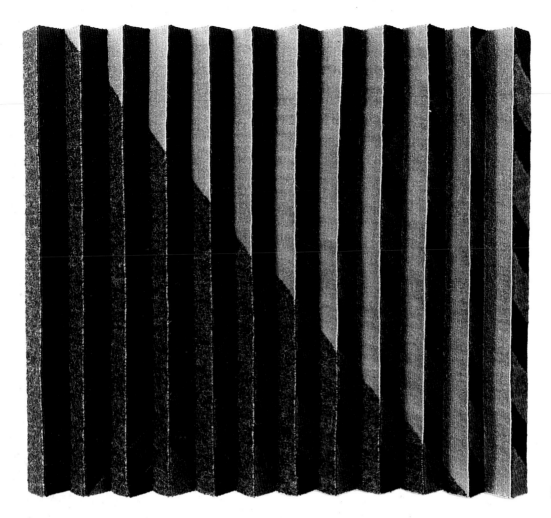

186 'Midnight'
Sisal, linen, wool
Adela Akers
USA, 1988

187 'Bull's Roar'
Acrylic paint on
synthetic felt and
linen
Anne Wilson
USA, 1986

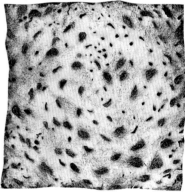

188 'Les Berniques'
Installation of folded
and painted paper
Théa Bernard
France, 1989/90

189 'Gaming Field'
Acrylic paint on
synthetic felt and
linen
Anne Wilson
USA, 1986

Page 145:
185 'Reflection'
Salt, pine needles, wire,
parcel tape
Claire Barber
UK, 1994

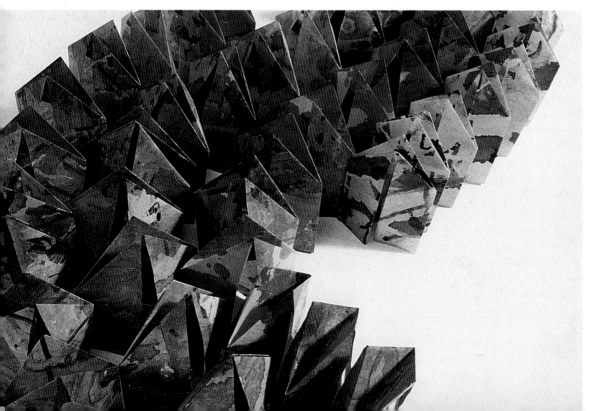

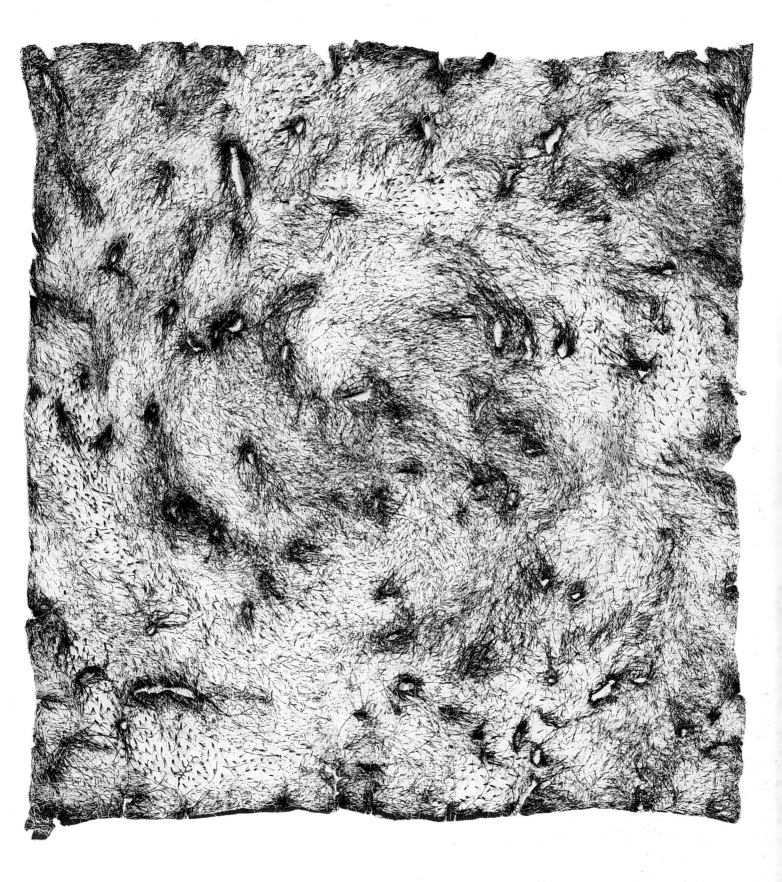

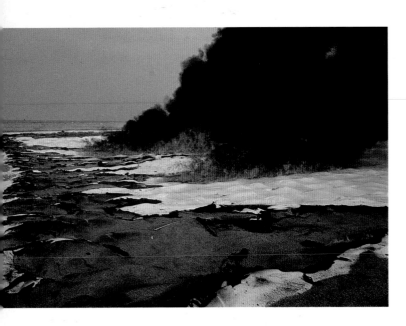

190 'Scorched Earth'
Cotton sheeting
Hideho Tanaka
Japan, 1984

191 'Over the Rainbow'
Plimsoles, pigment
Mitsuo Toyazaki
Japan, 1987

192 'Kuu'
Woven stainless-steel
filaments
Kyoko Kumai
Japan, 1987

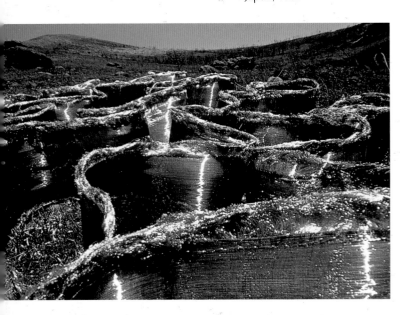

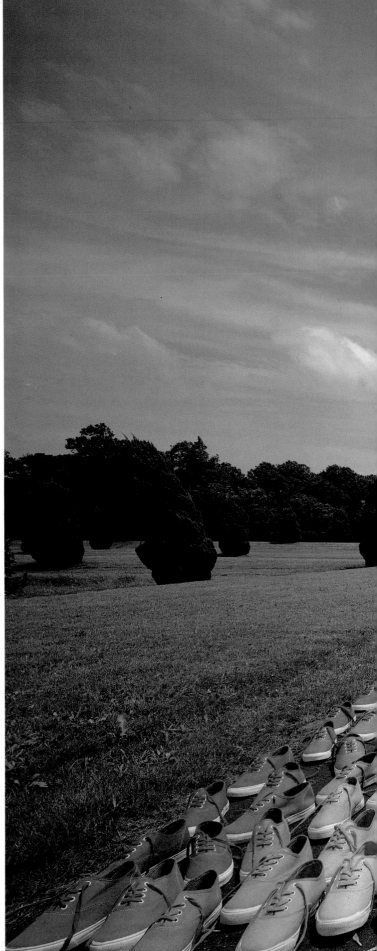

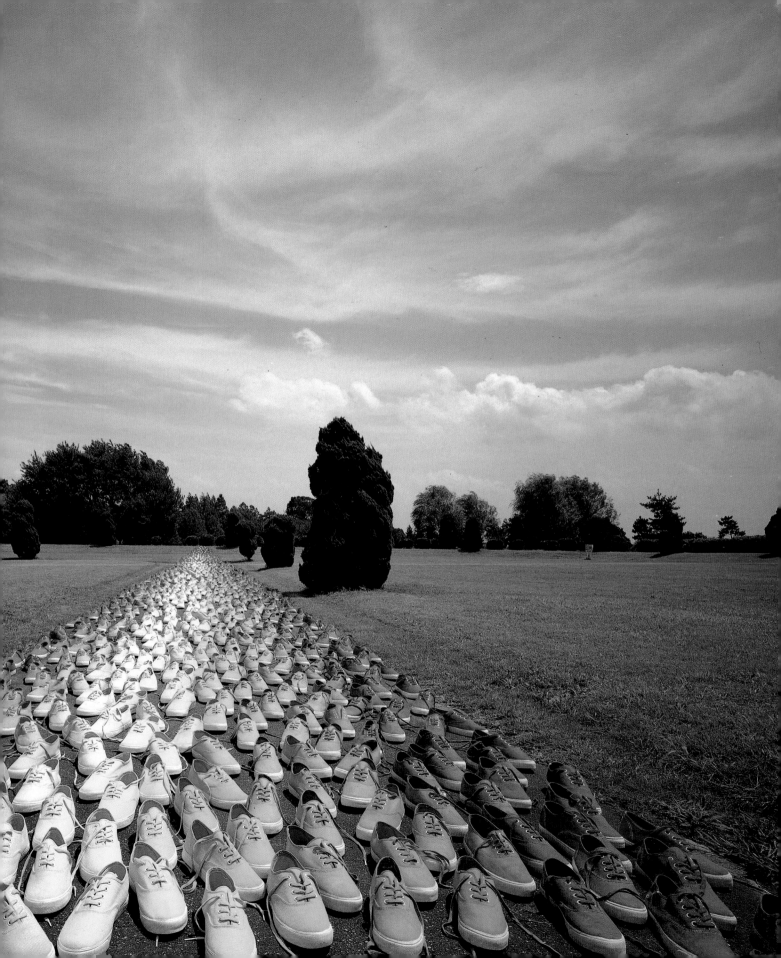

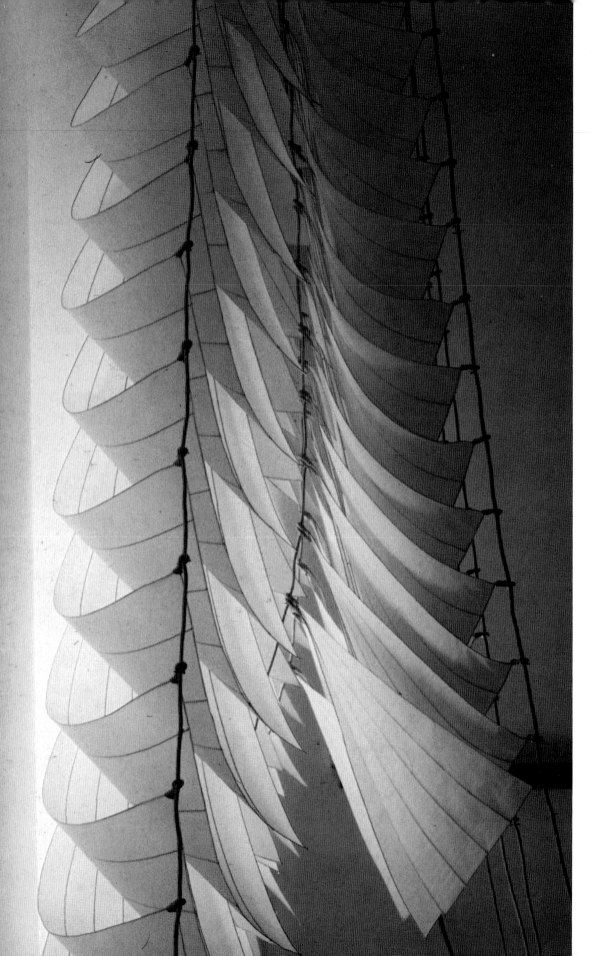

193 Constructed light wall
Shellacked fabric and
paper, cord
Patricia Campbell
USA, 1979

195 'White Arc III'
Silk organza, lime
Sally Freshwater
UK, 1989

194,196
Structures under
tension
Polyester canvas
reinforced with fibre
glass
Vera Svekely
France, 1985/6

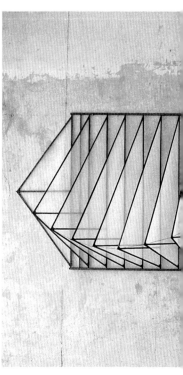

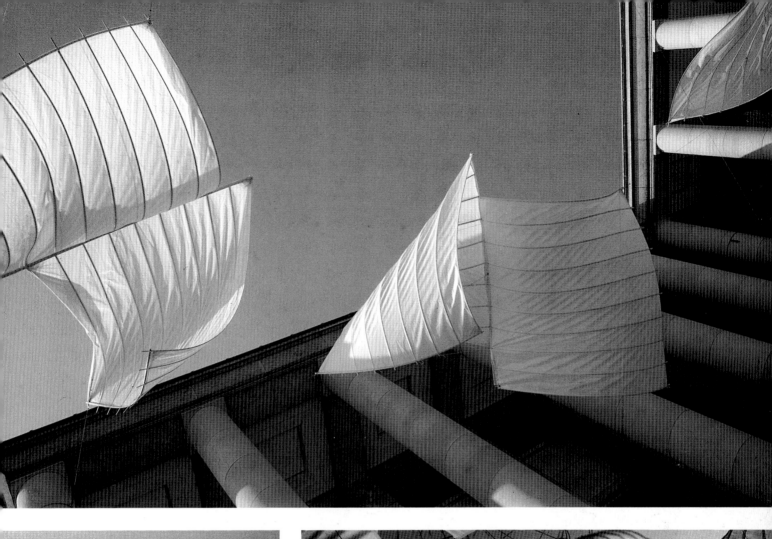

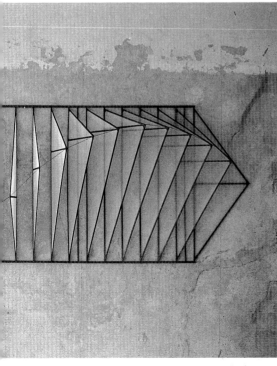
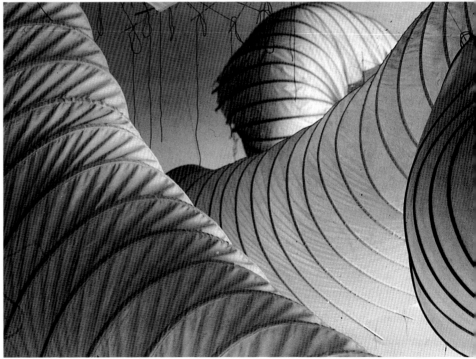

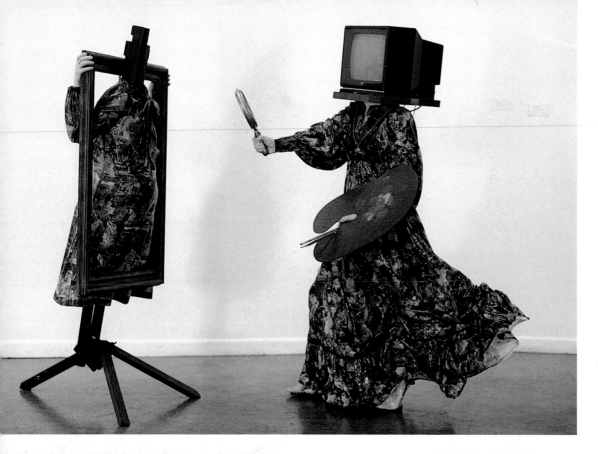

197 'La Pittura, the Spirit of
     Painting Reclaimed'
     Installation using nylon
     dresses
     Rose Garrard
     UK, 1986

198 'Fall' (detail)
     Heat-transfer printed on
     synthetic net
     Patrice Hugues
     France, 1983

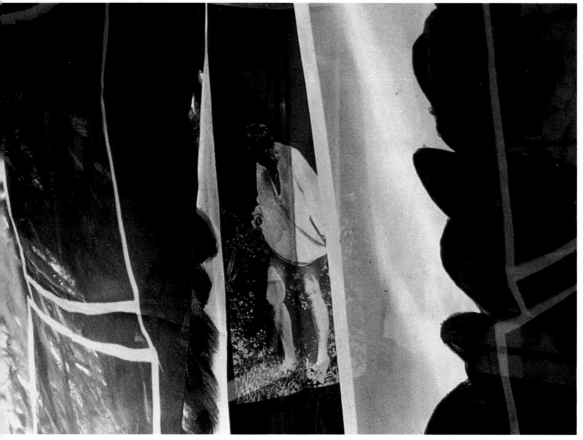

199 'Gilded by the Sun'
Felt
Maisa Tikkanen
Finland, 1988

200 'Est' (detail)
Rolled fabric
Sibyl Heijnen
Holland, 1989/90

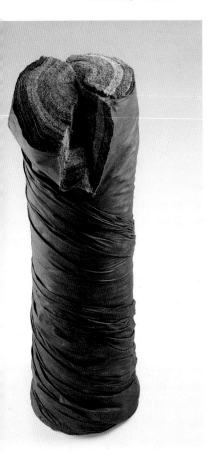

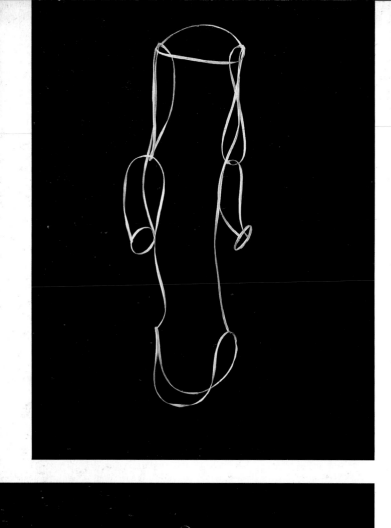

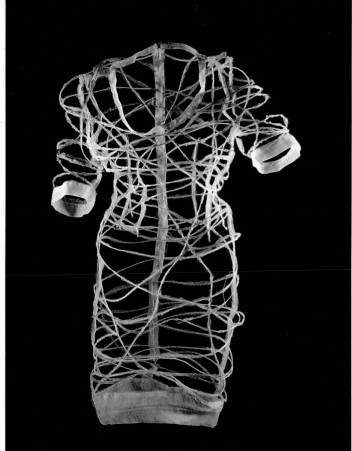

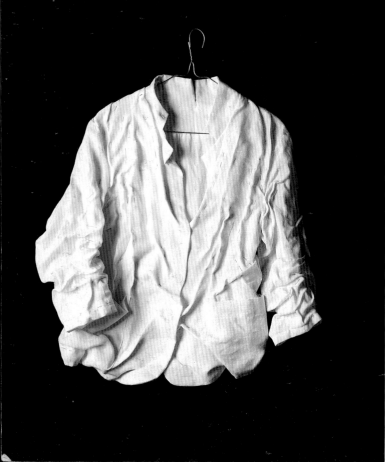

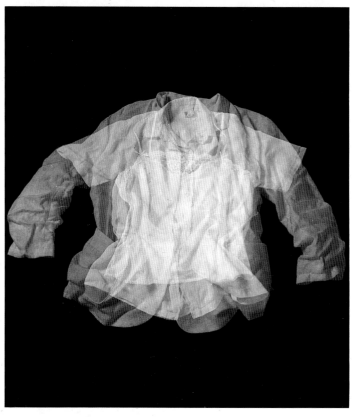

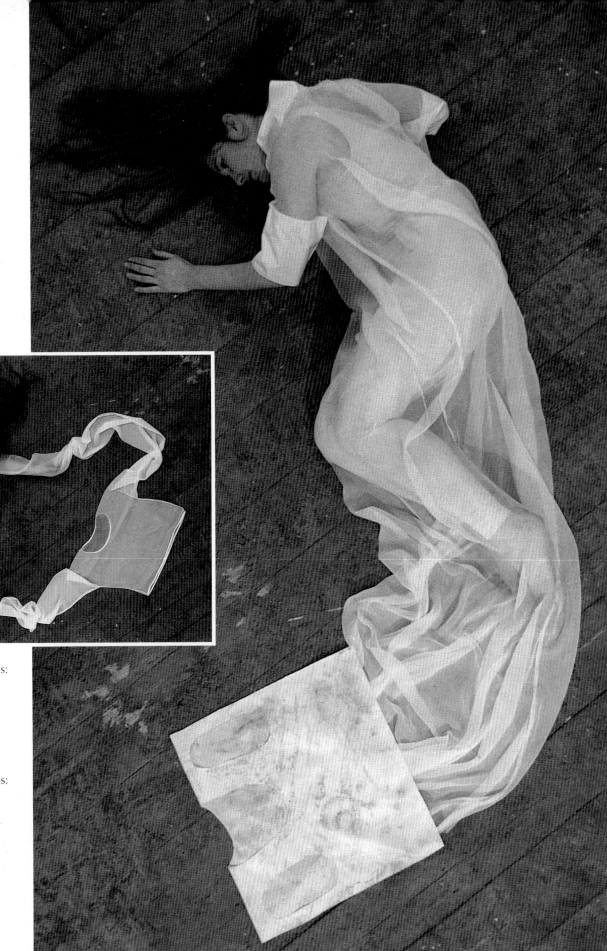

201 Seven Ages No. 7:
     'Seam'
     Machine-stitched
     cotton and nylon
     Caroline Broadhead
     UK, 1986

202 'Web'
     Machine-stitched
     cotton and nylon
     Caroline Broadhead
     UK, 1989

203 Seven Ages No. 6:
     'Crumple'
     Linen, pins
     Caroline Broadhead
     UK, 1986

204 'Layers'
     Photomontage of
     garments
     Caroline Broadhead
     UK, 1990

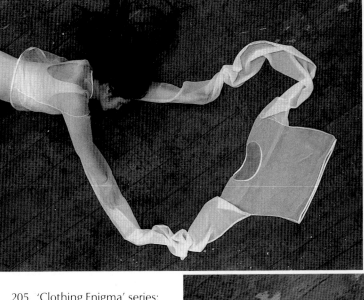

205 'Clothing Enigma' series:
     'Failure of Character,
     Static Performance',
     double shirt
     Silk mousseline, taffeta
     Marian Schoettle
     USA, 1985

206 'Clothing Enigma' series:
     'Inside and Out of
     Traditional Dress'
     Silk mousseline, taffeta
     Marian Schoettle
     USA, 1985

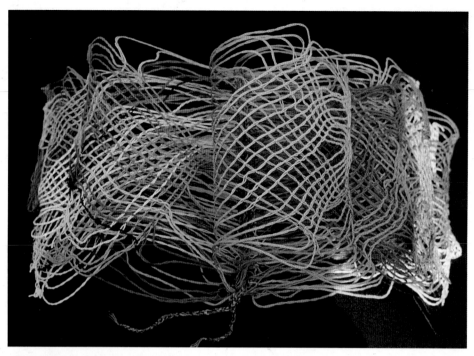

207 'Textile Book'
Cotton sprang
Teresa Pla
Spain, 1989

208 'Ronds'
Oil paint on canvas
Daniel Chompré
France/Finland, 1985

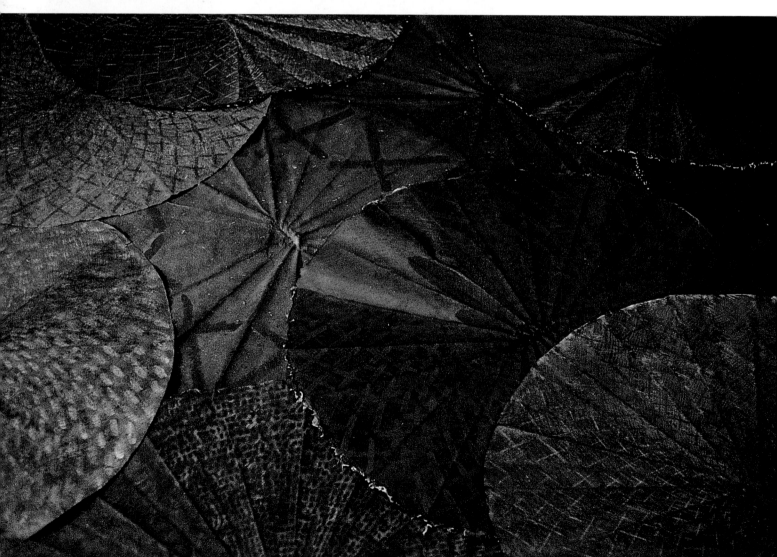

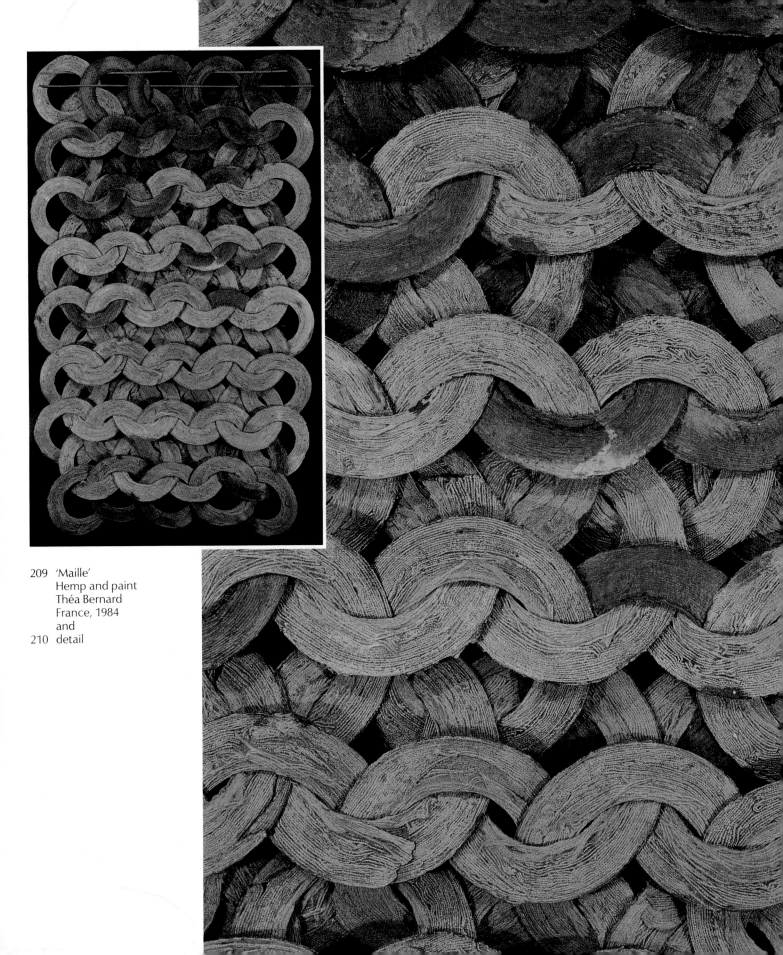

209 'Maille'
Hemp and paint
Théa Bernard
France, 1984
and
210 detail

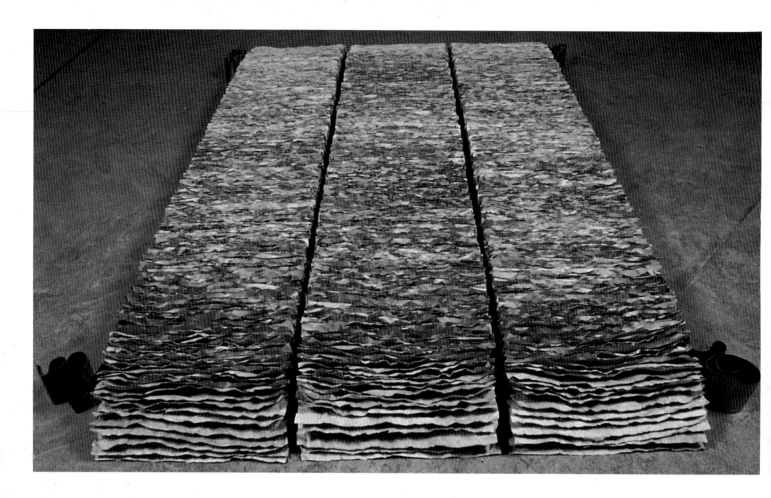

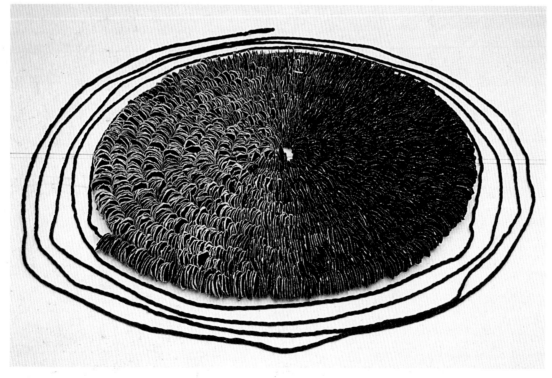

211 'Floating Blue'
Paper installation
Maryan Geluk
Holland, 1988

212 'Black Pool'
Paper installation
Maryan Geluk
Holland, 1988

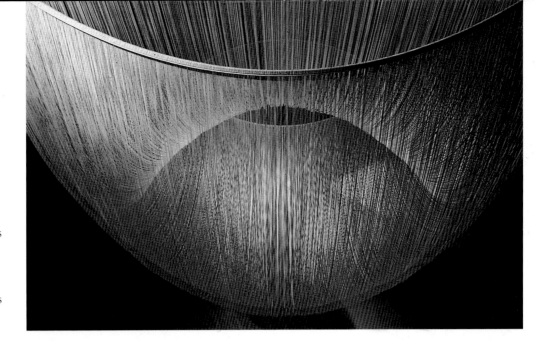

213 'Wings 5'
Rayon filaments
Akio Hamatani
Japan, 1990

214 'White Arc 3'
Rayon filaments
Akio Hamatani
Japan, 1983

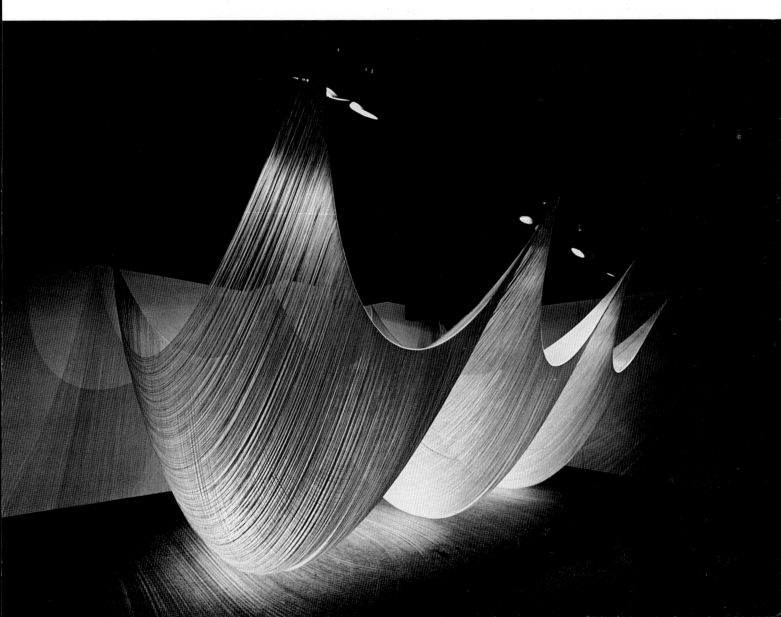

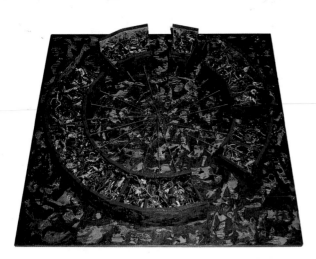

215 'Cast of Thousands'
Mixed media
   installation
Michael Brennand
   Wood
UK, 1987

216 Wall piece
Willow sticks, dyed and
   bound felt
Odile Levigoureux
France, 1988

217 'Our Bones Are Made of
   Stardust'
Carol Shaw-Sutton
USA, 1988

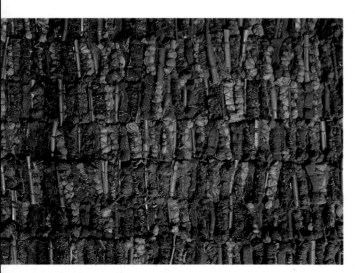

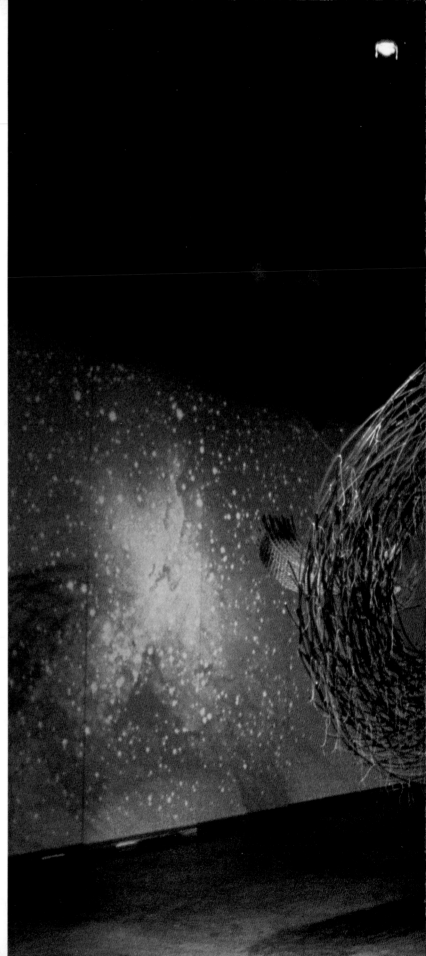

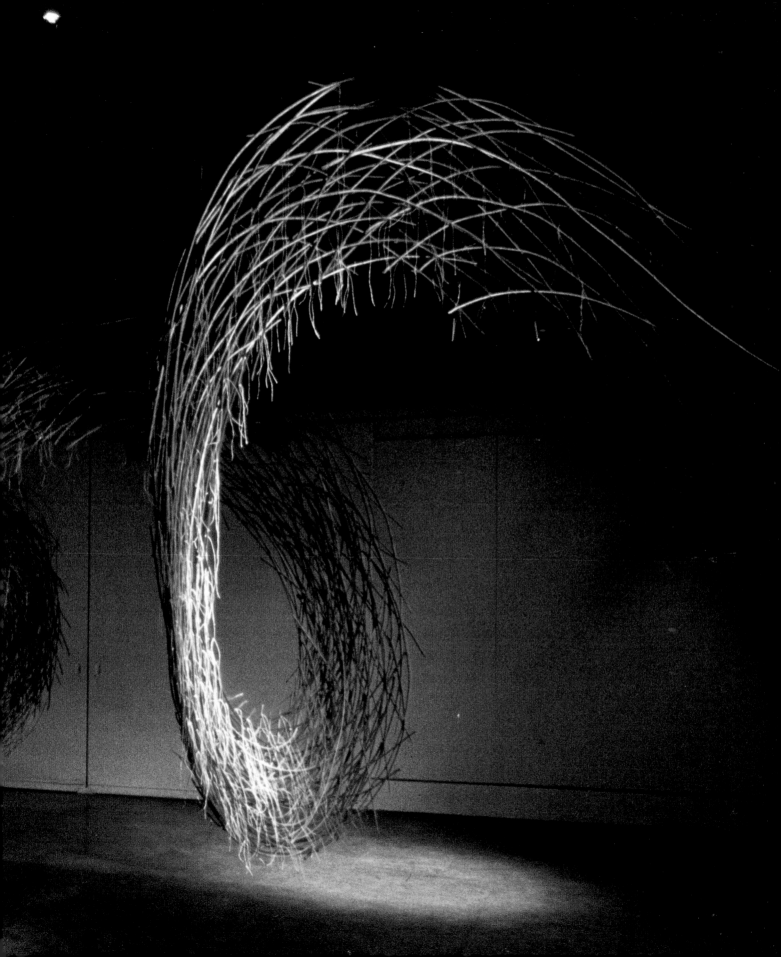

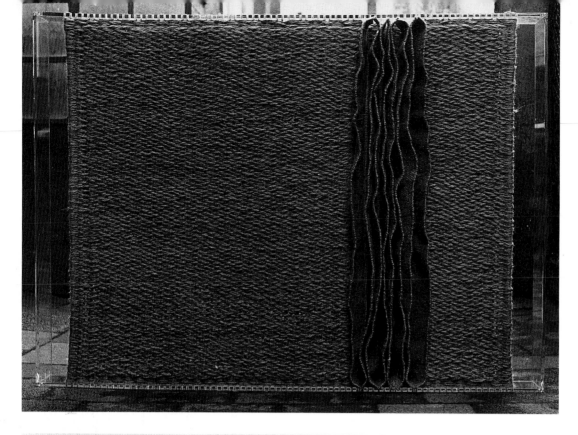

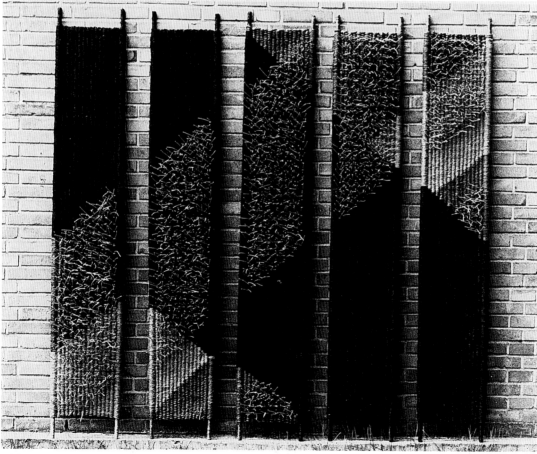

218 Hanging
   Jute in acrylic glass
      frame
   Elfi Knoche Wendel
   West Germany, 1987

219 'Colour Overlay'
   Jute
   Elfi Knoche Wendel
   West Germany, 1986

220 'Romanica I'
   Goat hair, paper,
      graphite
   Ritzi and Peter Jacobi
   West Germany, 1978

221 Hanging
   Cotton, sisal paper
   Ritzi Jacobi
   West Germany, 1989

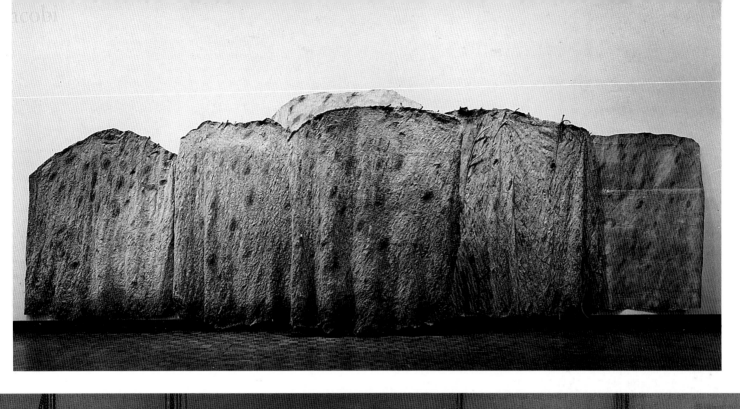

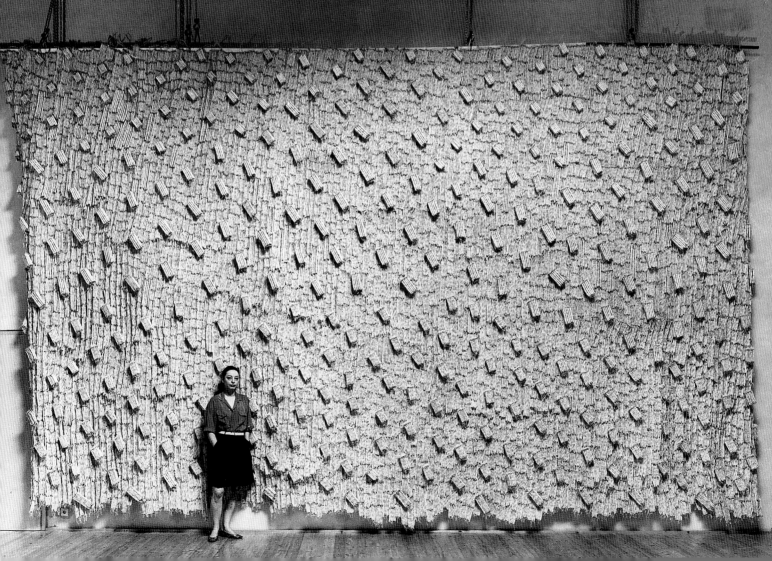

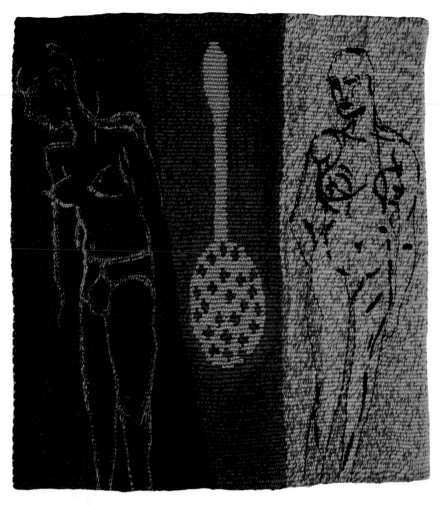

222 'Eshbeheble'
     Tapestry
     Discharge-printed wool,
        silk and linen
     Shelly Goldsmith
     UK, 1988

223 'From Above'
     Tapestry
     Hand-woven wool and
        linen
     Cynthia Schira
     USA, 1989
     and
224 detail

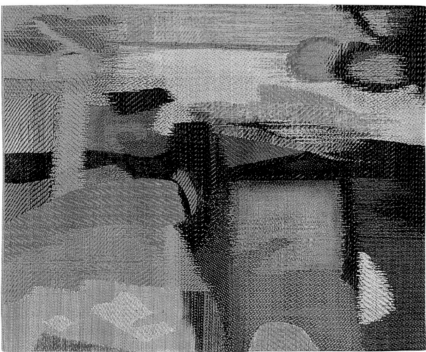

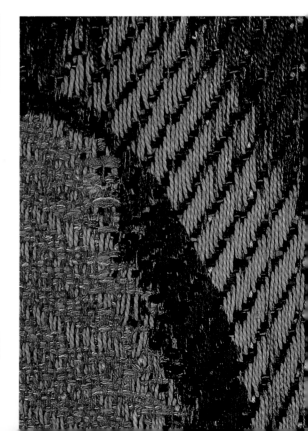

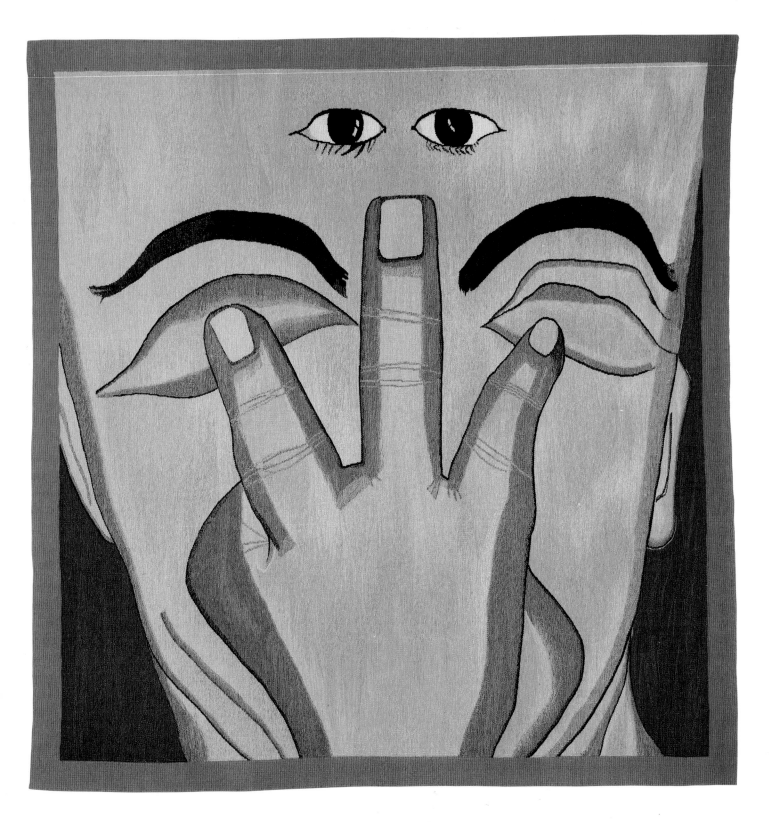

225 'Three' by Francesco Clemente
100% wool on a cotton web
Hand-woven using the 'Gobel' technique
Taller Mexicano de Gobelinos, Italy/Mexico, 1989

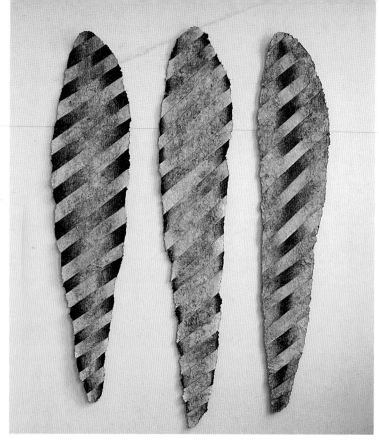

226 'Paper Shields'
Papier-mâché, gouache
Ady Comou
Holland, 1987

227 'Winged Form'
Woven and knotted
hemp and wool
Kathleen McFarlane
UK, 1986

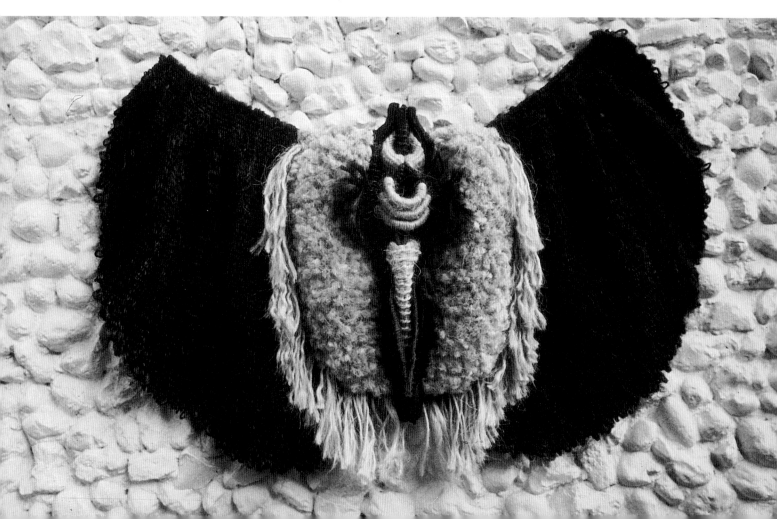

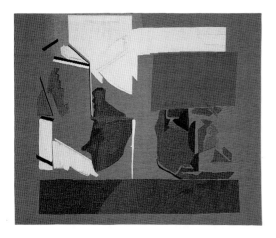

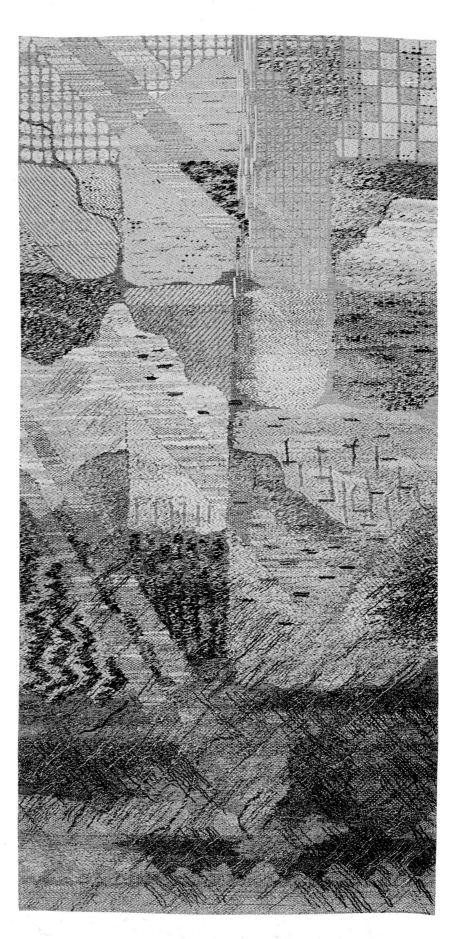

228 'Still life with table and
     bowls'
     Hand-woven wool
     tapestry
     Martha Kreutzer-
     Temming
     West Germany, 1987

229 'Eroded Memory'
     Hand-woven wool
     tapestry
     Harumi Isobe
     Japan, 1988

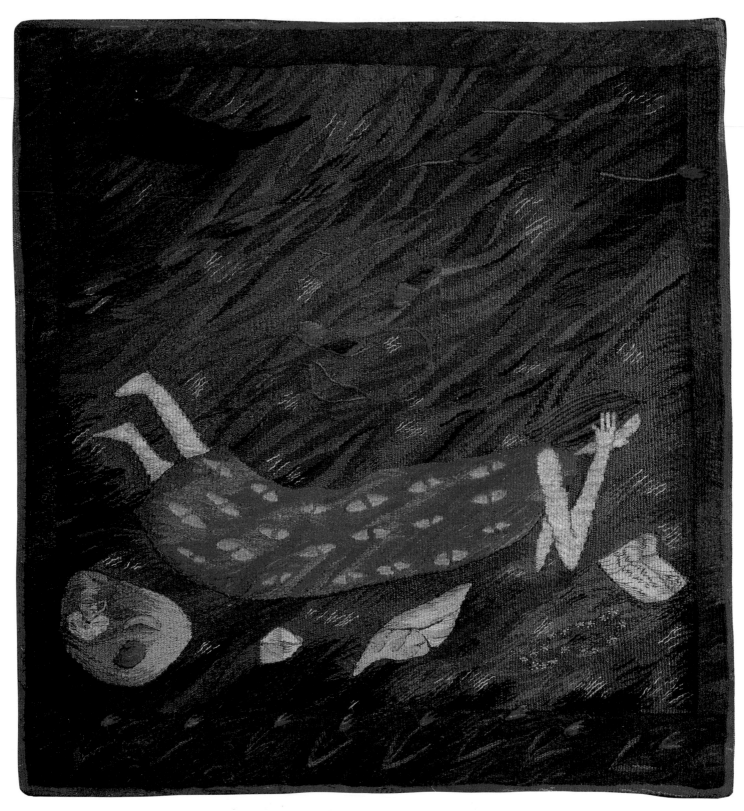

230 'The Billet Doux' by Lynne Curran
Hand-woven wool and linen tapestry
UK, 1982

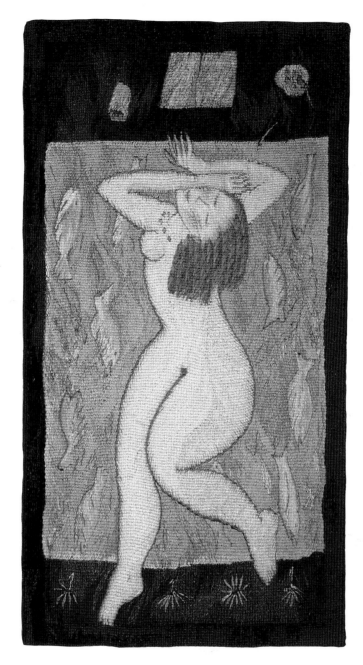

'Take me to the Hallbankgate'
Tapestry
Lynne Curran
UK, 1985

Biographies

Galleries and Museums

Exhibitions

Publications

Glossary

Index

Biographies

Abild, Helle b. Denmark 1965. Studied at the School of Arts, Crafts and Design at Copenhagen. Since graduating Abild has created one-off fabrics for fashion designers. Her designs feature in the *International Design Yearbook 1991*.

Akers, Adela b. Spain 1933. Studied at Cranbrook Academy, and currently teaches at the Tyler School of Art, Philadelphia.

Albers, Anni b. Germany 1899. Albers took up weaving at the Weimar Bauhaus with some reluctance – it was the only course open to women. Albers later described it as a 'creative vacuum'; she had to rely on her fellow students, such as Gunta Stölzl, for both inspiration and technical advice. She went on to succeed Gunta Stölzl as the director of the weaving workshop at Dessau. However, it was only some years after she had left the Bauhaus and was living in America that her weavings and her achievements at the Bauhaus were given the recognition they deserved. Throughout her career Albers explored weaving both as an aesthetic and functional medium. Her influence in the field of industrial design was considerable. In 1949, she was the first weaver to be given a solo exhibition at the Museum of Modern Art in New York. In her books *On Designing* and *On Weaving* Albers argued convincingly for the need for craft-based design. By encouraging designers to handle the materials they worked with, she hoped that they would stop thinking of design as a purely graphic process. She also asked weavers to recognize the thread as the basic unit of structure and pattern. In the 1950s, these ideas went on to foster a trend in textured, architectonic fabrics which exposed their structure. Her work and ideas on weaving and design have had an enduring influence on designers as varied as Jack Lenor Larsen and Junichi Arai. Albers was both a champion of new synthetic materials and an expert in, and collector of, pre-Columbian textiles; this duality was a key feature of her work. Since her work is not sculptural, Albers is rarely credited for influencing the development of the fibre art movement. However, her own textile hangings, with which she aimed 'to let threads be articulate again to no other end than their own orchestration', form some of the most satisfying contemporary works in this medium and may prove to be more influential than has hitherto been acknowledged. See *The Woven and Graphic Art of Anni Albers*, published on the occasion of the major retrospective of her work at the Renwick Gallery in 1986. Samples of Albers' work can be seen in several public collections including the Bauhaus Archiv Museum für Gestaltung, MOMA in New York and the Victoria and Albert Museum, London.

Al-Hilali, Neda b. Czechoslovakia 1938. Lived in Baghdad and moved to the USA in 1961 where she studied at the University of California, Los Angeles. In the late 1970s Al-Hilali started to weave fabrics from recycled, bunched and interlaced paper, painted with gestural patterns. Al-Hilali's approach is contemporary, her patterns are about textiles, they describe the way fabrics bunch and crumple when they are seen in relief. See *The Art Fabric: Mainstream*, by Mildred Constantine and Jack Lenor Larsen.

Arai, Junichi b. Japan 1932. Arai comes from Kiryu, a traditional craft weaving centre to the north of Tokyo. In the past few years, Arai's exuberantly sculptural woven fabrics have made him an international celebrity but have also done much to promote interest in textile design. His family has a traditional involvement in weaving, from which Arai derives an exceptionally thorough understanding of his craft; he is famous for being able to 'design by telephone', selecting the yarn and weave from his own formidable memory banks. During the 1980s he ran a business called 'Anthologie', based on a network of small, family-run specialist weaving and finishing businesses in the Kiryu district, and supplied extraordinary, image-building fabrics to Japan's fashion designers, and to Issey Miyake in particular. Anthologie's bankruptcy, ironically the same year that Arai was made a Royal Designer for Industry, forced him to change gear and in 1987 he became a full-time partner of Nuno, the design team and cult Tokyo fabric store managed by Reiko Sudo. This has also marked a change of direction, and now he designs contemporary furnishing fabrics.

Nuno fabrics are sold through Ilana Goor in New York and will be sold through Liberty's in London. His work can be seen at the Victoria and Albert Museum, London, and at the Cooper-Hewitt Museum in New York. See Peter Popham's article 'Man of the Cloth' (*Blueprint*, Spring 1987).

Atkinson, Nigel b. UK 1964. Studied textile design at the Winchester School of Art. Atkinson's work reveals a rare combination: an understanding of new printing techniques combined with a strong sense of design, rhythm and pattern. He uses a technique that involves printing a heated rubber paste on to fabric, enabling him to sculpt his fabrics into relief. His designs, inspired by marine animals, plants and fossils, have been used by leading architects and fashion designers including Nigel Coates, Issey Miyake, Martine Sitbon and Romeo Gigli. Since 1989 Atkinson has also designed a collection of fabrics available by the metre which are manufactured in London by Jamison Print and Padgett and Grey.

Awatsuji, Hiroshi b. Japan 1929. Studied printing at the Kyoto University of Arts and founded his own textile design studio in 1958. His major commissions include decorating the Japanese Government Pavilion for the Japanese Trade Fair, 'Expo '70', and a series of tapestries for the Keiro Plaza. Since the early 1970s Awatsuji has supplied designs to Fujie Textiles. His work was included at the exhibition 'Japan Style' at the Victoria and Albert Museum, London, and at 'Design Since '45' at the Philadelphia Museum of Modern Art. He founded his own manufacturing company, Awa, in 1988. See *The Textile Design of Hiroshi Awatsuji* (Japan 1990).

Bailey, Bridget b. UK 1960. Studied at the West Surrey College of Art and Design. Bailey creates steam-moulded and pleated fabrics whose forms are highlighted with strategically placed prints. Since the mid-1980s she has produced a line of scarves and hair accessories for Liberty's and Bloomingdales amongst others and has also designed hats for Jean Muir's collections. In 1990 she formed her own hat company, Bailey Tomlin, in partnership with the milliner Anne Tomlin. Bailey's work was featured in the 'New Faces' exhibition at the Victoria and Albert Museum and in the International Textile Design Contest in Tokyo in 1989.

Bellinger, Gretchen b. USA 1946. Studied at the Cranbrook Academy of Art. Founded in 1976, Gretchen Bellinger Inc.'s textile collection has become internationally renowned for its precise, understated fabric designs for both the contract and domestic markets. Bellinger anticipated the revival of natural fibres and a more muted palette after the 1970s synthetics boom. Most of her fabrics are in solid colours; a purist and a modernist, she relies on weave structure to animate the surface – pattern is never applied. Her work is texturally interesting, illustrated by the fact that her fabrics photograph so well in black and white. Her work is featured in the Metropolitan Museum of Art and the Art Institute of Chicago.

Bernard, Théa b. USA 1947. Studied at the Ecole Supérieure des Arts Décoratifs in Paris. Bernard became a fibre artist in the 1970s before starting to work in paper in the mid-1980s. She has exhibited widely in France – her group exhibitions include 'Comparaisons '90' at the Grand Palais.

Blaisse, Maria b. Holland 1944. Studied at the Gerrit Rietveld Academy where she later became a professor of textile and flexible design (1974–87). Since 1982 Blaisse has explored the industrial potential for creating flexible clothing using rubber laminates, synthetic foams, non-wovens and other new fibre technologies. Blaisse's designs are lucid and minimalist; her most famous design is the envelope hat which she designed for Issey Miyake in 1987, made from a square envelope of neoprene rubber with a single incision in it. More recently Blaisse has designed costumes for dance and opera. She was awarded a prize for the most innovatory design by the Dutch Ministry of Economic Affairs in 1989. Her work attracted considerable attention in the International Textile Exhibition in Kyoto in 1989. See *Imitation and Inspiration: the Japanese Influence on Dutch Art*, edited by Stephen van Ray, 1989.

Bosence, Susan b. UK 1913. Bosence went to teach at Dartington Hall (the experimental school founded by Leonard and Dorothy Elmhirst in the 1930s) where she developed her ideas on progressive education and the rural revival. Bosence came across some block-printed curtains made by the pioneer British craftswomen Phyllis Barron and Dorothy Larcher in the early 1950s and, with their encouragement, took up block printing herself. She went on to become extremely knowledgeable about not just block printing but also both traditional and synthetic dye recipes and resist-dyeing techniques from the Asian subcontinents, and her book *Handblock Printing and Resist Dyeing* is a classic on the subject. Bosence's influence as a teacher at Dartington, the Camberwell School of Arts and Crafts and, above all, at the West Surrey College of Art and Design, is evident in the work of a number of her students featured in this book. A functionalist and to an extent a historicist-craftswoman, Bosence is a strong believer in the value of individual workmanship of quality. Her style is economic, sometimes almost to the point of austerity, but her colours are rich and true and her sense of rhythm – an important element of block printing – is amazingly acute. Her work can be seen at the Craft Study Centre in Bath. Also, see Deryn O'Connor's article in *Crafts* (May/June 1982) and Rosemary Hill's article 'Friends of the Earth' (*Crafts* No. 100, 1990).

Brennand Wood, Michael b. UK 1952. Studied textiles at Birmingham and Manchester polytechnics and is currently a senior lecturer in textile art at Goldsmiths College, London. A mixed-media artist, Brennand Wood's wall pieces probe the surface of textiles. His works are frequently assembled from superimposed painted wooden grids interlaced with threads, remnants of fabric and elements of text. Brennand Wood is interested in archaeology and likes the idea that his work should seem partly eroded, as if the skin of things has been peeled away to reveal some inherent structure beneath. He is one of Britain's few internationally known textile artists, and he won the Creative Concept Award at the 1987 International Textile Competition in Kyoto.

Brero, Mary b. USA 1949. A self-taught needlework and mixed-media artist, Brero claims that her lack of formal training was an advantage, since it meant that she had less to unlearn. Her style, which reflects her interest in tribal folk art, has been described as 'neo-naive'. Since the early 1980s Brero has been at the forefront of the new embroidery movement in America. Her work is urban, contemporary and fun and has done much to challenge the genteel, historicist aesthetic conventions of embroidery and needlework. See the essay on her work by Neda Al-Hilali in the catalogue to 'Fiber R/Evolution' (1986).

Brink, Renata b. West Germany 1960. Studied in England at the Harrogate College of Arts. Brink is content to describe herself as a craft weaver – quite a rarity today. She specializes in dip-dyed double-cloth scarves embellished with woven patterns. Her work can be seen at the Museum of Decorative Arts in Hamburg.

Broadhead, Caroline b. UK 1950. Studied at the Central School of Art and Design, London, and currently teaches at Middlesex Polytechnic. In the early 1980s she created some of the most radical pieces of jewelry 'in the new tradition' which rejected the decorative conventions and the traditional use of expensive materials for personal ornamentation. Broadhead was one of the first European new jewelers to use textiles; since the mid-1980s she has created a series of pieces that explore ideas and meanings in clothing. Her work was featured in the exhibition 'Conceptual Clothing' at the Ikon Gallery, Birmingham, in 1986, and in another exhibition of the same name that was held in Philadelphia in 1989. Her work can be seen at the National Museum of Modern Art in Kyoto, the Crafts Council in London and the Stedelijk Museum in Amsterdam.

Burch Cochran, Jane b. USA 1943. Studied at the Cincinatti Art Academy. Burch Cochran is a contemporary quilter who has developed a strongly personal iconographic style within the nineteenth-century tradition of crazy quilting. Her work was featured in the exhibition of contemporary American quilts 'Americana Enshrined' (1989) and in the International Contemporary Quilt Art Exhibition held in the United States in 1988.

Cook, Lia b. USA 1942. Studied textiles at the University of California, Berkeley, with Ed Rossbach, and has been Professor of Art at the California College of Arts and Crafts in Oakland since 1976. In the late 1960s much of the new American fibre art was sculptural; woven hangings were considered passé. In the mid-1970s Cook was one of the first fibre artists to start working again with flat fabrics, often beetled or pounded flat, and pattern. Describing her own work, she has written: 'I have used the fabric image as both the subject and object of my work. In creating a series of curtains I want to isolate a particular moment of a familiar piece of fabric with all its inherent associations.' Important exhibitions include 'Woven Structures in the Computer Age' (1989) and 'Craft Today: The Poetry of the Physical' (1986). Her work features in public collections including New York's Museum of Modern Art, Metropolitan Museum of Art and American Craft Museum.

Corben, Carolyn b. UK 1963. Studied at the Royal College of Art, London. Corben's machine-knitted and em-broidered one-off clothes combine decoration with political comment. She has designed knitwear for Paul Smith, Katherine Hamnett and Georgina Godley and has created stage clothing for Sinéad O'Connor and Paul McCartney. She is currently part of the New Renaiscance, a group of designers and craftspeople who create experimental fashion from recycled and reworked clothing. Her work was included in the exhibition 'Image and Object' at the Pompidou Centre in Paris in 1990.

Création Baumann Switzerland. A third-generation family business, Création Baumann produces furnishing fabrics for the top end of the contract and domestic markets. Every stage of textile manufacture, from yarn twisting to design and distribution, is housed within the same factory complex. Création Baumann differs from many textile companies in that it promotes team effort rather than individual design; the fabrics it creates are the result of a collaboration between design and technical staff. It has a reputation for being technologically advanced, and its fabrics are typically 'clean modernist'.

Crow, Nancy b. USA 1943. Studied at the Ohio State University. Crow is one of the leading figures in the quilt art movement in America. She is skilled at patchwork and has developed a different approach to pattern from the traditional heritage styles, largely inspired by Mexican textiles. Crow has done a great deal to change the way in which contemporary quilts are valued and perceived. She was a key figure behind the instigation of the first juried exhibition of contemporary quilts, 'Quilt National', in 1979, which has gone on to become an international biennial event. She recently completed a lavish monograph, *Nancy Crow: Quilts and Influences*. Her work was recently featured in the exhibition 'Americana Enshrined' (1989), and the international touring exhibition 'Design in America' (also 1989).

De Amaral, Olga b. Colombia 1932. Studied at the Cranbrook Academy of Art, Michigan. De Amaral made her name as a fibre artist in the late 1960s with a series of textile hangings which revived ancient plaiting techniques indigenous to the Americas. She was made Director for Latin America at the World Craft Council from 1970 to 1978. She is a recognized expert in various techniques of interlacing and used this technique to make a series of sumptuous gilded hangings during the 1980s. In the past twenty years her work has been extensively exhibited all over the world. See the book that accompanied 'Interlacing: The Elemental Fabric' (1987) curated by Jack Lenor Larsen. Her work can be seen in numerous public collections including the Metropolitan Museum of Art, New York, the Musée d'Art Moderne de la Ville de Paris and the National Museum of Modern Art, Kyoto.

Di Mare, Dominic b. USA 1932. Self-taught. Di Mare was made a fellow of the American Crafts Council in 1987. In the mid-1970s Di Mare's delicate, decorative fetishes, frequently constructed from willow twigs and twisted hand-made paper, made him a key figure in the neo-primitive movement in America. Important exhibitions featuring his work include 'Contemporary Arts: An Expanding View', curated by Helen Drutt in 1986, and 'Architextures' at the Musée des Arts Décoratifs, Paris, in 1985.

Duc, Christian b. South Vietnam 1947. Studied at the Université de Paris VIII. A furniture and lighting designer, Duc started to design carpets in the mid-1980s. In the past three years he has produced three best-selling collections for the Belgian carpet manufacturer Toulemonde Bochard. Christian Duc has received numerous awards for his work including the 'Grand Prix de la Création de la Ville de Paris' in 1990.

Du Pasquier, Nathalie b. France 1957. After travelling in the Americas and India, du Pasquier arrived in Milan in 1979 and has lived and worked there ever since. It was there that she first came into contact with the Memphis group. With George Sowden, another member of Memphis, du Pasquier developed a decorative language of pattern which they applied to a variety of objects including textiles, ceramics, carpets and clocks. She has worked for clients such as Fiorucci, Lorenz and Esprit.

Dupeux, Geneviève b. Belgium 1924. Served a traditional apprenticeship of weaving at the J. Plasse-Lecaisne Studios. Founded the Atelier National d'Art Textile in 1976 for research into textile art, craft and design, which moved to the top floor of Les Ateliers in the early 1980s. Geneviève Dupeux is both a textile designer and a contemporary textile artist. She has designed upholstery fabrics for the national train company SNCF, for Renault and for Air Inter. Her interest in new fibre technologies is evident in both her design and art works. Her work was featured in the exhibition 'French Design 1940–1990' at the Pompidou Centre in Paris.

Efstratiou, Alida b. 1963. Studied at the Royal College of Art, London. Efstratiou won an award for outstanding work from the Worshipful Company of Gold and Silver Wire Drawers in 1987. Efstratiou's art and one-off design pieces are created from fine, hand-woven lamé which she moulds into sculptural forms with her fingers. Her work was included in the travelling exhibition 'British Fashion in the '80s' and in the 'Cross Threads' exhibition in Bradford, England, in 1990.

Eliakim b. Israel 1954. Studied painting on cloth at the Ecole des Beaux Arts de Paris. In 1978 he joined Pierre Cardin's design studio and created a collection of hand-painted scarves for Ted Lapidus. From 1980, Eliakim supplied textile designs to the leading fashion houses in Paris, and since 1987 he has designed his own line of furnishing fabrics, tableware, furniture and carpets which he sells through his shop on the Rue de Lappe.

Fisher, Sharon b. Denmark 1959. Studied at the School of Decorative Art in Copenhagen. Fisher forms part of a group of young Danish designers who have returned to their native tradition of craft-based designs. Fisher's clean geometric patterns are woven using an ikat resist technique. She has recently been invited by the leading Danish furnishing fabric manufacturer Kvadrat to become a consultant designer.

Freeman, Susie b. UK 1956. Studied at the Royal College of Art, London. Freeman's gauze-like fabrics are knitted into pockets which contain shells, shiny buttons and other small bits of ephemera. She was appropriately commissioned by the Geffrye Museum in the East End of London, where she was born, to create a contemporary suit for a Pearly Queen. Her work can also be seen at the Victoria and Albert Museum and at the Whitworth Art Gallery in Manchester.

French, Stephen b. UK 1953. Studied fine art at the Duncan of Jordanstone College of Art. French was an award-winning artist, but a serious motorcycle accident in 1983 forced him to abandon painting. Since then he has turned his attention to the application of new technologies such as etched PVC lenses and fibre-optics to everyday objects. French pioneered research into the application of holograms to venetian blinds in the mid-1980s. His work was featured in the exhibition 'The Plastic's Age' at the Victoria and Albert Museum in 1990 and in the touring exhibition 'Image and Object', also in 1990.

Freshwater, Sally b. UK 1958. Studied at Goldsmiths College and the RCA, London. Freshwater's art works quote from the craft traditions of kite, parasol and Japanese screen making. They are typically constructed from opalescent membranes of paper or fabric stretched taut over a geometrical framework. Freshwater's work recently appeared in the exhibition 'New British Textile Art' in Tokyo and Kyoto in 1990. Her work can be seen at the Whitworth Art Gallery in Manchester and at the Crafts Council in London. See 'In Full Flight' (*Crafts*, 1987).

Geluk, Maryan b. Holland 1947. Studied at the Gerrit Rietveld Academy, Amsterdam. Geluk creates soft sculptures made from layers of fabrics and torn paper. She has exhibited widely in Holland as well as Japan, where her work has been warmly received. As an indication of the developing links between artists in these two countries, the book *Imitation and Inspiration: the Japanese Influence on Dutch Art* (edited by Stephan van Ray) was published in 1989, in which her work is discussed.

Gordon, Joanna b. UK 1967. Studied at the West Surrey College of Art and Design. Since leaving college, Gordon's jewel-coloured, hand-painted and discharged patterns have attracted considerable attention. She has designed furnishing fabrics for the interior designer Mark Brazier Jones. Her work was also featured in the exhibition of avant-garde British design 'Image and Object' in 1990.

W. L. Gore USA 1958. Founded by Mr and Mrs W. L. Gore. Continuing research into the characteristics of Polytetra-fluorothylene, used to insulate electric cables, led to the invention of the microporous Gore-tex membrane in 1976. This membrane has been developed as an oil, water- and wind-proof laminate which can be bonded to other fabrics but allows the skin to breathe. It permits the passage of water-vapour in protective clothing such as surgical gowns. The microstructure of Gore-tex makes it highly compatible with the body for vascular grafts and ligament replacements. Gore Associates currently have about thirty plants spread across the United States, and in France, Germany, Britain, India and Japan.

Grau-Garriga, Josep b. Spain 1929. Studied at the Higher School of Fine Arts in Barcelona. In 1958 he went to join the studio of Jean Lurcat, a leading figure of the tapestry revival in France, which inspired him to return to Spain and to help establish the Catalan tapestry school in Barcelona. Grau-Garriga went on to become the champion of the contemporary tapestry movement in Spain. Since 1960 he has created vast fibre installations in the squares and churches of Spain. He is most famous, however, for his baroque, visceral tapestries. These are rampantly organic – they frequently incorporate found objects, often lace and clothes, which are worked into tumescent relief. Grau-Garriga's work was included in the exhibition '45 Ans de la Tapisserie' held in Paris in 1985. His work features in a number of public collections including the Metropolitan Museum of Art, New York, and the Textile Museum Terrassa in Barcelona. See *Grau-Garriga* (1985) by Arnaud Puig and *Grau-Garriga* by Pilar Parcerisas (1990).

Greaves Lord, Sally b. UK 1957. Studied at the West Surrey College of Art, and at the Royal College of Art, London. Sally Greaves Lord was a prominent part of an outbreak of talent in printing at the RCA which included The Cloth and Timney Fowler. She prints abstract, symbolic patterns on to cloth. Her silk banners are finely crafted, her palette derives from a carefully timed chemical reaction between black procion dyes and bleach. In 1983 she was commissioned by Powell Tuck, Conner and Orefelt to design a painted interior and furnishing fabrics for Research Recordings Ltd, and has since collaborated with architects, creating murals and banners on a number of projects. She was made creative director of Issey Miyake UK in 1985 and subsequently made the windows of his Sloane Street shop a forum for contemporary experimental craftwork.

Hamatani, Akio b. Japan 1947. Hamatani became a fibre artist in the 1970s. His graceful, curved forms are made from a single filament of white rayon wound back and forth over a frame. His work has been widely exhibited in Europe and Japan, and he recently held a one-man show at the Hillside Gallery in Tokyo, 1989. See Janet Koplos' articles on new Japanese textile art in *Sculpture*, May/June 1989.

Hegelund Sørensen, Bitten b. Denmark 1960. Studied at the School of Arts, Crafts and Design in Copenhagen. Sørensen is one of a new generation of designer-makers who have recently emerged in Denmark. Her work was featured in the exhibition of new Danish craft-based design 'Møbiler Tekstiler' (1990) and can be seen in the public collection of the Danish Museum of Decorative Arts.

Hishinuma, Yoshiki b. Japan 1958. Studied design at the Bunka Fashion Institute in Tokyo. Hishinuma worked for the Issey Miyake Design Studio in 1978 and is now a freelance designer of fashion textiles and accessories. His approach to pattern is figurative, punchy and graphic. He launched his own label for fashion clothing in 1984, and in the same year he was awarded the prize for new designers in the Manichi Fashion Grand Prix in Tokyo.

Hodge and Sellers, UK. Victoria Hodge and John Sellers met whilst studying at the Royal College of Art, London, and formed their partnership, Hodge and Sellers, in 1983. Compared to many of the bold, not to say burlesque, art-based prints that emerged during the London print revival in the early 1980s, Hodge and Sellers' print designs are understated, finely detailed and graphically precise. A reverence for Japanese textiles, their precise patterning and minute observation of surface texture in the natural world is reflected in their work. Their designs are popular with leading international fashion designers because they are both interesting and diplomatically understated – they reward, but don't demand, closer inspection. As well as selecting and promoting British textile students and matching them to specific clients, they have produced exclusive designs for several of Azzedine Alaïa's collections and have been commissioned by designers such as Issey Miyake, Marithe and François Girbaud, Cerruti and Geoffrey Beene to supply designs.

Hugues, Patrice b. France 1930. Studied painting under the artist Fernand Léger. Since the early 1970s Hugues has worked with a technique called 'heat-transfer printing' which enables him to create high-fidelity monoprints on sheer fabric. Hugues' multilayered images are collages of pattern, photography and, more recently, text which are loosely assembled together. His work reflects his main interest in the contemporary and historical cultural meanings of textiles and motifs. He wrote a vast catalogue to an exhibition on the subject called 'Le Language du Tissu' in 1980. His work is held by numerous public collections including the Musée National d'Art Moderne and the Musée des Arts Décoratifs, Paris.

Ishimoto, Fujiwo b. Japan 1941. Studied design and graphics at the Tokyo National University of Art, and worked as a commercial artist and designer in Japan before moving to Finland to become an award-winning designer of printed furnishing fabrics for Marimekko in 1974.

Itter, Diane USA 1946–90. Studied at the Indiana University, Bloomington. Itter was a great collector of indigenous Indian artefacts, an interest reflected in her work. Itter's miniature fringed fibre pieces, impeccably crafted from knotted linen, are amongst the most skilfully made and charming pieces of contemporary miniature textiles to have come from America. See the article by Janet Koplos in the *American Crafts Magazine*, March 1980, and the book *Miniature Fiber Arts: A National Exhibition*, published by the University of North Dakota Press in 1980.

Jacobi, Ritzy b. Ritzi Gavrila, in Rumania 1941. Studied textiles at the Institut de Arte Plastice in Bucharest. A husband and wife team, Ritzy and Peter Jacobi were at the forefront of the Central European New Tapestry Movement during the 1960s and 1970s.

Jacobs, Ferne b. USA 1942. Studied at the Art Center College of Design in Los Angeles. Jacobs' forms are made from hundreds of coils of waxed cotton which she binds tightly together – a time-consuming process which results in surprisingly clearly defined, sometimes almost sharp, objects. Jacobs' approach is contemporary, her vessels comment on other vessels, passive domestic objects and weapons. She has had a number of solo exhibitions in the US and her work has been included in crafts exhibitions which have helped to establish new basketry in America, such as 'The Modern Basket: A Redefinition' (1987) and 'Basketry: Tradition in New Form' (1982). Her work can be seen at the American Craft Museum in New York.

Kallesøe, Else b. Denmark 1949. Studied at the Pratt School of Art and Design in New York. Kallesøe is a freelance textile designer and a maker of one-off fabrics; she is celebrated in Denmark for her clever, modular, geometric designs. Her fabrics were included in the important exhibition 'Design Textile Scandinave 1950/1985' at the Musée de L'Impression sur Etoffes, France.

Klomp, Maryan b. Holland. Studied at the Academy for Industrial Design in Eindhoven, Holland. Worked as a freelance textile and carpet designer, and in 1974 became the executive manager and designer for Wikkel, a small independent company of casual clothing that produces many printed fabrics of original designs through its sibling company, Zeebra. Klomp's prints are experimental, graphic and often feature unorthodox subject-matter

such as carp, marbles and stone carvings. Her work was featured in the Cooper-Hewitt exhibition of new textiles, 'Colour, Light, Surface' (1990).

Larsen, Jack Lenor b. USA 1927. Studied at Cranbrook Academy of Art. Jack Lenor Larsen has been a dominant figure in American textile art and design for nearly forty years; his writings and exhibitions have also established him as an authority on both subjects. Larsen opened his own design studio in New York in 1952. A strong advocate of the craftsman-designer, he modelled his practice on the great craft workshops – Morris, Fortuny, Tiffany – of the nineteenth century, whilst looking to pre-Columbian and Sassanid textiles for decorative and technical inspiration. From the beginning of his career he started exploring methods of transferring the vivacity and irregularities of hand-woven samples to machine-woven products. His earliest successful collections, such as The Andean (1956), The African (1963) and The Irish (1969), were all inspired by textiles from other cultures – he is known to be an obsessive collector of fabrics. He has worked on a number of overseas projects, which have included consultancy work for the US Department of State on grass-weaving projects in Taiwan and Vietnam.

One of his major contributions to textile design lies in the way he has used new technology to transform archaic craft techniques to create designs for the luxury modern interior furnishings market. Despite his interest in craft, Larsen remains a designer of his time, and he has used his extensive knowledge of man-made fibres and powerloom weaving techniques to transform these influences into a sophisticated brand of modernism.

Lesage, François b. France 1929. Lesage was apprenticed to his father and inherited the family business, Albert Lesage et Cie, in 1949. Since the death of his main competitor, Rebe, in the late 1960s, François Lesage has manned the leading French company of *paruriers* (embroiders and embellishers) to supply the Parisian couturiers. During the late 1980s the boom in the art market and the return of female power-dressing found its expression in Lesage's sequinned copies of Van Gogh's painting *The Irises* for Yves Saint Laurent, and his copy of the decoration of a Ming vase for the bodice of a Chanel dress. As part of the spirit of *glasnost* that swept through the French couture system in the 1980s, Lesage was finally awarded the 'Dé d'Or' in 1986 – only six years after he had first been allowed to give press interviews. His leading embroideress was invited to a couture show for the first time in 1988. The Fashion Institute in New York staged a major retrospective of his work in 1987. Recently Albert Lesage et Cie, renamed Lesage S.A., has expanded into costume jewelry and embroidered furnishings.

Lundberg, Tom b. USA 1953. Studied painting at the University of Iowa, and textiles at the Indiana University, Bloomington. He is currently the Associate Professor of

Fiber at the Colorado State University. With Mary Brero, Lundberg is a leading figure in the new embroidery movement. His small, pictorial embroideries marked a return towards narrative content and smaller-scale work in American fibre art in the late 1970s. Exhibitions include 'Threads' at the Renwick Gallery, Smithsonian Institution (1982–84), 'Modern Master Tapestries' (New York, 1985) and 'Filaments' (Chicago, 1986).

Marieta Textil A small textile-printing company which produces experimental furnishing fabrics, founded by Maria Cardoner in 1974. Since 1978, Cardoner has included playful graphic, almost cartoon-like, designs from artists and designers such as Javier Mariscal, Silvia Gubern, Perico Pastor and Maarten Vrolijk. Marieta is an indication that textile design is an integral part of the Catalan design movement of the 1980s.

Marimekko Oy Finland 1951. Marimekko prints fashion and furnishing fabrics and has its own fabric store – it has become internationally well known for its bright, bold fabrics. In 1951 Armi Ratia joined her husband's company, Printex, and revitalized its production by asking artist friends to come up with designs. In the 1950s bold geometric patterns seemed daringly modern and refreshingly bright. Marimekko has proved that it is strong enough to incorporate designers' individual styles without threatening its own identity, and, on its fortieth anniversary, it remains at the leading edge of print design.

Minagawa, Makiko b. Japan. Makiko Minagawa has been the leading researcher and designer of woven fabrics at the Issey Miyake Design Studio since it was opened in 1971. Like Junichi Arai, Makiko Minagawa's work draws on two particular strengths of Japanese textile production: its active rural craft tradition and its sophisticated industrial manufacturing base. That said, her work is subtly different from his; compared with the boisterous exuberance of his fabrics, hers are of a much lower key, and they are therefore arguably more wearable as a result. Her designs tend to be minimalist and very understated; they work because her sense of surface pattern and rhythm is amazingly acute. In 1990 Minagawa received the Amiko Kujiraoka prize of Manichi Fashion and had a one-woman show of fabrics at Gallery Ma, Tokyo.

Minkowitz, Norma b. USA 1937. Fibre artist who studied at the Cooper Union Art School, New York. Minkowitz started making art clothing in the late 1970s and has gone on to make sculptural vessels. She is currently considered to be one of the leading figures of new basketry in America, and her work was included in the exhibition on 'The Tactile Vessel', curated by Jack Lenor Larsen in 1988. Other exhibitions include 'Fiber R/Evolution' (Wisconsin, 1986). Minkowitz's work is held in several public collections including the American Craft Museum and the Metropolitan Museum of Art in New York.

Miyamoto, Eiji b. Japan 1948. Miyamoto was born in Hachioji, a city well known for its textile industry, and studied at the Hosei University. Miyamoto started to develop and design fashion fabrics for his father's textile company Miyashin Co. Ltd, where he became a managing director in 1975. The company has supplied leading Japanese fashion designers, including Issey Miyake, ever since.

Moore, Rosemary b. UK 1959. Studied at the RCA, London. In 1984, whilst still a student, she issued a patent for her invention 'Maxxam', a tube-knitted jersey lycra fabric with a crinkly surface, made famous by the swimwear designer Liza Bruce. Moore refined her invention for use in the fashion market by using CAD to experiment with textural and tonal pattern. In 1986, she was awarded a prize for the most innovative fabric at the first International Textile Design Competition in Tokyo. Since 1988 she has had her fabrics manufactured under licence by the Japanese company Nittobo Seki. In the late 1980s Moore became disheartened by the fact that leading fashion designers failed to credit her for her contribution to their designs. She therefore now designs her own lines of sports and activewear for the British and Japanese markets. Her Maxxam fabrics are manufactured under licence in Australia, America, Japan and the UK. She plans to issue two new patents for fabric inventions in 1991.

Nagin, Risë b. USA 1950. Trained as fine artist. Nagin's work is a hybrid, decorative art that embraces patchwork, kimono-making, painting, pattern and figuration. Frequently made from translucent superimposed layers of silk organza, her 'fabric paintings' describe interior and exterior worlds simultaneously – often with reference to the female body and the home. Much of Nagin's work hovers between pattern and figuration; her sense of space is almost cubist, objects and the space between them are flattened into the geometric patterning of patchwork quilting. Her work acts as a commentary on the traditional, feminine and domestic associations of her media. She has long been supported by the American gallery owner Helen Drutt who recognized the originality of her work early on. She has exhibited widely in America; important exhibitions include 'The Contemporary Crafts: A Concept in Flux' (1986) and 'The Art Quilt', Municipal Art Gallery in Los Angeles, 1987.

Olszewski, Michael b. USA 1950. Studied at Cranbrook Academy of Art. Olszewski uses various needlework techniques such as embroidery, patchwork and pleating to construct abstract symbolic compositions that are a comment on his personal feelings. Olszewski's work is proof that the qualities of softness, expressiveness and delicacy, so often attributed to women's work, can also apply to a man. Olszewski's work has been described by Richard Flood in *Artforum* as being 'very like Anne, the heroine of Jane Austin's *Persuasion*, extremely pretty …

with gentleness, modesty, taste and feeling'. His exhibitions include 'Art Against Aids' (1987) and 'Michael Olszewski' at the Helen Drutt Gallery.

Pla, Teresa b. Spain 1947. Studied interior design at the Academy of Fine Arts in Barcelona. Pla uses a plaiting technique called 'sprang' to create delicately assembled constructions. She has exhibited widely in Spain.

Richards, Ann b. UK 1947. Studied hydrobiology before going to the West Surrey College of Art and Design to become a weaver. Richards is content to describe herself as a craftweaver. She works with natural materials, especially cotton, cashmere, wool and silk 'because of the wide variety of physical properties they offer when used in different weave structures'. She is currently engaged in an investigation of the possibilities of combining different materials, yarn twists and weave structures to produce texture and elasticity. The International Wool Secretariat have recently recognized the value of her work and have invited her to experiment at their research laboratory. Her work was awarded a prize at the International Textile Design Contest in Tokyo, 1990. See Ann Sutton's *Ideas in Weaving* for more information.

Richards, Victoria b. UK 1964. Studied at the West Surrey College of Art and Design. A designer-maker, Richards started her business on a stall in London's Camden Lock market. She now has her own label of scarves and ties which are sold through Bloomingdales, Liberty's, Paul Smith and Valentino in Rome. Her work can also be seen at the Victoria and Albert Museum, London.

Rivas Sanchez, Luiven b. Venezuela 1957. Printed and embellished fabrics for fashion design. Studied medicine at the University of Maracaibo and oceanography at University College London before doing a degree in textiles at St Martin's School of Art, London. His work offers an original perspective on the natural world; his art-based prints display motifs based on the rayographs of objects, plants and marine microbiology. Supplied distinctive prints to fashion designers such as John Galliano, Katherine Hamnett and Jasper Conran, who achieved an international reputation during the London style-boom in the early 1980s. More recently Rivas Sanchez has supplied designs to Rei Kawakubo and Nino Cerruti. A collection of his fabrics is currently being manufactured by Bianchini-Férier.

Robert le Héros France 1986. A group of four designers, Corinne Helein, Cristelle le Dean, Blandine Lelong and Isabelle Rodier. All four graduated from the Ecole des Arts Décoratifs in 1985, worked independently as freelance designers and reunited to form Robert le Héros in 1986. Their work is a good example of the new movement in the applied arts that quotes from expressionism and the baroque. Their designs are drawn freehand, and are printed to their specifications, often with thick impasto

inks on wild linen or rough cotton, which gives a painterly effect. They are both printed and distributed by the French manufacturer Nobilis Fontain.

Santagata, Sabrina b. Italy 1964. Studied painting at Brera Academy, Milan. Santagata was awarded first prize for printed fabric design at Idea Como in 1986 and in the same year was also awarded first prize at the first International Textile Design Competition in Tokyo. Since then, she has worked as a designer for Pierre Cardin in Paris. She creates art works incorporating textiles in her spare time, which she has exhibited in Paris.

Schira, Cynthia b. USA 1934. Studied at the Rhode Island School of Design and at the University of Kansas. Currently Professor of Design at the University of Kansas. She was awarded an honorary Doctorate of Fine Arts for her work by the Rhode Island School of Design in 1989. Schira is one of the most influential tapestry weavers in America – she has evolved her own approach derived from the traditional Gobelin technique. Her tapestries combine semi-figurative images with woven texture. Schira's work has been widely exhibited in America, Europe and the Far East, and recently at 'Craft USA' in Frankfurt and at the International Textile Competition held in Kyoto, Japan in 1989. Her work is held by several public collections in America including the Metropolitan Museum of Art and the Cooper-Hewitt Museum at the Smithsonian Institution, New York. See 'Image Into Structure', by Nancy Corwin, in the *Surface Design Journal*, Volume 14, No. 1 (Fall 1989).

Schoettle, Marian b. USA 1954. Studied sociology at the Colgate University, Hamilton. Schoettle worked as a printing technician for the Fabric Workshop in Philadelphia in the late 1970s. She began to create sculptural clothing and moved to London in the mid-1980s. Schoettle has collaborated with the performance artist Richard Layzell and co-curated the seminal exhibition on 'Conceptual Clothing' (Birmingham, 1986–88) with the British performance artist Fran Cotell. Since 1986 Marian Schoettle has lived in Paris. Her work is in the collection of the Victoria and Albert Museum, London.

Scott, Joyce J. b. USA 1948. Studied at the Rochester Institute of Technology, New York. An Afro-American and a feminist, Joyce Scott works in media such as African beadwork, quilting and performance which reflect her political views and her solidarity with her cultural roots. Her work is both political and decorative and has been exhibited widely in America. Key exhibitions to do with the craft aspects of her work include 'African American Art 1986' at the Smithsonian Institution, Washington (1987), 'Explorations: The Aesthetics of Excess' at the American Craft Museum (1990) and 'The Eloquent Object' (1987). For further information see the book that accompanied 'The Eloquent Object', *The Art of Politics in Contemporeana*

International Art Magazine Nov/Dec 1988, Vol. 1, No. 4 and 'Feminist Rituals of Re-membered history' by Arlene Raven in *Feminist Americana*, Vol. 4, No. 1, Issue 7.

Shaw-Sutton, Carol b. USA. Studied at San Diego University and is currently an assistant professor at the California State University, Long Beach. Shaw-Sutton's fibre sculptures, frequently made from wands of willow shaped into graceful forms, occupy a shady area, half way between craft and art. She has exhibited widely in the US and represented America in the fourteenth Tapestry Biennale at Lausanne. See the article about her work 'The Other Gods', in *Artforum*, June/July 1986.

Sisson, Karyl b. USA 1948. Studied at the University of California, Los Angeles. Sisson's work is based on transforming common-or-garden domestic materials into intricate organic structures. She has become affiliated with the new basketry movement in America. Her work was included in the exhibition 'Within and Beyond the Basket'. See the catalogue to 'Fiber R/Evolution', 1986 and Neda Al-Hilali's article 'Fibre as Structure' in *Artweek*, Dec. 11, 1982.

Skinazi, Sylvie b. France 1958. Studied mural painting at the Ecole des Beaux Arts in Paris where she was talent-spotted by Christian Lacroix, who invited her to become his assistant when he became head couturier at Patou. Her most interesting work has been achieved using heat-transfer printing. Some purists disapprove of this method, basically a high-fidelity, monoprint technique, as it involves none of the traditional printers' skills such as registration and colour overlay. For couture purposes, however, it is ideal. Because each transfer only works once, each print is guaranteed to be a one-off; a handmade dress therefore becomes doubly exclusive. Whilst Yves Saint Laurent was commissioning the embroiderer Lesage to make beaded copies of Van Gogh's *Irises*, Lacroix and Skinazi, with their large-scale printed pastiches of Matisse's *Veuve Noir*, staged something of a coup. Their method was not only quicker and cheaper but also preserved the vitality of the artist's gesture.

Skinazi's position was something of an anomaly in the couture world. Although she shares Lacroix's taste for neo-primitivism, peasant costumes, theatricality and the baroque, she has a strongly defined style of her own – traditionally, assistant craftsmen in couture are meant to interpret the house style but not impose their own creative ideas. As well as interpreting the works of past masters, Skinazi created fabrics to her own dramatic designs and in doing so transgressed the laws of couture hierarchy. Part of Lacroix's post-modern, patchwork attitude to fashion embraced this but eventually it led to a clash of creative wills and Skinazi left the house in 1988 to become a theatrical designer. She now designs scarves for Lacroix on a freelance basis. Of late, she has designed costumes for the Rameau opera/ballet at the Opéra Comique in Paris (1988) and for a circus production at the Cirque d'Hiver called 'Folies' (1989).

Svekely, Vera b. Czechoslovakia. Studied graphic arts in Budapest with Gustave Vegh, but then moved to Paris. Svekely's fabric installations, which she describes as 'Tension Structures', are inspired by the forms of sails filled in the wind. Recent exhibitions of her work include her installation in the Musée d'Art Moderne de la Ville de Paris in 1988 and the exhibition 'Soft Art' at the Barbican Centre, London, in 1989.

Szerszynska, Jasia b. UK 1955. Studied at Goldsmiths College, London. Szerszynska is a designer-maker who creates one-off screen-printed fabrics. Her designs reflect the influence of Paul Klee, and feature abstract elements.

Tanaka, Hideho b. Japan 1945. Studied at the Musashino Art University in Tokyo. Tanaka worked at the Jack Lenor Larsen Design Studio in the late 1970s and in the 1980s became an important textile artist in Japan. Many of Tanaka's sculptures are made from unlikely conjunctions of materials such as sisal and stainless steel moulded into basic geometric forms. As well as exhibiting in Japan, Tanaka has represented Japan at the twelfth and thirteenth International Tapestry Biennales in Lausanne and was also included in Jack Lenor Larsen's exhibition 'The Tactile Vessel' (Pennsylvania, 1989).

Tastemain and Riisberg A craft-based design studio of six designers: Sophie Bernard, Sophie Duval, Anne Lesobre and Anne Tastemain, led by Sylvie Tastemain (b.1954), and Vibeke Riisberg (b.1951) who is also an influencial teacher at the Copenhagen School of Arts, Crafts and Design. Tastemain and Riisberg offer textile manufacturers and designers high-calibre design research and consultancy; their work is both contemporary and technically experimental. Their thorough understanding of their craft, contemporary manufacturing techniques and the international textile market means that their design solutions are a good deal more than mere surface styling. Their list of clients spans both fashion and furnishings and includes Issey Miyake, Jean Passot, Jogan, Multipla, Texunion and Renault.

Tawney, Lenore b. USA 1925. After the death of her first husband, Tawney studied at the American Bauhaus, the school of design at the Illinois Institute of Technology, where she was taught drawing by László Moholy-Nagy and sculpture by Alexander Archipenko. In the early 1960s Tawney's silhouetted weavings inspired the title 'Woven Forms' for the exhibition that was said to have launched the fibre art movement in America. There is something atavistic about much of Tawney's work, heightened no doubt by her reverence for ancient indigenous American Indian textile artefacts and her interest in Indian mysticism and Jungian symbolism. Meditation is also an important part of her life and this has helped her to create her 'Clouds', fibre installations made from several thousand strings which had each to be knotted in turn from the ceiling. Tawney's work can be seen at numerous public collections including the Museum of Modern Art in New York and the American Craft Museum. See the catalogue to the retrospective of her work in 1990 at the American Craft Museum.

Tikkanen, Maisa b. Finland 1952. Studied at the University of Industrial Arts, Helsinki. Russia and Sweden have an ancient tradition of felt-making as this material provided good insulation from the cold. Tikkanen draws on this tradition as an appropriate medium for describing the Finnish landscape, using felt as if she were working with watercolour. Her hangings are 'giant washes' which she believes to be intimately related to the colours in Finland's lake district. The London Crafts Council held an exhibition of her work in 1989. It was also included in the travelling exhibition 'Scandinavian Craft Today', and in the permanent collection of the Museum of Applied Arts in Finland.

Toyazaki, Mitsuo b. Japan 1955. Studied at the Tokyo University of Art, Japan. Toyazaki's father worked in the rag trade in Japan and his early memories are of sitting on warehouse floors surrounded by piles of clothing. These early experiences have clearly influenced his later work. Toyazaki creates installations by filling rooms with identical basic-commodity products, such as women's tights or respiratory masks, which he embellishes with dye and paint. Toyazaki has exhibited widely in Japan. He had a one-man show at Gallery Gallery in Kyoto. His work is held in a number of public collections including the Azabu Museum of Arts and Crafts in Tokyo.

Von Etzdorf, Georgina b. Peru 1955. Studied at Camberwell School of Arts and Crafts, England. Von Etzdorf is one of the most enduringly successful and perhaps more conservative print designers to have emerged from the London fashion boom of the mid-1980s. Von Etzdorf started business by designing and making exclusive prints in her parents' garage near Bath, but by the end of the 1980s she and her partners Jonathan Docherty and Martin Simcock were running their own printing workshop and had expanded their line into fashion, furniture and ceramics.

Von Etzdorf has developed a strong, independent style that pays little attention to the vagaries of the fashion market. Her jewel-coloured prints belong within the tradition of British romantic naturalism, although the influence of Paul Klee and Richard Burra is also reflected in her work. Her swirling aqueous patterns, assembled from half-tone screens over-printed on damask cloth, demonstrate the intricacy of her craftwork. It is significant that Von Etzdorf is the only new British print designer to have developed a following in Italy.

Vorwerk & Co., Germany. Vorwerk has manufactured wall-to-wall carpets for over one hundred years. Recently, following the lead of smaller companies who made such a success of issuing small editions of artists' and designers' carpets, Vorwerk has decided to apply the same principle to wall-to-wall carpeting, until then one of the most low-profile areas of the textile design industry. In late 1988, they invited a selection of leading artists and designers, including David Hockney, Sol LeWitt, Arata Isozaki and Matteo Thun, to create designs for a selection of carpets. Two other collections have followed. In 1991 Vorwerk also issued a collection, called 'Vorwerk Classic', which comprised designs from the turn of the century found in the archives of Peter Behrens, Henry van de Velde and others.

Wilson, Anne b. USA 1949. Studied art and then textiles at the Cranbrook Academy of Art, and since 1979 she has been Associate Professor of the Fiber Department at the School of the Art Institute of Chicago. Wilson's work questions the link which has persisted since the 1960s between fibre art and nature. Like the Japanese textile artist Mitsuo Toyazaki, Anne Wilson uses synthetic materials to ape the organic and so express the tension between nature and contemporary urban and industrial society and its products. Since 1983, Wilson has used synthetics to simulate animal and more specifically human hair of various sorts. Wilson describes her hirsute hangings as 'urban furs' and certain pieces which resemble ragged hides do powerfully suggest the mutability of the animal world. She has been inspired by animal hair, pubic hair, fur, animal hides and radical hair styles, and the tattered surfaces of her rampantly visceral sprouting tufts reflect an equally tattered and fragile natural world in peril. Wilson's work was included in the important exhibition of fibre art 'Fiber R/Evolution' in 1986 and in 'Craft Today: The Poetry of the Physical'.

Zeisler, Claire b. USA 1903. Studied at the American Bauhaus, the school of design at the Illinois Institute of Technology. She was taught by the Russian avant-garde sculptor Alexander Archipenko, who opened up her ideas about sculpture. Zeisler was one of five artists chosen to exhibit in the so-called first fibre art exhibition in America, 'Woven Forms' in 1963. Zeisler has been described as one of the 'revolutionaries who broke through the constraints separating craft technique from self-expression'. In the 1970s Zeisler was one of the first fibre artists to experiment with fibre as free-standing sculpture. Her 'fibre forms', based on cascades of knotted sisal, asserted the independence of fibre as a medium worthy of consideration. Her work can be seen in numerous public collections including the Art Institute of Chicago and the Stedelijk Museum, Amsterdam. See the introductory essay to the 'Fiber R/Evolution' catalogue and the catalogue to 'Claire Zeisler: A Retrospective' at the Art Institute of Chicago, 1979.

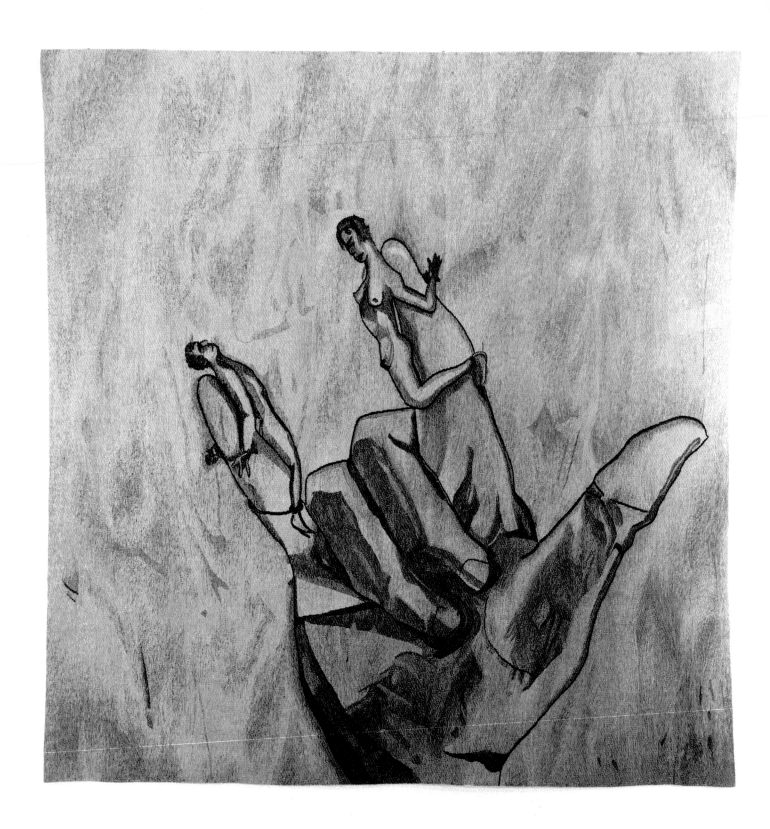

'Two' by Francesco Clemente
100% wool on a cotton web
Hand-woven using the 'Gobel' technique
Taller Mexicano de Gobelinos, Italy/Mexico, 1989

Galleries and Museums

The following list provides a selection of galleries and museums which house collections of contemporary textiles – it is not a comprehensive directory. Many other worthwhile galleries and museums can be discovered through the specialist magazines listed on page 187.

Australia

Art Gallery of South Australia, North Terrace, Adelaide 5000, South Australia

Aspect Design, 79 Salamanca Place, Hobart 7000, Tasmania

Australian Craft, 2 Waitomo Plaza, South Port 4215, Queensland

Australian Craftworks, The Old Police Station, 127 George Street, Sydney, New South Wales

The Western Australian Art Gallery, Beaufort Street, Perth 6000, Western Australia

Belgium

Centre de recherche Fondation de la tapisserie, des arts du tissu et des arts muraux de la Communauté Culturelle Française de Belgique, 82 boulevard des Combattants, 7500 Tournai

Galerie Philharmonie, 7bis, rue de Bénédictines, 4000 Liège

La Main, 215, rue de la Victoire, 1060 Brussels

Denmark

Arhus Kunstmuseum, Vennelystparken, 8000 Arhus Den Permanente, Vesterport, 1612 Copenhagen

Kunstindustrimuseet, Bredgade 68, 2100 Copenhagen

Nationalmuseet, Vestergade 10, 1260 Copenhagen

Stadsbiblioteket i Lyngby, Lyngby Hovedgade 28, 2800 Lyngby

Nordjyllands Kunstmuseum, Konig Christians, Alle 50, 9000 Aalborg

Finland

Didrichsen Taidemuseo, Kuusilandenkuja, 3 Helsinki

Kansallismuseo, Mannerheimintie, 34 Helsinki

Taideteollisuusmuseo, Hogbergsgatan 23A SF 001, 30 Helsinki

France

Atelier 10, 10, rue Pernety, 75004 Paris

Centre Culturel et Artistique Jean Lurçat, Avenue des Lissiers, 23200 Aubusson

Galerie Alain Blondel, 4, rue Aubry-le-Boucher, 75004 Paris

Galerie Alain Oudin, 28 bis, boulevard de Sébastopol, 75004 Paris

Galerie Baudoin Lebon, 34, rue des Archives, 75004 Paris

Galerie de l'Espace Malraux, Parc de Bretonnières, Jouel-les-Tours

Galerie des Femmes, 74, rue de Seine, 75006 Paris

Galerie Jean-Claude David, 1, rue Saint-Hughes, 38000 Grenoble

La Licorne en Montgolfière, 27, rue de Montreuil, 75011 Paris

Galerie la Margelle, 26, rue des Cordeliers, 13100 Aix-en-Provence

Galerie Neotu, Rue du Renard, 75004 Paris

Galerie Noëlla Gest, 5, rue de la Commune, 13210 Saint-Rémy-de-Provence

Galerie l'Œil écoute, Quai Romain-Rolland, 69000 Lyon

Galerie du Poisson d'or, 7, rue des Prêcheurs, 75001 Paris

Galerie Trente, 30, rue Rambuteau, 75003 Paris

Grenier de Villâtre, 18330 Nançay

Librairie Teepee, Espace Basfroi-Roquette, 48–50 rue Basfroi, 75011 Paris

Musée d'Art Moderne de la Ville de Paris, 11, avenue du Président Wilson, 75016 Paris

Musée d'Art Moderne de Villeneuve-d'Ascq, 59650 Villeneuve-d'Ascq

Musée des Arts Décoratifs, Château des Ducs de Bretagne, 44000 Nantes

Musée des Arts Décoratifs, 107, rue du Rivoli, 75001 Paris

Musée des Beaux-Arts, 10, rue du Musée, 49000 Angers

Musée-Château d'Annecy, 74000 Annecy

Musée des Gobelins, 42 avenue des Gobelins, 75013 Paris

Musée de L'Impression sur Etoffes, 3, rue des Bonnes Gens, 68100 Mulhouse, Alsace

Musée de Jean Lurcat, Angers

Musée de la Mode, 107, rue du Rivoli, 75001 Paris

Musée National d'Art Moderne, C.N.A.C. Georges Pompidou, 75004 Paris

Musée Réattu, rue du Grand Prieuré, 13200 Arles

Musée des Tapisseries, place des Martyrs de la Résistance, 13100 Aix-en-Provence

Musée de Tissus, 30–32, rue de la Charité, 69002 Lyon

Musée de la Villette, Cité des Sciences et de L'Industrie, Parc de la Villette, 75019 Paris

Place des Arts, 8, rue de l'Argenterie, 34000 Montpellier

Germany

Badisches Landesmuseum, Schloss 7500 Karlsruhe

Bundesverband Kunsthandwerk, Bleichstrasse 38a D–6000 Frankfurt

Design Centre, Stuttgart, Landesgewerbeamt Baden-Württemberg, Willi-Bleicher Strasse 19, D–7000 Stuttgart

Deutsches Textilmuseum, Andreasmarkt 8, 4150 Krefeld-Linn

Forum Kunst-Handwerk, Alte Schmiede am Lappan Lappan-gasse 2900 Oldenburg

Galerie Droysen, Droysenstrasse 17, 1000 Berlin

Galerie Margot Kreth d'Orey, Handschulheimer 71, 6900 Heidelberg

Galerie Meru, Querallee 13, 3500 Kassel

Galerie Metta Linde, Dr Julius Leberstrasse 49, 2400 Lübeck

Galerie Smend, Mainzerstrasse 28, 5000 Cologne

Galerie für Textilkunst, Brunnenstrasse 65, 4830 Gütersloh

Germanisches Nationalmuseum, Nurenberg
Handwerkform, Berliner Allee 17, 3000 Hanover
Handwerkskammer, Neumarkt 12, 5000 Cologne
Haus Kunst und Handwerk, Koppel 66, 2000 Hamburg
Kulturgeschichtliches Museum, Rissmüllerplatz, 4500 Osnabrück
Kunst und Handwerk & Galerie Terra, Heidelberger Strasse 104, 6100 Darmstadt
Das Landatelier, Ruschwedelerstrasse 42, 2165 Harsefeld-Ruschwedel
Linner Galerie, Margaretenstrasse 24, 4150 Krefeld-Linn
Museum für Kunsthandwerk, Schaumainkam 15, 6000 Frankfurt-am-Main
Museum für Kunst und Gewerbe, Steintorp Platz, D–2000, Hamburg
Staatliches Museum für Völkerkunde, Maximilianstrass 42, 8000 Munich
Städtische Galerie Peschkenhaus, Meerstrasse 1, 4130 Moers
Städtisches Museum Schloss Rheydt, 4050 Mönchengladbach
Textilkunst Galerie Rasmussen, Pariserstrasse 40, 1000 Berlin
Textilmuseum, Brahms 8, Heidelberg
Textil Werkstatt, Kleperstrasse 23, 6000 Frankfurt
Textil Werkstatt, Lütticherstrasse 48, 5000 Cologne
Württembergisches Landesmuseum, Schillerplatz 6, 7000 Stuttgart 1

Holland

Boymans van Beuningen Museum, Mathenesserlaan 18–20, 3015
De Rozengang, De Vos van Steenwijkerstraat 29, De Wijk
Galerie Detail Folkingestraat 53, Groningen
Galerie Dubbelzeven, Kamp 77, Amersfoort
Galerie Ja, Rielsedijk 2, Eindhoven
Galerie de Ploegh, Breestraat 18, Amersfoort
Galerie Gaaf Stoeldaaierstraat, 56a Groningen
Galerie Het Kapelhuis, Breestraat 1, 3811 BH Amersfoort
Galerie Kathareze, Nieuwlandstraat, 31 Tilburg
Galerie Ra, Vijzelstraat 80, Amsterdam
Galerie van Mourik, Rotterdam
Gemeentesmuseum, Kasteelplein 1 Helmond
Het Provinciehuis, Brabantlaan 1 5216 TV's-Hertogenbosch
Historisch Kostuum Museum, Loeff Berchmakerstraat 50, Utrecht
Intermezzo, Voorstraat 176, Dordrecht
Museum ter Zijde, Schoolstraat 3 Wouw
Nederlands Texteilmuseum, Goirkestraat 96 50–46 GN Tilburg
Stedelijk Museum, Paulus Porterstraat 13, Amsterdam
Stov, Lange Leidsedwarsstraat 208, Amsterdam
Zidjar Galerie, Schoolsteg 1, Franeker

Japan

Fashion Foundation 3–6–1, Kita-Aoyama, Minato-ku, Tokyo 107
Gallery Gallery, 5F Kotobuki Building, Shijyo-Kawaramachi Sagaru, Shimogyo-ku, Kyoto 600
Gallery Ma, 3F ToTo-Nogizaka Building, 1–24–3 Minami-Aoyama, Minato-ku, Tokyo 107
Gallery Maronie, Kawaramachi-Shijyo Agaru, Nakagyo-ku, Kyoto 604
Gallery Muu, Aya-Nishi Koen, Ayanokohji-Sagaru, Nishinotoin, Shimogyo-ku, Kyoto 600

Gallery Shinanobashi, B1 Tojiki-Kaikan, 1–3–4 Nishimoto-cho, Nishi-ku, Osaka 550
Hillside Gallery, Hillside Terrace A-1, 29–18 Sarugaku-cho Shibuya-ku, Tokyo 150
Isetan Museum, 8F Isetan-Shinkan, 3–14–1 Shinjyuku, Shinjyuku-ku, Tokyo 160
Kyoto Municipal Museum, 124 Enshoji-cho, Okazaki, Sakyo-ku, Kyoto 606
Meguro-ku Museum, 2–4–36 Meguro, Meguro-ku, Tokyo 153
Mingeikan (Japan Folk Crafts Museum), 4–3–33 Komaba, Meguro-ku, Tokyo 153
Museum of Modern Art, Tokyo, 1–1 Kitanomaru-Koen, Chiyoda-ku, Tokyo 102
Plus Minus Gallery, 8–8–5 Ginza, Chuo-ku, Tokyo 104
Sogestu Gallery, 7F Sogetsu-kaikan, 7–2–21 Akasaka, Minato-ku, Tokyo 107
Spiral Garden (Wacoal Art Center), 5–6–23 Minami-Aoyama, Minato-ku, Tokyo 10-7
Tokyo Metropolitan Art Museum, 8–36 Ueno-koen, Daitoh-ku, Tokyo 110
Wacoal Ginza Art Space, B1 Daiichi-Miyuki Building, 5–1–15 Ginza, Chuo-ku, Tokyo 104

Spain

FAD Gallery, AAFAD Brusi 45, Barcelona
Fondacion Joan Miró, Place de Montjuic 4, Barcelona
Museo de Arte Moderno, Palacio de la Ciudadela, Barcelona
Museo Papelero Capellade, Barcelona
Museo Provincial Textil, Calle, Cervantés Tarrasa, Barcelona

Sweden

Nationalmuseum, 103, 24 Stockholm

Switzerland

Centre Genevois de l'Artisanat, 26 Grande Rue, 1204 Geneva
Centre International de la Tapisserie Ancienne et Moderne (CITAM), 4 avenue Villamont, 1005 Lausanne
Forum, Galerie Jakob, Feldballe, Zurich
Galerie Alice Pauli, 7 avenue de Rumine, 1005 Lausanne
Galerie Faust, 25 Grande Rue, Vieille Ville, 1204 Geneva
Galerie Filambule, 4 rue de la Tour, 1004 Lausanne
Galerie Focus, 18 rue Madeleine, 1003 Lausanne
Galerie Jonas, 2016 Cortaillod
Galerie Littmann, Bäumleingasse 16, CH-4051 Basel
Galerie Maya Behn, Neumarkt 24, 8001 Zurich
Minigalerie, Neustadt 9, 8200 Schaffhouse
Musée des Arts Décoratifs, 4 avenue de Villamont, 1005 Lausanne
Musée Bellerive, Höschgasse 3, Zurich
Musée cantonal des Beaux-Arts, Palais de Rumine, place de la Riponne, 1003 Lausanne

UK

Artizana, The Village, Prestbury, Cheshire 5K1 4DG
Bluecoat Display Centre, Bluecoat Chambers, School Lane, Liverpool
The Cecilia Colman Gallery, 67 St John's Wood High Street, London NW8 7NL
Cirencester Workshops, Brewery Court, Cirencester GL7 1JH
Conroy Foley, Designer Craft, 6 Merchant's Court, St George's Street, Norwich NR3 1AB

Contemporary Applied Arts, 43 Earlham Street, London WC2H 9LD

Contemporary Textiles Gallery, 6a Vigo Street, London W1X 1AH

Crafts Council, 12 Waterloo Place, London SW1

Crafts Study Centre Collection, Holburne of Mentrie Museum, Gt Pulteney Street, Bath

Dartington Craft Shop and Cider Press Gallery, Shimmers Bridge, Dartington, Totnes, Devon

Laurimore Gallery, Swan Street, Boxford, Suffolk

Mostyn Art Gallery, 12 Vaughan Street, Llandudno, LL30 1AB

New Ashgate Gallery, Wagon Yard, Farnham, Surrey, GU9 7JR

New Craftsman, 24 Fore Street, St Ives, Cornwall

New Elvet Gallery, Durham DH1 3AQ

Primavera, 10 Kings Parade, Cambridge

Public Art Development Trust, 1a Cobham Mews, Agar Grove, London NW1 9SB

The Royal Exchange Craft Centre, Royal Exchange Theatre, St Ann's Square, Manchester M2 7DH

The Scottish Craft Centrer, 140 Canongate, Edinburgh, EH8 8DD

The South Bank Centre and Craft Shop Gallery, London SE1

The Victoria and Albert Museum and Craft Council Shop, Cromwell Road, London SW7

The Whitworth Art Gallery, Oxford Rd, Manchester

USA

The Allrich Gallery, 251 Post Street, San Francisco, CA 94108

The American Craft Museum, 73 West 45th Street, New York, NY 10019

The Art Institute of Chicago, Michigan Ave at Adams St, Chicago, IL 60603

Art Wear, 409 West Broadway, New York, NY 10013

Bellas Artes, New York, 584 Broadway, New York, NY 10012

Braunstein Quay Gallery, 254 Sutter Street, San Francisco, CA 94108

Brooklyn Museum, Eastern Parkway, Brooklyn, New York NY 11238

California Crafts Museum, Ghirardelli Square, North Point and Larkin Street, San Francisco

Center for Tapestry Arts, Cooper-Hewitt Museum of Decorative Arts and Design, Smithsonian Institution, 9 East 90th Street, New York, NY 100193

Clay and Fiber, North Pueblo Road, Taos, NM OI733

Cleveland Art Centre, Cleveland, Ohio

Contemporary Crafts, 3934 SW Corbett Avenue, Portland, OR 97201

Craft and Folk Art Museum, 5814 Wilshire Bd, Los Angeles, CA 90036

Elaine Potter Gallery, 336 Hayes Street, 94102 San Francisco

The Esther Saks Gallery, 311 West Superior Street, Chicago, IL 60610

Franklin Parrasch, 584 Broadway, New York, NY 10012

Hadler Gallery, 35 East 20th Street, New York, NY 10003

Helen Drutt Gallery, 1721 Walnut Street, Philadelphia, Pennsylvania 19103

Heller Gallery, 71 Green Street, Soho, New York, NY 10012

Julie Artisan's Gallery, 687 Madison Avenue, New York, NY 10021

Miller Brown Gallery, 355 Hayes Street, San Francisco, CA 94102

Metropolitan Museum of Art, 5th Avenue and 82nd Street, New York, NY 10028

Modern Master Tapestries, 11 East 57th Street, New York, NY 10022

The Museum of Modern Art, 11 West 53rd Street, New York, NY 10019

The Museum of Modern Art, Rhode Island School of Design, Providence, Rhode Island

The Philadelphia Museum of Art, Parkway at 26th Street, Philadelphia, PA 19130

The Renwick Gallery, National Museum of American Art (Smithsonian Institution), Pennsylvania Avenue at 17th Street, NW, Washington, DC 20560

Southeastern Ohio Cultural Arts Centre, Athens, Ohio

Twining Gallery, 33 Bleeker Street, New York, NY 10012

The Textile Museum, 2320 South Street NW, 2008 Washington, DC

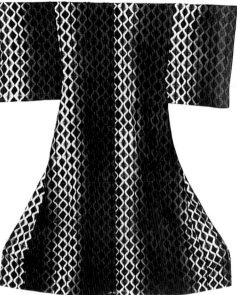

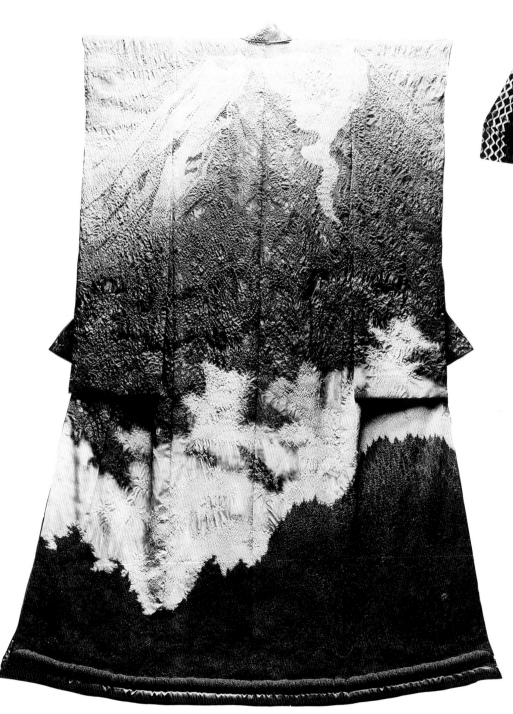

Kimono
Shibori on silk with natural indigo
    dyes
Hiroyuki Shindo
Japan, 1989

'Mount Fuji after the Rain'
Kimono
Silk hand-dyed using the Itchiku
    Tsujigahana
Itchiku Kubota
Japan, 1988

Exhibitions

A selected list of important exhibitions of textile art, craft and design, with catalogues.

1962 First Biennale Internationale de la Tapisserie, Musée Cantonal des Beaux Arts, Lausanne, Switzerland

1963 'Woven Forms', Museum of Contemporary Crafts of the American Crafts Council, New York. First exhibition of New Fiberworks in America

1967 'Funk Art', University of Art Museum, Berkeley, California

1969 'Objects USA', Johnson Collection of Contemporary Crafts. Inaugural exhibition.

1972 'Sculpture in Fiber', Museum of Contemporary Crafts of the American Crafts Council, New York

1972 International Tapestry Triennale, Lodz, Poland

1974 First exhibition of Miniature Textiles, Crafts Council Gallery, London

1977 'Fiberworks', Cleveland Museum of Art, Ohio

1979 'Craft Horizons', American Craft Museum, New York

1979 'Quilt National', South-Eastern Ohio Cultural Arts Center, Athens, Ohio

1980 'American Fiber Art: A New Definition', University of Houston, Texas

1980 'Le Langage du Tissu', Hôtel de Ville, Le Havre

1981 'Thirty Years of Creative Textiles', Musée des Arts Décoratifs, Paris

1982 'Scandinavian Design 1880–1980'

1982 'Basketry: Tradition in New Form', Institute of Contemporary Art, and national tour of USA

1983 'Design Since '45', Philadelphia Museum of Art, Pennsylvania

1983 'The Quilt: New Directions for an American Tradition'

1985 'Architextures: Fibre Art '85', SNAC, Paris

1985 '45 Ans de la Tapisserie', Ecole des Beaux Arts, Paris

1985 'Textiles for the Eighties', Museum of Art, The Rhode Island School of Design, Providence, Rhode Island. International exhibition of contemporary furnishing fabrics.

1986 'The Woven and Graphic Art of Anni Albers', Smithsonian Institution, Washington, DC

1986 'The Art Quilt', Los Angeles Municipal Art Gallery, California

1986 'Conceptual Clothing', Ikon Gallery, Birmingham

1986 International Textile Design Contest, organized by the Fashion Foundation, Tokyo. The annual juried exhibition of experimental textile designs for fashion travels to Europe for the first time in 1991.

1986 'La Mode: Une Industrie de Pointe', Cité des Sciences et de l'Industrie, La Villette, Paris

1986 'Fiber R/Evolution', Milwaukee Art Museum and University of Art Museum, University of Wisconsin, Milwaukee

1986 'Craft Today: The Poetry of the Physical', American Craft Museum, New York

1986–87 'Design Textile en Scandinavie 1950/1985'; Musée de L'Impression sur Etoffes, Mulhouse, France

1987 'Interlacing: the Elemental Fabric', American Craft Museum, New York

1987 International Textile Competition, Kyoto, Japan. Juried competition of textile art, craft and design.

1987 'Quilts: Tradition and Innovation', Society for Arts and Crafts, Pittsburgh, Pennsylvania

1987 'The Eloquent Object', Philbrook Arts Center, Tulsa, Oklahoma

1988 'Textsyles' at the Smiths gallery, London. Round-up of young contemporary designers

1988 'The Subversive Stitch', Whitworth Art Gallery and Cornerhouse Gallery in Manchester, UK

1989 International Textile Competition, Kyoto, Japan

1990 'Lenore Tawney: A Retrospective', American Craft Museum, New York

1990 'Colour/Light/Surface', Cooper-Hewitt Museum, New York. International exhibition of contemporary fabric design from the Cooper-Hewitt public collection, no catalogue.

1990 'Texteil', Nederlands Beeldende Kunst, Amersfoort, Holland

1990 'Sport '90', Design Museum, London

1990 'A Primal Spirit, Ten Contemporary Japanese Sculptors', Los Angeles County Museum of Art, California

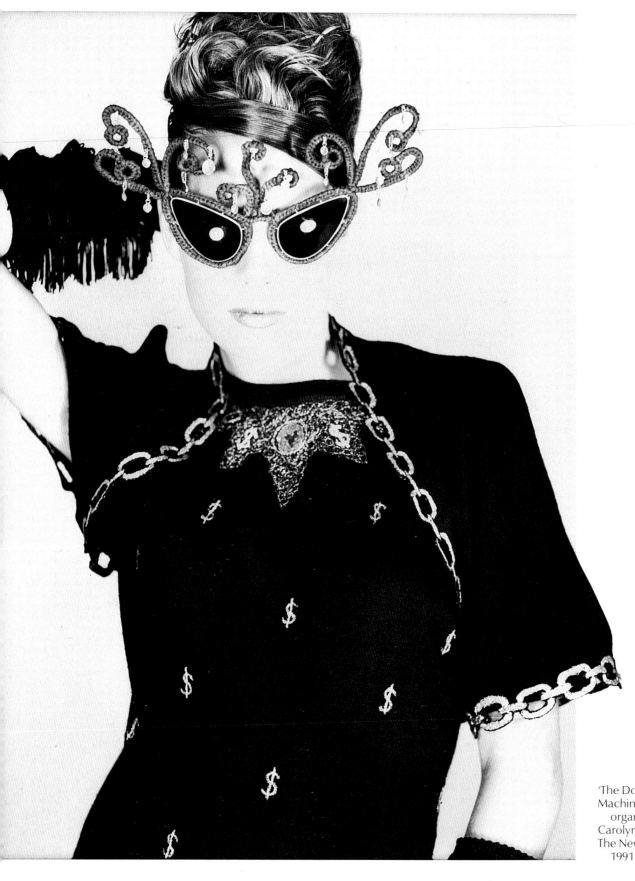

'The Dollar-Shirt'
Machine-embroidered
organza
Carolyn Corben
The New Renaissance, UK,
1991

Publications

Books

Albers, Anni, *On Designing* (Wesleyan University Press, Middletown, 1971)

Albers, Anni, *On Weaving* (Wesleyan University Press, Middletown, 1974)

American Fabrics Magazine, Encyclopedia of Textiles (Doric Publishing Company, 1972)

Bosence, Susan, *Handblock Printing and Resist Dyeing* (David and Charles, Newton Abbott, 1985)

Centro Design Montefibre, Decorattivo 1 (Idea, Milan, 1976)

Centro Design Montefibre, Decorattivo 2 (Idea, Milan, 1977)

Constantine, Mildred, and Jack Lenor Larsen, *The Art Fabric: Mainstream* (Kodansha International Ltd, Tokyo, 1985)

Constantine, Mildred, and Jack Lenor Larsen, *Beyond Craft: The Art Fabric* (Van Nostrand Reinhold, New York, 1973)

Hollander, Anne, *Seeing Through Clothes* (Viking Penguin, London, 1978)

Koren, Leonard, *New Fashion Japan* (Kodansha International Ltd, Tokyo, 1985)

Larsen, Jack Lenor, *Furnishing Fabrics* (Thames and Hudson Ltd, London, 1989)

Larsen, Jack Lenor and Betty Freudenheim, *Interlacing: the Elemental Fabric* (Kodansha International Ltd, Tokyo, 1987)

Manguy, Christine, Sophie Pommier and Michel Thomas, *Textile Art* (Rizzoli, New York, 1985)

Manzini, Ezio, *The Material of Invention* (the MIT Press, Cambridge, 1989)

Mayer, Barbara, *Contemporary American Craft Art* (Gibbs and Smith, USA, 1988)

McDermott, Katherine, *Street Style* (The Design Council, London, 1986)

Parker, Roszika, *The Subversive Stitch: Embroidery and the Making of the Feminine* (The Women's Press Ltd, London, 1984)

Parker, Roszika, and Griselda Pollock, *Old Mistresses: Women, Art and Ideolog* (Pandora, London, 1981)

Storey, Joyce, *Textile Printing* (Thames and Hudson Ltd, London, 1974)

Sutton, Anne, and Diane Sheehan, *Ideas in Weaving* (Batsford, London, 1989)

Van Ray, Stephen, *'Imitation and Inspiration: the Japanese Influence on Dutch Art'* (Art Unlimited, Amsterdam, 1989)

Vincent Ricard, Françoise, *Clefs pour la Mode* (Seghers, Paris, 1987)

Magazines

American Craft, 401 Park Avenue South, New York, NY 10016, USA

L'Atelier, 41 Rue Baurault, 75013 Paris, France

Driade, 3 Rue Felix Faure, 75016 Paris, France

Fiberarts, Lark Communications, 50 College Street, Asheville, 28801 USA

Form and Function, Finnish Society of Craft and Design, Erottajankatu 15–17, A502, 00130, Helsinki 13, Finland

From Australia, PO Box 74 Chippendale, New South Wales 2008, Australia

International Textiles, ITBD, 33 Bedford Place, London WC1, UK

Kunsthandwerk, Norske Kunsthandverkeres Formidlingssentral Arbeiengst 7, 0253 Oslo 2, Norway

Shuttle, Spindle and Dyepot, Handweavers Guild of America, 998 Farmington Avenue, West Hartford, CT 06107, USA

Surface Design Journal, Surface Design Association, 311 Washington Street, Fayetteville, TN 37334, USA

Textile Art 3 Rue Felix Fauré, 75015 Paris, France

Textile Fibre Forum, The Australian Forum for Textile Arts, PO Box 77, University of Queensland, Brisbane, Queensland, Australia

Textilforum, Friedenstrasse 1, Postfach 5944, D–3000, Hanover 1, Germany

Textilkunst, Verlag M & H Schaper, Grazer Strasse 20, Postfach 81 06 69, D–3000 Hanover 81, Germany

Textile Outlook International (London, Hong Kong, New York, Tokyo), The Economist Intelligence Unit Limited, 40 Duke Street, London W1A 1DW, UK

Articles

Abrams, Janet, 'Adressing the Body', *Blueprint*, London, July 1990

Alexander, Jane, 'Vital fabrics, Ripping yarns' *iD*, Life and Soul Issue, May 1990

Corwin, Nancy, 'Cynthia Schira: Image Into Structure', *Surface Design Journal*, Autumn 1989

Corwin, Nancy, 'Fiber R/Evolution', *American Craft*, Vol. 46n, No. 3, June/July 1986

Davies, Stan, 'Silk Like Breatheable and Other Microfilament Fabrics', *Textile Outlook International*, Jan. 1990·

Freudenheim, Betty, 'Interlacing: The Elemental Fabric', *American Craft*, April/May 1987

Hill, Rosemary, 'Friends of the Earth', *Crafts*, No. 100, Sept./Oct. 1989

'Issey Miyake: Sewing a Second Skin', *Art Forum*, Feb. 1982

Koplos, Janet, 'Spirited Away: The Japanese Folkcraft Tradition', *Crafts*, No. 10, Sept./Oct. 1989

Koplos, Janet, 'The Many Forms of Fiber', *Sculpture*, May/June 1989

'The Man-Made Fibre Industry in Japan', *Textile Outlook International*, March 1989

Nectoux, Pascale, 'La banque des imaginaires', *Textile Art Industries*, Nov. 1986

Popham, Peter, 'Junichi Arai: Man of the Cloth', *Blueprint*, Spring 1987

Smith, Paul J., 'Craft Today: The Poetry of the Physical', *American Craft*, Vol. 46, No. 5

Thomas, Michel 'La Mode et les Trois Vagues', *Textile Art Industries*, 1987

Wimmer, Gayle, 'Polish Textile Art: Photo Realism in the Three Second Generation', *American Craft*, Vol. 46, No. 1, Feb./Mar. 1986

Glossary

batik   Technique involving the application of wax paste or starch to fabric in order to resist dye.

beetling   Method of finishing cloth by pounding the fabric surface with a mallet or stone.

block printing   Technique for hand-printing patterns on to cloth using a carved wooden or linoleum block.

calendering   Industrial ironing finishing technique achieved by passing cloth between a heated and a padded roller. Calendering can be used for aesthetic effect, to smooth materials into a high polish (friction calendering) or to create watered or moire effects by folding the material.

chiné (also clouding, warp- or weft-printing)   Technique that imitates ikat, invented in the eighteenth century.

cloqué   General term for fabrics with a blistered surface, sometimes achieved by weaving a double cloth from yarns with differing degrees of shrinkage.

combination fabrics   Hybrid fabrics that combine two or more different types of yarn. This is by far the most popular way of using the new high-tech fibres to add performance qualities, such as stability, anti-crinkle, stretch or water-proofing.

combination jacquard   A recent sophistication of the jacquard weaving process by programming computer, to create highly complex jacquard patterns. It is capable of placing various yarns of differing degrees of thickness and twist into cloth.

core-spun yarns   Yarns consisting of a central filament surrounded by staple fibres, e.g. lycra and cotton.

crêpe plissé   Effect achieved by applying an acid solution to cloth which elongates fibres, creating a puckered surface.

deposit printing   Technique for printing patterns in light relief on the fabric surface.

devoré   From the French for 'devour'. General term for a patterning technique whereby solutions are applied that etch or burn out the pattern. Often used on combination cloths.

direct jacquard   Automated process for translating photographic images into jacquard-woven fabric.

discharge printing   The application of bleach paste for bleaching out patterns of previously dyed, printed or woven cloth. Used in conjunction with certain dyes, the bleach may react to give different colours.

double cloth   Fabric made of two (or more) superimposed layers of interwoven cloth.

finishing   General term that describes a variety of treatments after weaving, including bleaching, lacquering and calendering.

geotextile   Polyester fabric used for earthworks on engineering projects.

Gore-tex   Microporous membrane derived from Polytetrafluorothylene, invented (1976) and manufactured by W. L. Gore (USA). Gore-tex can be laminated on to any traditional textile material, it is wind-proof, water-proof and bacteria-proof but allows for the passage of water vapour, thus enabling skin to breathe.

half-tone screens (Also nickel-coated mesh galvano screens) These screens enable colours to be screen-printed on to fabric in graduated strengths.

heat-reactive fibres Fibres based on a liquid crystal component. This reflects a narrow wave-band of light in between certain temperatures. Colours vary from red through the spectrum to blue and ultimately violet as the temperature increases.

heat-transfer printing High-fidelity monoprint technique. Solvent-based varnishes applied to waxed paper are passed through heated rollers (170–220°C) and are sublimated, vaporized on to the cloth. Recently this method has been developed as a means of transferring painting on to cloth.

hemp Strong bast fibre from the hemp plant, usually used in rope.

high-shrink yarns Yarns that shrink to such an extent during the finishing processes that they distort the surface of the cloth. This property may be used by weavers to create specific tactile effects.

high-twist yarns Assembled from two elements with a high degree of ('s' or 'z') twist.

ikat Resist technique achieved by binding and dyeing warp or weft threads (or both) prior to weaving.

leno weave Ancient Peruvian weaving technique which involves twisting the warp threads together between sections of weft.

microencapsulation Technique for enclosing a variety of substances (e.g. heat-reactive liquid crystals, perfume, bactericides) in micron-sized bubbles which can be attached along the length of a yarn.

microfibres Extremely fine synthetic fibres generally of less than one decitex in diameter (roughly sixty times finer than human hair).

microfinishes Tactile aesthetics possible with microfibre monofilament yarns, which make up fabrics such as 'peach skin' and 'moist touch' surface effects.

non-wovens Textile structure generally made from fibres rather than yarns. 'Non-woven' is a general term that covers a broad variety of techniques such as wet-laying, thermal bonding, fluid-jet entanglement, stitch-bonding etc. Non-wovens are used for a broad variety of purposes from nappies and battery interlinings to surgical gowns and carpets.

overspun yarns Yarns spun with a higher degree of twist than is necessary for tensile strength, which tend to distort when woven.

pigment print Insoluble powdered colouring agent carried in a liquid binder that can only be printed on to the surface of the cloth.

procions Family of synthetic dyes manufactured by ICI.

raschel lace Fabric produced on a raschel-warp knitting machine.

resist General term for creating patterns on cloth by either binding, stitching or treating the fabric with a dye-resistant substance prior to dyeing the cloth.

rubber printing Form of deposit printing using a latex solution which can be used to transform the fabric surface.

screen printing A printing technique based on stencilling colour on to cloth. A metal, silk or synthetic screen may be used, which may either be flat or cylindrical (rotary).

Shibori General Japanese term for tie-dye, stitch- and pleat-resist techniques.

sisal Strong, coarse fibre from the leaf of the sisal plant.

slit film Very fine film cut from plastic or metallic film.

space dyeing General term for creating multicolour yarns by warp printing or by dyeing yarns with spray jets.

sprang Ancient method for creating fabrics by interlacing parallel warps, creates a very elastic fabric.

spun bonding A technique for making a non-woven fabric by extruding filaments that are laid down in the form of a web and then bonded.

vacuum bonding Technique for applying a metallic coating, typically titanium or aluminium, to polyester yarns or fabrics in a high vacuum.

Wilton carpet Jacquard-woven patterned carpet which may be woven face to face and separated by a bladed wire.

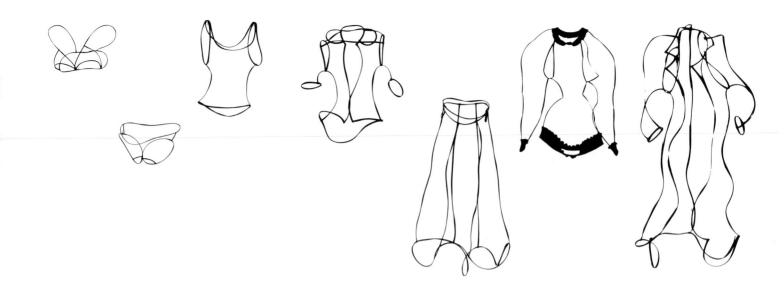

'Skeleton Clothes'
Machine-stitched cotton
Caroline Broadhead
UK, 1986–91

'Stretch'
White cotton shirt
Caroline Broadhead
UK, 1988

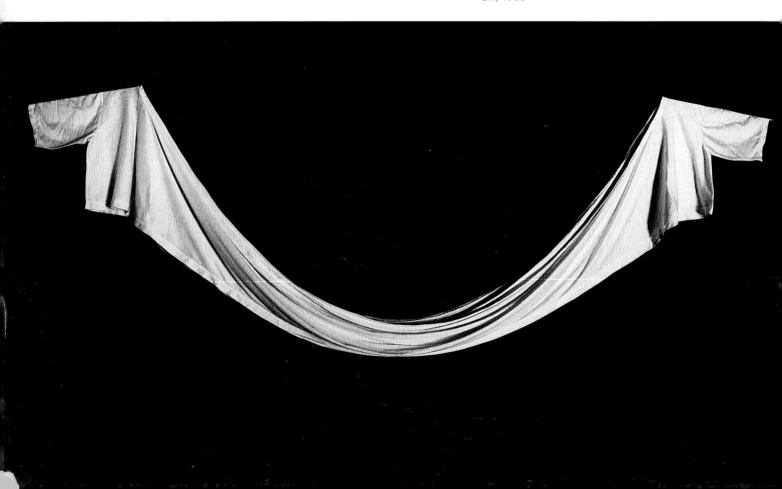

Index

Numerals in italics refer to plate illustration numbers

Aalto, Alvar 30
Abakanowicz, Magdalena 143
Abild, Helle *47–52*
'Abstract Design in American Quilts' (exhibition) 106
Agnès B. *72*
Akers, Adela *186*
Alaïa, Azzedine 24; *28*
Al-Hilali, Neda 140; *166*
Alland, Micheline 13
Almedahls 30
Aquator 26
Arai, Junichi 19, 20, 27, 39, 40; *61–3, 117, 119*
Ascher, Lida and Zika 29
Atkinson, Nigel 21, 24; *1, 2, 37*
Aust, Rushton 140
Awatsuji, Hiroshi *96–101*

Bailey, Bridget 21; *13–18*
Balinari, Arlette *120*
Barber, Claire *185*
Barnes, Jhane 26
basketry 105, 110–11
Bauhaus 27, 29, 138
B. D. Ediciones de Diseño 33; *91, 133, 134*
Bedin, Martine *91*
Bellinger, Gretchen 39; *106–9*
Bernard, Théa 140; *188, 209, 210*
Beytebiere, D'Arcie 22
Blaisse, Maria 27; *23, 24*
block printing 112; *136, 152–5*
Body Map 16, 24
Bonas 40
Bonfante, Paola *173*
Borås 30
Bosence, Susan 112; *154, 155*
Brennand Wood, Michael 140; *215*
Brero, Mary 109, 110; *178*
Brink, Renata 140
British fashion textiles 15–17
Broadhead, Caroline 141; *201–4*
Burbidge, Pauline 108
Burch Cochran, Jane 108; *157*

Calatroni, Sergio *92*
Campbell, Patricia 140; *193*
carpets 32–4
Cerruti, Nino 23
Chicago, Judy 106
Chompré, Daniel 140; *208*

Ciba Geigy 15
Classic Contemporaries Collection *114, 126*
Clemente, Francesco *225*
Coleridge, Nicholas 20
Collingwood, Peter 139
'Colour, Light, Surface' (exhibition) 38
combination jacquard technique 19, 21; *117*
Comou, Ady 144; *226*
Constantine, Mildred 138
Cook, Lia *159, 160*
Corben, Carolyn 15
craft textiles 105–35
Création Baumann 38, 39–40; *89, 90, 120*
Crow, Nancy 108, 109
Curran, Lynne *230*

Day, Lucienne 29
De Amaral, Olga *168*
Delaunay, Sonia 143
Denni Vee Sportsclothing 45
devoré printing 38; *75*
Di Mare, Dominic *167*
discharge printing 22; *55–9, 103, 104, 113*
Do Modo *30*
Dorner, Marie Christine 33
Doyle, Kris 109
Duc, Christian 33; *93*
Dupeux, Geneviève *161*
Du Pont de Nemours 24

Edinburgh Tapestry Company 143
Efstratiou, Alida 22; *32–5, 43, 44*
Eliakim *75*
embroidery 13–14, 105, 106; *9, 10, 147, 157, 177, 178*
Enghoff, Ulla *150, 151*
English Eccentrics 16
Esprit 37

Fabric Workshop *176*
fashion textiles 12–27, 141; *41–75*
felting 105
Fischbacher, Christian 39
Fisher, Sharon 30; *115*
Freeman, Susie *156, 180*
French, Stephen 38; *81, 83–6*
Freshwater, Sally 140; *194*
Fujie Textiles 96, 100
furnishing textiles 28–40; *76–104*

Galliano, John 16
Garrard, Rose 141; *197*
Geluk, Maryan 140; *211, 212*
General Dourking Collection *94*
geotextiles 27
Gigli, Romeo 21
Girbaud, François 12, 13
'Gobel' technique *225*
Gobelin tapestries 139, 143
Godley, Georgina 23, 24; *54, 64*
Goldsmith, Shelly *222*
Gombrich, Ernst 34
Gordon, Joanna 17; *57, 59*
Gore-tex 25–6; *54*
Gore, W. L. 25, 27
Graffin, Daniel 140
Gråsten, Viola *126*
Greaves Lord, Sally 39; *113*
Gubern, Silvia 36

Hadid, Zaha 33
Hamatani, Akio 142; *213, 214*
Hamnett, Katherine 17
haute couture 13–15
heat-moulded fabrics *1, 2*
heat-reactive dyes 20, 26; *20*
heat-transfer printing 15; *3–8, 198*
Hegelund Sørensen, Bitten *103, 104*
Heijen, Sibyl *200*
Herman, Nancy *137*
Hicks, Sheila 139
Himanuki, Akiko *165*
Hishinuma, Yoshiki 29; *66–8*
Hodge and Sellers 16, 23, 24; *28*
Hugues, Patrice 141; *198*

Ikea 30
Intair 39
International Exhibition of Miniature Textiles (1974) 108
Ishimoto, Fujiwo 30; *122*
Isobe, Harumi *229*
Isozaki, Arata 33; *131*
Itter, Diane *143–5*

Jacobi, Peter and Ritzi 143; *220, 221*
Jacobs, Ferne 110–11; *169, 170*
Jacobsen, Arne 30
Japanese fashion textiles 18
Jean Passot 24

Kallesøe, Else 30; *129*
Kandlbinder, Eva 139
Kawakubo, Rei 18, 20
Kettle, Alice *175*

kimonos 18
Kinnasand 30; *118*
Kiryu, Japan 20
Kivalo, Inka 30
Kjaerholm, Kristine *116*
Klomp, Maryan 37; *123*
Knoche Wendel, Elfi 144; *218, 219*
Knodel, Gerhardt 143
Koren, Leonard 20
Kreutzer-Temming, Martha 144; *228*
Kubota, Itchiku 112
Kumai, Kyoko 142; *192*
Kummer, Christine *184*
Kvadrat 30; *110, 111*

Lacroix, Christian 11, 15; *3–8*
Lagerfeld, Karl 14
Larsen Design Studio 82
Larsen, Jack Lenor 38, 138
laser-beam printing 18
Laurent, Yves Saint 14; *9*
Lausanne Contemporary Tapestry Biennales 108
Lesage S.A. 13; *9, 10*
Lesage, François 13
Levigoureux, Odile *216*
LeWitt, Sol 33; *130*
Lichtenstein, Roy 33
light-reactive dyes 26
Lipman, Helen 16
Littell, Ross *110*
Ljunbergs, Eric 30; *114, 126*
Lorenz 36
Lundberg, Tom 109; *177*
lycra 24; *36, 45, 46, 50–4*

McAsh, Jim *19, 20*
McFarlane, Kathleen 227
McLaren, Malcolm 15
Malcolm, Lyn 107–8
Marieta Textil 36; *88, 124*
Marimekko Oy 30; *122*
Mariscal, Javier 37; *88, 121, 124*
Modennini, Doriano 28
'La Mode: Une Industrie de Pointe' (exhibition) 13
Memphis 31, 34, 35; *77–9*
Minagawa, Makiko 18; *38, 39*
Minkowitz, Norma 111; *171, 172*
Miyake Design Studio 18; *38, 39*
Miyake, Issey 18, 20, 21, 27
Miyamoto, Eiji *25, 27*
Miyashin Co. Ltd *25, 26, 27*
Mobilier National 143
Møller, Anne Fabricius *102*
Montana, Claude *31*
Moore, Rosemary 27; *36*
Morris, William 13, 37

Nagin, Risë *181*
neoprene *46*
Neville, Bernard 31
Nittobo Seki *36*
Nobilis Fontain 32
Nordiska Kompaniet 30
Norelene *136*
Nouvel, Jean *132*
Nuno Co. 19, 40; *40, 41, 61–3, 87, 105, 117, 119*
Nurmesniemi, Vuokko Eskolin 30
nylon 25, 26; *201, 202*

Olesen, 'Colil' C. *152, 153*
Olzewski, Michael *179*
Oxido 33; *95*

Pallucco 32
Palmissano Edizioni Tessili 34, 36; *80*
Pasquier, Natalie du 35, 36; *79, 80*
Peeters, Liesbeth *146*
Pentagon Peace Ribbon 107
Petrossian, Karen 31
Pinon, Patrick 22; *69–72*
Pinton, François 143
Pla, Teresa *207*
Polytetrafluorothylene 25
Putman, Andrée 9, 32, 33; *94*

Ratia, Armi 30
Restieaux, Mary *135*
Richards, Ann *141, 142*
Richards, Victoria 17; *55, 56, 58*
Riisberg, Vibeke *125, 127, 128*
Ringgold, Faith 107; *176*
Rivas Sanchez, Luiven 17; *11, 26*
Robbins, Freddie 12
Robert le Héros 34, 35
Rothstein, Scott *147*

Sampe, Astrid 30; *114*
Santagata, Sabrina *148, 149*
Scandinavian textile printing 29–30
Scheuer, Ruth 7, 143
Schira, Cynthia 143–4; *182, 183, 223, 224*
Schoettle, Marian 141; *205, 206*
Scott, Joyce J. 107; *174*
screen printing 29; *11, 20, 26, 29, 31, 60, 67, 70, 72–4, 76–8, 99–101, 114, 121–3, 125–9, 131, 132, 138, 150, 151*
Seelig, Warren 140, 143
Severinsson, Anna *118*
Shaw-Sutton, Carol *217*
Shibori resist-dyeing 21, 112
Shindo, Hiroyuki 112
Sisal Collezione 92, 95

Sisson, Karyl 111; *162–4*
Sitbon, Martine 21
Skinazi, Silvie 11, 15; *3–8*
Sködt, Finn 111
Smith, Hilde 16
Smith, Paul 16, 137
Sonday, Milton 38
Sowden, George 34, 35, 37; *77–9*
Studstill, Pamela 108; *158*
Sudo, Reiko 40; *41, 105*
Sutton, Ann 108
Svekely, Vera 140; *194, 196*
Szerszynska, Jasia *73, 74, 76*

Tactel 26
'tactile' design 26
Taller Mexicano de Gobelinos *225*
Tanaka, Hideho 142; *190*
tapestry 142–4; *185, 222–4, 228–30*
Tastemain and Riisberg 24; *21, 22*
Tawney, Lenore 137, 138, 139
Teijin 26
three-dimensional fabrics 21
Thun, Matteo 33
Tikkanen, Maisa *199*
Tino Cosma *77, 78*
Toulemonde Bochard 33; *93, 94*
Toyazaki, Mitsuo 141, 142; *191*
Toyobo 26
Traficó de Modas 36; *121*
Transtam 36, 37
Treacy, Philip *42*
Trend Union 70
Troll *46*
Tsujigahana kimono-dyeing 112
Tusquets, Oscar 33; *133, 134*

Vionnet, Madeleine 18
Von Etzdorf, Georgina 17; *60*
Vorwerk 33, 34; *130–2*
Vuokko Oy 30

Weisz, Renata 40
Westwood, Vivienne 15, 18; *65*
Whitney Museum of American Art 106
Wilson, Anne *187, 189*

Yamamoto, Yoji 18, 20

Zanotta 28
Zeebra 37; *123*
Zeisler, Claire 137, 139
Zimmer und Rohde 40; *112*
Zumsteg et Fils 39